LOGIC OF DISCOVERY

AND

LOGIC OF DISCOURSE

LOGIC OF DISCOVERY

AND LOGIC OF

DISCOURSE

Edited by

Jaakko HINTIKKA
Fernand VANDAMME

PLENUM PRESS ● NEW YORK AND LONDON

COMMUNICATION AND COGNITION ● GHENT

Distributed in the U.S.A. and Japan by

Plenum Press,
a Division of Plenum Publishing Corporation, 233 Spring Street, New York 10013
ISBN 0-306-42157-7

Printed in Belgium

CONTENTS

PREFACE

This book reflects the main papers which were discussed at the Ghent-Helsinki Conference on the theme, The Logic of Discourse and The Logic of Scientific Discovery.

In fact this meeting was the setting for a successful confrontation of the scientists of the Helsinki Center with those of the Center for Communication & Cognition. All share an interest in formal logic and language and a conviction that logic and language are important for a better understanding of epistemology and methodology, and vice versa.

This book illustrates the possibilities and perspectives of the union of formal, logical, linguistic and epistemological methods and interests.

We hope that this approach will lead to a better knowledge of the world, for a better mankind.

J. Hintikka, F. Vandamme

INTRODUCTION

LOGIC OF DISCOVERY AND LOGIC OF DISCOURSE : WHY ?

F. Vandamme

Why to try to relate discovery and discourse, and more peculiarly what link can there exist between a logic of discovery and a logic of discourse ? It is not at all our intention to answer this question here in this introduction. This is rather the task of the several contributors to this book.

What we want to do is firstly to bring to the fore some interesting historical impulses to the rising awareness of the interrelation between discovery and discourse.

Secondly to throw light on several aspects of these logics, which are put forward in the following papers.

Trirdly to comment on the social and scientific importance of the theme of this book.

In this short introduction it is not our intention to dwell extensively on how the Aristotelian, and most of all the Averroistic traditions of approaching discovery and its logic implicitly refer to discourse. Following the wake of the Averroistic tradition, the discovery and its discourse have played without doubt an important role in the development of western science in the sixteenth and seventeenth century. The study of this role would be very useful for a better understanding of the development and structure of modern science.

Today it is Hanson who is mostly credited for the revival of the logic of discovery, and also in his approach discourse is implicitly important. But the several discussions following Hanson's 1958 paper illustrate that the notion of logic was rather loose.

I myself believe that Hintikka's provoking paper "Sherlock Holmes confronts Modern Logic: toward a theory of information seeking through questioning" (Hintikka 1982) is a real turning point.

It brings us a system and an explanation of how a logic of discovery, in the strict sense of logic, is possible. But what is more, it also relates this logic of discovery, by way of the dialogue system, with a kind of logic of discourse. For, does a dialogue logic not presuppose at least a minimal logic of discourse? And is it not true that the more elaborate the dialogue logic is, the more elaborate the implied discourse logic has to be? We obtain an important argument for this view when we consider the relation between answers and questions. So for instance Hintikka argues, that — and I quote — "there is no need that a question is answered on the basis of information that is specifiable in some given language even when both the question and its answer are formulated in that language" (Hintikka and Merrill, 1982, p. 60). Another of his points is that the process of activating tacit knowledge is controlled by the questions which serve to elicit it to actuality (ibid., p. 59). Hintikka also considers observations to be answers to questions.

What does interest us most of all in this paper of Hintikka is his view on the interrelations between a) questions, b) answers, that is premisses, and c) inferential conclusions. These interrelations can be of a very complex nature (See Hintikka and Merrill, 1982, pp. 60–61).

A certain answer may be partially based on an earlier inferential conclusion and a question. In other words, as Hintikka argues, answers to questions do not always precede (temporally or logically) deductive inferences. Why is this remark important for us here? First of all such a process of producing answers to questions which result in deductive inferences have at least something to do with a type of discovery. In the weakest interpretation it is relevant for the discovery of tacit information. But the ideas quoted are relevant for our topic for still another reason.

Discovery (new information, answers) seems to be dependent on questions and inferential conclusions. Inferential conclusions in turn seem to be dependent on answers and questions. But questions, on what are they dependent?

Perhaps Karin Knorr's book *Manufacture of Knowledge* is rather relevant here. She starts the discovery with an answer. Questions with inferential conclusions are used for realising an answer, they are used to transform the un-realised answer, which starts the discovery process, into an answer which fits. Such an unrealised answer is not a hypothesis. For the answerer is really engaged to his answer. He will use all means he has in his power: questions, deductions, observations, authority, power, to realise his answer.

What this story suggests is that in the discovery we have three important tools, namely questions, answers and inferential conclusions. Perhaps none of them are methodologically, temporally or logically more fundamental than the others. It will depend on the discourse, on the construction one is making, what the role will be of the different mentioned components. But the structure and characteristics of the discourse themselves are dependent on many things. The cultural, the social, the psychological characteristics of the situation, where the discourse is to be produced or analysed, determine the structure of the discourse to a high degree.

Does this mean that the peculiar process of discovery will be dependent on those factors controlling the discourse ? If the answer is positive, then certainty the work of Jean-Blaise Grize, of Foucault, of Bourdieu, is relevant for the development of a logic of discourse and for a logic of discovery. This together with the whole modern development of the study of discourse in all its aspects.

The papers in this book give us certain answers and projects of study for aspects of the problems raised concerning discourse, discovery and its interrelations. The contributions to this book can be classified into five main topics, we believe. It is however evident -- and this is the case with all attempts at classification -- that our classification will do wrong to certain important features of the contributions. The classification we propose is the following one.

1. There is a first set of papers treating implicitly or explicitly of the integration of a logic of discovery and a logic of discourse. Hintikka, Pearce and Sintonen, and my own paper are here relevant. Hintikka in his paper discusses certain competing views on the logic of scientific discovery and develops the leading ideas of his own approach. Sintonen treats of the problem of the embedding of scientific problems in their background and ways of isolating them. An erotetic logic is used for this task. In my paper, I dwell somewhat on the historical antecedents of the logic of discovery, and, in their perspective, some attention is paid to the logic of discourse and more peculiarly to the relevance of dialogue logic. In this frame a relative differentiation between logic of proof and logic of discovery is suggested.

2. The second set comprehends contributions to an elaboration of a logic and/or a general theory of discourse. We would like to mention here the papers of Hintikka and Kulas, Taiminen and Komlosi. Hintikka and Kulas illustrate how functional a pragmatical game approach is for a better understanding of the functioning of the definite article. Taiminen's paper elaborates on Frege's content principle and the consequences of it for Frege's view on logic: logic as language and language as the universal medium. Komlosi in his paper argues in favor of relating psychological representation theories and discourse interaction with linguistic parsing.

3. The third set of contributions contains case studies, namely on the interrelations between discourse and discovery. F. Hallyn, De Waele and Vervenne, Niiniluoto, and Kuipers must be mentioned here. Hallyn elaborates on the role of metaphor in the work of Kepler and its connection with manneristic aesthetics. De Waele and Vervenne introduce their observational study in a scientific laboratory. They discuss some possible projections which can be made and which are relevant for theories on scientific discourse, on scientific discovery

and scientific justification. Niiniluoto investigates the development in operational research and relates this development with the Kuhnian and the Laudanian approach. The Laudanian problem-solving activity, present in operational research, conflicts in his view with the cognitive and truth-seeking features of science. Pearce and Rantala in their paper "Ramsey eliminability revisited", review briefly this already "classic problem" and they try to show how, in the light of some new developments in mathematical logic, a fresh outlook on this topic can be made. Kuipers scrutinizes the discovery problems in intentional explanation and intentional behaviour.

4. Last but not least we want to mention the set of contributions containing elaborations of discourse and the logic of justification. We believe that the papers of Dacey, Phalet, Van Bendeghem and Batens could be classified under this heading. Dacey introduces a very interesting game-theoretical approach to the logic of scientific discourse. The actors are man and nature, and the prupose is to evaluate hypotheses. His conclusions are at the least very striking. Let us mention only that he maintains that with act-independent detections the scientist is capable of protecting himself from deception. But in a realistic model of the scientists, the scientist is incapable of doing so. Phalet dwells extensively on Kepler's development of his system of planetary motion. He does this in function of elaborating a dynamic logic, as a logic of evolving theories, aimed at controlling discovery in science and aimed at making possible true axiomatisations of theories. Batens pays much attention to the problem of inferences from inconsistent premises and to some extent also to the enrichment which may arise from the removal of inconsistencies.

This in a nutshell is a perspective on the contributions of the papers in this book to the general problem of logic of discovery and logic of discourse. But still some will ask "What is the relevance of this topic for science and its development and for society and its development?" We believe that a better knowledge of the logic of discovery, logic of discourse and their interrelations is a sine qua non for a better and more efficient understanding and control of science, and its role in nature and society.

For knowledge in general (and scientific knowledge in particular), nature and society are interdependent. In this view we follow the strict nominalism of the sofists, of Frege in certain interpretations, and perhaps even Averroism, at least in its antiplatonic development. Consequently, a rational science policy and a rational methodology presuppose a better knowledge of the interrelations between discourse, discovery, justification and their respective logics. In order more consciously to make decisions for the realisation of a better mankind, a better world and a better man in a better world, we need to be aware of the functioning and the integration of the logics of discourse, discovery and justification, used by man for making his construction of his world, his tools, his action strategies. Having knowledge of this integration we have a better chance for a more efficient coordination and cooperation in order to realize progress. Progress in method, progress in knowledge, but anyway progress for a better and therefore for a more pluralistic world.

REFERENCES

FOUCAULT, Michel, 1971, *L'ordre du discours.* Paris, Gallimard.

GRIZE, Jean-Blaise, 1980. Pour aborder l'étude des structures du discours quotidien. In: Boriocha et Portine, *Langue française, argumentation et énonciation.*

HANSON, N. R., 1958. The logic of discovery. *Journal of Philosophy*, Vol. IV, pp. 1073–1089.

HINTIKKA, J. and Merrill B. HINTIKKA, 1982. Sherlock Holmes confronts modern logic: toward a theory of information seeking through questioning. In: Barth & Martens, *Argumentation, approaches to theory formation,* Vol. 8, SLCS, Benjamins BV, Amsterdam.

1

LOGIC OF DISCOVERY AND LOGIC OF DISCOURSE

TRUE AND FALSE LOGICS OF SCIENTIFIC DISCOVERY

Jaakko Hintikka

1. Introduction

This paper is a first step in a larger enterprise. The ultimate aim of my enterprise is to uncover the logical structures, in a strict sense of the word "logic", typically involved in scientific enterprise, not just in the justification of already obtained results but in the acquisition of new information.

Needless to say, such an enterprise is too large to be carried out in one paper. For those reason I shall in this paper restrict myself to a couple of partly preliminary matters. They include a discussion of certain competing views on the logic of scientific discovery and an acknowledgement of the most important existing treatments which partly anticipate the leading idea of my own approach.

In the title of this paper and in the paper itself, it is important to keep in mind that the word "logic" is to be taken quite seriously. The structures I am concerned with uncovering are intended to be of the same kind as the structures studied in mathematical logic and foundations of mathematics. I have a great deal of sympathy with the intentions of those philosphers who speak of "informal logic", but I don't think any clarity is gained by using the term "logic" for what they are doing.

2. False logics of discovery

But hasn't the logic of discovery already been discovered ? Indeed, speaking of the true logic of scientific discovery presupposes that there are false ones on the market. This is in fact the case. Indeed, misconceptions concerning the subject are many and ripe. For instance, there are those who declare any logic of scientific discovery impossible, on the ground that there are no mechanical rules for the "lucky guesses" that are required for the advance of science. Their premise may be right, but the conclusion does not follow. For by the same token there could not be any logic of deductive inference either, for it is well known that there are no mechanical procedures for finding desired logical proofs outside the most elementary department of logic.

In fact, if the philosophers who believe that there are no mechanical rules for scientific discovery want to prove their thesis instead of holding it as an unexamined dogma, they very likely will have to resort to some explicit formulation of the logic of inquiry themselves. Ironically, it is the logicians of science — that is, the philosophers who use explicit logical tools in their theories of the scientific procedure — who are in the best position to answer the question whether scientific discovery can be subjected to rules, to answer it negatively, and to actually *prove* their answer.

Some philosophers base the same impossibility claim on Thomas Kuhn's theory of scientific revolutions which is supposed to show that a major scientific breakthrough is not subject to logic because it means a shift in the "paradigm" which guides an entire research tradition and is not a subject of rational choice (1). But an appeal to Kuhn's actual views doesn't help them at all. In this matter, Kuhn is not a Kuhnian. Not only has he renounced the term "paradigm"; he is on the record as saying that the first people to take his theoretical ideas seriously were those philosophers, especially Sneed and Stegmüller (2), who have built formal models of theory change by means of set-theoretical conceptualizations (3). Indeed, the rise of this so-called structuralist school was the most important development in the philosophy of science in the seventies.

Unfortunately, the conception of the logic of science represented by the structuralist school also leaves a great deal to be desired. The main novelty of the structuralist approach is usually explained by saying that it lies in the replacement of the *statement view* of theories by a *structuralist view*. According to the former, so the story goes, theories are conceived of as sets of statements, whereas in the latter theories are characterized by their models.

This characterization is nevertheless misleading to the point of being perverse. It reduces the difference between the two views very nearly to a purely conventional choice of a jargon. On the one hand, in any view a set of statements specifies a set of models. This determination can in fact vary a great deal. For instance, a scientist might very well choose to accept only certain special models as the intended realizations of his assumptions. Moreover, and most importantly, the properties of statements studied in formal logic include those that serve these statements to determine (partly) their models (including certain aspects of the structure of those models). Even as simple a concept as logical implication has a neat model-theoretical import : X implies Y if and only if all the models of X are among those of Y. Hence the "statement view" is in reality perfectly compatible with the idea that theories are to be characterized in terms of their models.

If there is a real weakness in the so-called statement view, it is not that it operated with statements, but that the properties of statements it operated with were few and far apart and insufficiently grounded on model-theoretic considerations. One of those restrictions was the identification of a scientific theory with a deductive system. In brief, the logic of science of the statement view was wrong, not because of the role of statements, but because the logic this view presupposed was too poor.

The real question is therefore not whether the statement view should have been rejected but what the richer logic is that it should be replaced by. Some of the representatives of the so-called structuralist view answer this question in effect by going to the other extreme and using the full force of unrestricted set theory — to all practical purposes, the full force of classical mathematics — in theory conceptualizations. This is a very questionable procedure. It runs the risk of committing one of the same mistakes as the statement view committed, viz. severing the connection between, on the one hand, the actual formulation of a theory in some language or other, and the properties of its models on the other hand. For the model-theoretical properties of full set theory are extremely tricky, as is illustrated by the difficulty of various consistency and relative consistency problems. The "classical" structuralist view thus also fails to give a satisfactory answer to the question : What is the true logic of scientific theorizing".

Another way of looking at the predicament of the hard-line structuralists is the following : One important motive they have had is to keep their dscussion independent of commitments to one particular language, and to concentrate simply and solely on the intended models of a theory. I find this idea very suspect. It is simply an illusion to think that we can deal with the models of a theory directly, without the help of some language or other. The real problem is not to dispense with references to a language, but to find the most suitable language to operate with one. The choice of this language is a delicate matter. It should be rich enough to do justice to actual scientific theorizing, and at the same time it should be simple enough so that its model-theoretic behavior can be mastered. It seems to me that even though the proper choice may be difficult, the resources of model theory and abstract logics have not been harnessed to the use of the philosophy of science in the way they would and should.

The illusion of language-independence is generated in the "structuralist" work by ample use of set theory without explicit reference to its axiomatization. This is not a satisfactory procedure philosophically, and I don't think that it is the best approach technically, either. Unrestricted (unaxiomatized) use of set theory is a difficult and untidy subject. Set theory is hence not the true logic of scientific inquiry.

Indeed, these viewpoints even suggest an answer to the question : if first-order languages are not rich enough, where should we look for richer ones ? The kind of answer my remarks bring close is to say : some extension of first-order languages which does not make the model theory of the outcome language hopelessly difficult. Candidates for this role include some of the simpler infinitary languages, for instance L_{w1w} in which one can for instance develop a neat model theory of probability theory (4). Other candidates which have not received sufficient attention include the outcome of imposing some further model-theoretical restraints on models of first-order sentences, e.g. restriction to saturated models or to prime models. Such restrictions add a great deal of expressive power, messing up the model theory of one's language.

An interesting fresh answer to this question has been put forward recently by Veikko Rantala and David Pearce (5). They propose to view scientific theorizing from the vantage point of recently developed theories of abstract logic and abstract model theory. This approach to the logic of science is very interesting and promising. We can expect that it will soon produce enough specific results to estimate its true worth.

I have a suspicion that there is ample room for further approaches, however. More specifically, I suspect that somewhat older and less fancy logical tools than those wielded by Rantala and Pearce can still give us plenty of mileage. It has become fashionable to criticize old-fashioned logic of science because it relied on first-order languages, and to criticize first-order languages as being too poor for the representation of actual scientific theories. This view may very well be true, but I doubt very much that it catches the most important parameter. I suspect that old-fashioned philosophy of science was relatively fruitless, not because the languages it dealt with were too poor, but became the model-theoretic and even proof-theoretic concepts it applied to these languages were too poor. This opens the door once again with vengance to the question : What are the richer concepts we should use ? What is the true logic of scientific discovery ?

3. Popper's non-logic of scientific discovery

In trying to answer this question, we don't get much help from Sir Karl Popper, either (6). According to his own principles, there is in the literal sense of the word no logic of scientific discovery. Not only is the title of his best known book a solecism according to his own principles, what is worse, Popper's constructive suggestions, whether we choose to pidgeonhole them under the heading "logic" or not, simply are not very helpful. In criticizing Carnap, Popper makes much of the inverse relation of probability and information. Since in the scientific enterprise we are seeking information (knowledge). Popper's advice for ascientist faced with the choice of a hypothesis or theory is : Be bold ! Choose the most improbable hypothesis !

Unfortunately, this is a seriously oversimplified picture. What is true is that the prior probability of a hypothesis and its absolute information are inversely related. However, hypotheses are never judged on the basis of their prior probability, but on the basis of their posterior probability (probability on evidence), while high information can very well mean high absolute one. A much better candidate for the role of an index of high informativeness is *expected* absolute information of a hypothesis. But if so, Popper's thesis is not generally valid. Given a suitable prior probability distribution, high posterior probability and high expected absolute information can very well go together (7). There simply does not exist the kind of inverse relation Popper believes in for the most interesting kinds of information and probability.

There exist mathematical results which show that boldness is one's best strategy if the odds are long against oneself (8). Such results may offer a way of vindicating partly some of Popper's ideas. This would make little difference to our overall evaluation of Sir Karl's non-logic of scientific discovery, however. It nevertheless enables me to formulate compactly what is wrong with Popper's philosophy of science. What the results I referred to mean is that it can be not only argued, but in a certain sense proved, that Popper's philosophy of science is, if not a counsel of despair, then a counsel of desperation.

4. Scientific procedure as information-seeking by questioning

Can we do better ? Yes, I believe that there were very good answers available to the question : What is the true logic of scientific discovery ? In order to find some of them, I start from an old idea which has never been exploited properly. The idea was put forward by Kant in the preface to the second edition of his *Critique of Pure Reason* (B xiii). In the scientific enterprise, Kant says there, reason "must not allow itself to be kept, as it were, in nature's leading-strings, but must itself show the way with principles of judgment based upon fixed laws, constraining nature to give answer to *questions* of reason's own determining." (Emphasis added.) In other words, the idea is to think of the scientific procedure as a series of questions the investigator puts to nature. By choosing these questions a scientist can direct the course of inquiry according to plans and principles of his or her own, like "an appointed judge who compels the witness to answer questions which he has himself formulated" (loc. cit.).

This idea of the scientific method as information-seeking by questioning has cropped up repeatedly in the literature. The best, and the best known, case in point is, undoubtedly Larry Laudan's book *Progress and its Problems* (9). Laudan rejects there all the traditional measures of the worth of theories, such as explanatory power, deductive power, high degree of confirmation, etc. In their place, Laudan puts a new criterion, the *problem-solving power* of a theory. As Laudan puts it himself in the first and foremost thesis of this book (p. 13),

> The first and essential acid test for any theory is whether it provides *acceptable answers to interesting questions* : whether, in other words, it provides satisfactory solutions to important problems. (Emphasis added.)

It seems to me that Laudan is here right in an important and fundamental way. However, I don't see that he explains the nature of this problem-solving or question-answering power as fully as one might hope. Laudan gives us a wealth of historical examples and explains carefully many qualifications which are important in applying the idea to actual historical material, such as the dependence of the class of relevant problems (questions) on pragmatic and historical factors. All this nevertheless leaves a philosophically demanding reader with a problem. What is this mysterious problem-solving power, anyway ? What are its structural characteristics, and how is it related to the logical structure of the theory in question? One way of looking at what I am trying to do here is to see my enterprise as an attempt to provide a real logic to spell out for the benefit of conceptually sophisticated philosophers what Laudan's ideas really amount to. In other words, I am trying to perform for Laudan the same service as Kuhn and Stegmüller sought to do for Thomas Kuhn, that is, to provide a real model for the suggestive but informal ideas put forward mostly in terms of historical examples.

In this spirit, then, my idea is to construe the scientific enterprise as a questioning procedure, as a series of questions put to nature or to some other source of information. There is much to be said about this model (or conceptualization) both on a general philosophical level and on a more detailed technical level. As my title indicates, I shall concentrate on one question only, which is : What kind of "logic" (in a fairly literal sense of logical structures involved) does the interrogative approach lead to ? What is on this model the real logic of scientific investigation ?

5. The logic of questions and answers

In a somewhat superficial sense, a partial answer is implicit in the basic idea of my entire approach. One kind of logic we clearly need here is the logic of questions and answers. Indeed, the reason why a questioning model of scientific inquiry has not been developed systematically before is that the crucial question-answer relation has remained almost completely unanalyzed. This has left in the air the precise issue which — as we in effect acknowledged above — is the nerve of the interrogative approach, viz. how a question conditions (partly determines) its answers. As the quote above shows, Kant was concerned with the way a researcher can by putting the right questions to nature guide her answers according to one's own plan.

In my theory of questions and answers, I offer an analysis of this crucial question-answer relation — both for conclusive (complete) answers and partial ones (10). Likewise, I have shown how the presuppositions of questions of different kinds are to be defined. This theory is here taken for granted. I don't have enough space here to expound it here. It is in any case only one ingredient in the logic of science on my interrogative model.

6. Logic of questioning and semantical tableaux

Another, still a somewhat superficial answer to the question as to what the logic of scientific investigation is, when it is construed as the logic of information-seeking by questioning, is obtained by considering what book-keeping methods one might use in one's questioning games against nature. The term "game" should be taken seriously here, for it turns out to be eminently useful to formulate our question-answer sequences in the form of games in the precise sense of the mathematical theory of games. One possible setup is the following : There are two "players" (parties) the scientist (also known as "my-self") and nature. I start out with an initial assumption T, known as the "theory", and a conclusion C I am trying to prove. The premises I am allowed to use are then essentially T and the answers to the questions I put to nature one by one.

In such circumstances, the natural book-keeping method is to use a mild extension of Beth's semantical *tableaux* (11). (Beth's method is of course related extremely closely to Hintikka's model set method and to Gentzen's calculus of sequents.) (12) In the initial situation, T is put into the left column of the *tableau* and C in its right column. In making a move I have a choice between carrying out one step of *tableau* construction according to the usual rules and putting a question to nature and entering the answer in the left column of the *tableau* in question. (More explicitly, the answer is put in the left column of the *subtableau* in question, for a question is always asked by reference to one particular *subtableau*.)

Another variant of my information-seeking games against nature — and in some ways an even more natural one — differs from the one so far presented only in that my aim in the game is to prove either C or $\sim$C. Then the semantical tableau used as our bookkeeping device is divided in two different ones, each having initially T in its left column, but the one having C in its right column while the other begins with $\sim$C in its right column. Thus this interrogative game consists essentially in my attempt to answer the "big" initial question "Is it the case that C or $\sim$C ?" by putting a number of "small" questions to my opponent.

Thus we have another relatively superficial answer to the question of what the logic of scientific information-seeking is on our interrogative model. It is an extension of the logic of Beth's semantical *tableaux*.

This answer is a step in the right direction. It enables us to formulate the explicit rules of the interrogative games of information-seeking, as we shall do below. It also enables us to show how actual examples of information-seeking by questioning can be "formalized", that is, represented in the canonical notation of semantical *tableaux*. (Of course, I am not "formalizing" them in the pejorative sense of turning them into uninterpreted calculi.)

7. The two roles of questions. Restraint on "small" questions

This does not yet close the question as to what the real logic of questioning and hence the real logic of scientific discovery is in the last analysis. The characterization given above of question-answer "games" is still incomplete in several crucial respects.

First and foremost, questions and answers enter into the scientific process in more than one way. Laudan is primarily emphasizing that the *aim* of a scientific theory is to solve important problems, to answer important questions. Kant's emphasis is on questions as a *means* of scientific inquiry. These two points are not incompatible, and are in fact combined in my *tableaux* formalization. When the aim of a questioning game is to prove C *or* ∼C, we can say that the aim of the game is to answer a "big" question ("Is it the case that C or that ∼C ?") by means of a number of "small" questions the investigator puts to nature.

The highlights the fact that certain restraints must be placed on the "small" questions (questions actually asked in the course of a game), lest the game be trivial. For if no restraints are imposed, a player can address at once to the source of information the question : "C or not ∼C ?" and thereby trivialize the whole process. It has been shown by Richard Robinson (13) that Aristotle's injunction against *petitio principii* was, as the term suggests, intended precisely as a way of avoiding the trivialization of academic question-answer dialogues precisely in the way indicated.

In order to discover the real logic of the scientific process, we thus have to discuss the nature of the restraints that have to be imposed on the "small" questions to yes-or-no questions concerning the truth of atomic sentences (14).

8. Presuppositions of questions and questioning

Another important aspect of the logic of knowledge-seeking by questioning is the role of presuppositions of questions. It was already mentioned above in section 5 that my theory of questions and answers provides a definition of the presupposition of different kinds of questions. Again, it would take me too far to enter the details here. Instead, I shall call attention to a general distinction, which is at the same time a comment on earlier theorists of questions and answers.

Presuppositions of questions can enter into the tableaux formalization through the requirement that I can ask a question if its presupposition occurs in the left column of my *tableau.* This means that they have an important role in the determination of the optimal questioning strategies. One important aim of asking questions can be to get an answer which can serve as presupposition for promising further questions.

Over and above the entries to the left column of my *tableau* which come about in the course of a questioning game, there is in it also the initial theoretical assumption T (cf. section 6 above). Its logical consequences can serve as a presupposition to a suitable question, and in general it serves as a kind of presupposition (in a non-technical sense of the word) to the whole questioning enterprise.

This role of the original theoretical assumption T has not always been appreciated. For instance, in Collingwood's approach the role of the basic theoretical assumption T is assimilated completely to that of the presuppositions of particular "small" questions (15).

One of the crucial aspects of any satisfactory logic of the scientific enterprise, conceptualized as a question-answer sequence, will be an analysis of the precise role of the basic theoretical presupposition T of one's questioning procedure. One important fact is that some nontrivial theoretical assumption is often unavoidable. For instance, if the "small" questions are limited so as to pertain to the truth of atomic sentences only, only a limited number of "big" questions can be eventually answered. In contrast, it is known that, even if the same restriction is imposed on "small" questions, *every* "big" question (in a natural sense of the term) can be answered on the basis of a suitable "theory" T. even when the theory itself does not entail these answers (16). This illustrates vividly the role of the theoretical assumption T.

NOTES

(1)   See T.S. Kuhn, *The Structure of Scientific Revolutions,* second ed., The University of Chicago Press, 1970; T.S. Kuhn, *The Essential Tension : Selected Studies in Scientific Tradition and Change,* The University of Chicago Press, 1977; Gary Cutting, editor, *Paradigms and Revolutions; Applications and Appraisals of Science,* University of Notre Dama Press,

12.

Notre Dame, 1980; Ian Hacking, editor, *Scientific Revolutions* (Oxford Readings in Philosophy), Oxford U.P., 1981.

(2)   See J.D. Sneed, *The Logical Structure of Mathematical Physics,* D. Reidel, Dordrecht, 1971; Wolfgang Stegmüller, *Theorienstruktur und Theoriendynamik,* Springer-Verlag, Berlin-Heidelberg-New York, 1973; Wolfgang Stegmüller, *Theory Construction, Structure, and Rationality,* Springer-Verlag, 1979. Useful surveys of the tradition Sneed and Stegmüller started are Ilkka Niiniluoto, The Growth of Theories : Comments on the Structuralist Approach in Jaakko Hintikka et al., editors, *Theory Change Ancient Axiomatics, and Galileo's Methodology,* D. Reidel, Dordrecht, 1980, pp. 3–47; and Ilkka Niiniluoto, "Scientific Progress", *Synthese* vol. 45 (1980), pp. 427–462.

(3)   See *Erkenntnis* vol. 10, no 2 (July 1976), with contributions by Sneed, Stegmüller, and Kuhn.

(4)   Cf. Dana Scott and Peter Krauss, "Assigning Probabilities to Logical Formulas" in Jaakko Hintikka and Patrick Suppes, editors, *Aspects of Indicative Logic,* North-Holland, Amsterdam, 1966, pp. 219–264.

(5)   See David Pearce and Veikko Rantala, "On a New Approach to Metascience", *Reports from the Department of Philosophy,* University of Helsinki, no. 1 (1981), pp. 1–42 (with further references).

(6)   Karl R. Popper, *The Logic of Scientific Discovery,* Hutchinson, London, 1959; Karl R. Popper, *Conjectures and Refutations,* Routledge and Kegan Paul, London 1963; Karl Popper, *Objective Knowledge,* Oxford U.P., 1972; P.A. Schilpp, editor, *The Philosophy of Karl Popper I–II,* Open Court, La Salle, Ill., 1974.

(7)   See Jaakko Hintikka and Juhani Pictarinen, "Semantic Information and Inductive Logic" in Jaakko Hintikka and Patrick Suppes, editors, *Aspects of Inductive Logic,* North-Holland, Amsterdam, 1966, pp. 96–112; Jaakko Hintikka, "Varieties of Information and Scientific Explanation", in B. van Rootselaar and J.F. Staal, editors, *Logic, Methodology, and Philosophy of Science III : Proceedings of the 1967 Congress,* North-Holland, Amsterdam, 1968. Of course we have to restrict our attention to a relevant range of hypotheses, but there is nothing *ad hoc* about such restrictions.

(8)   Cf., e.g., Lester E. Dubins and Leonard J. Savage, *How To Gamble If You Must : Inequalities for Stochastic Processes,* McGraw-Hill, New York, 1965.

(9)   Larry Laudan, *Progress and Its Problems : Towards a Theory of Scientific Growth,* University of California Press, Berkeley, 1977; Larry Laudan, *Science and Hypothesis,* D. Reidel, Dordrecht, 1981; Larry Laudan, "A Problem-solving Approach to Scientific Progress" in Ian Hacking, editor (note 1 above).

(10) Jaakko Hintikka, *The Semantics of Questions and the Questions of Semantics* (Acta Philosophica Fennica, vol. 28, no. 4), Helsinki, 1976; "New Foundations for a Theory of Questions and Answers", forthcoming; "Questions with Outside Quantifiers" in Robinson Schneider et al., editors, *Papers from the Parasession on Nondeclaratives,* Chicago Linguistics Society, Chicago, 1982, pp. 83–92.

(11) E. W. Beth, "Semantic Entailment and Formal Derivability", *Mededelingen van de Koninklijke Nederlandse Akademie van Wetenschappen,* Afd. Letterkunde, N.R. vol. 18, no. 13, Amsterdam, 1955, pp. 309–342; reprinted in Jaakko Hintikka, editor, *Philosophy of Mathematics,* Oxford U.P., 1969, pp. 9–41.

(12) One can construe a *tableau* construction as an attempt to construct a model set in which the entries in the left *tableau* column are all included but which does not contain any entries in the right *tableau* column. If you turn a closed *tableau* upside down you obtain a Gentzen-type proof of the desired sequent.

(13) Richard Robinson, "Begging the Question 1971", *Analysis,* vol. 31 (1971), pp. 113–117.

(14) If my questioning games are thought of as research games against nature, the motivation of this restriction is clear. Nature can directly tell us what is true or false in particular cases, not whether some complicated sentence involving nested quantifiers is true or false.

(15) Cf. R. G. Collingwood, *An Essay on Metaphysics,* Clarendon Press, Oxford, 1940; R. G. Collingwood, *An Autobiography,* Clarendon Press, Oxford, 1939; Michael Krausz, "The Logic of Absolute Presuppositions" in Michael Krausz, editor, *Critical Essays on the Philosophy of R. G.*

Collingwood, Clarendon Press, Oxford, 1972, pp. 222–240.

(16) This is shown by the existence of theories which are model-complete but not complete. Cf., e.g. Abraham Robinson, *Introduction to Model Theory and to the Metamathematics of Algebra,* North-Holland, Amsterdam, 1963.

CONTINUITY AND SCIENTIFIC DISCOVERY

David Pearce and Veikko Rantala

According to a common view in the traditional philosophy of science, scientific change is continuous and scientifid knowledge cumulative. Even in radical changes of theories, there obtains a natural connection between the supplanting and supplanted theories. This view has also been typical in science, especially among physicists. Sometimes this belief is formulated, after Nils Bohr, as the *Correspondence Principle* (CP) which says that in scientific change (concerning mature sciences) there obtains, at the very least, a *correspondence relation* between the old and the new theory. This means usually that the former is a *limiting case* of the latter. Typical cases can be found in physics. In the following list, a theory or law mentioned in the left column is thought of as being a limiting case of the one on the right :

Kepler's theory of planetary motion	Newton's theory of gravitation
classical particle mechanics	relativistic particle mechanics
,, ,, ,,	non-relativistic quantum mechanics
non-relativistic quantum mechanics	relativistic quantum mechanics
Boyle-Mariotte's law	van der Waal's law
geometrical optics	wave optics
phenomenological thermodynamics	statistical thermodynamics

etc.

Similar examples can be found in mathematics (e.g., Euclidean *vs.* non-Euclidean geometry). Whether there are analogous cases in other sciences is not clear.

The criticism that started in the sixties against the traditional view has challenged the assumption of continuity. Thus according to Kuhn, CP does not hold since in a scientific revolution the meanings of scientific terms change. Even though we can formally pass from the relativistic force law to Newton's second law by means of a limit procedure, there is no real correspondence between classical and relativistic particle mechanics; for instance, "mass" has different meanings in these two theories. Similar arguments have also been presented by some other critics, such as Hanson and Feyerabend.

On the other hand, there still are philosophers who defend continuity and CP and oppose Kuhn by claiming that there need not be any meaning variance in revolutionary scientific changes; rather it is the case that the two theories describe the *same* concept or entity in different, even incompatible ways. Thus according to Krajewski (1977), both classical and relativistic mechanics define "mass" similarly, as a measure of inertia; whence its meaning does not change. Even in a case where meaning may change, the change is not so radical that it would destroy correspondence; there is a relation between the new and the old meaning of the term.

In the light of this controversy, we can see that the debate of whether scientific change is continuous concentrates on the question of meaning variance. Although we shall not provide any explicit analysis of what meaning change would mean in this context, we claim that both parties are partly mistaken, but for opposite reasons. Kuhn and the others are wrong since, we claim, correspondence may hold in spite of meaning change; the opposing party is wrong since meaning change may take place in spite of correspondence. Actually, it even seems that in a general case, meaning change and correspondence belong rather naturally together. But this presupposes that the oversimplified deductive notion of correspondence which is typical for the debate is abandoned.

1. Correspondence and Discovery

Even from elementary textbooks of physics it can be seen that in many cases the derivation or formulation of a new, revolutionary theory or law is at least to some extent based on its predecessors. This may also be the way in which the new theory is originally invented. Thus, for instance, the force law of special relativity (the Minkowsky force law) can be derived from Newton's second law by replacing absolute time by local time; and the Lorentz transformation by combining the assumptions that the velocity of light is constant and that the *abstract form* of the Galilean transformation is preserved, in a relevant sense (see Eisele, 1969). Another way to derive the force law is to assume the Lorentz transformation plus the "classical" law of the conservation of momentum. This is close to Einstein's own procedure.

The discovery of special theory of relativity is of course an exceptionally clear-cut example of how a new theory can be grounded on the old one so that continuity will hold, in this case in the form of correspondence. But, as is well known, an analogous relationship obtains more generally in the developments of physics; at least it is often thought so (see above). Some philosophers of science even think that this kind of continuity provides general *heuristic principles* in the search for new theories. According to Post (1971), and Nickles (1980), these principles provide *guiding* and *constraining* rules rather than any logic of discovery (in some strict sense of logic). It is equally important that they provide a way of *appraising* and theoretically "testing" the new theory, thus a method of justification.

In this paper, we shall only consider how such heuristic rules can be associated with CP and a closely related principle concerning symmetries.

It is suggested in Post (1971) that one heuristic rule which can be obtained from CP is that a new theory T' should *explain* its predecessor theory T, and, especially, T' should explain the *success* of T. Thus, e.g., special theory of relativity explains the success of classical mechanics concerning the motion of particles having relatively slow velocity. This is a way to appraise T'. The role of CP as a guiding principle is especially clear if T is to be a limiting case of T'. This is exemplified by the derivation of special relativity mentioned above.

Since symmetries and invariance principles have a crucial and explicit role in physics, an important question is how the symmetries of T and T' are possibly related in their correspondence. This question has been discussed by some philosophers of physics (e.g., Post, 1971; Redhead, 1975). If an invariance principle is thought of as an acceptable or universal "superprinciple" governing the laws of nature, it is assumed to hold for the new theory (cf. Wigner, 1967). Then it is clear that it plays a role of heuristic constraint: the laws of the theory have to be invariant with respect to the accepted symmetry transformations. But, on the other hand, whether such an invariance principle is ultimately acceptable may depend on continuity considerations: the structural features of relevant symmetries are to be *preserved* in the correspondence.

In the rest of this paper, we shall discuss these ideas and claims in terms of our reconstructed notions of theory and correspondence, introduced in our earlier papers (see Pearce and Rantala, 1983a, 1983b). This will provide an exact meaning for them.

2. Correspondence Reconstructed

Our view of theories is *structural.* By a *theory* we mean a structure

$$T = <\tau, N, M, R>$$

where

(i) τ is a similarity type;

(ii)   N is a class of models of type τ;

(iii) $M \subseteq N$;

(iv)   R is a collection of relations of the form $R = \{<M_1,...,M_n; h>,...\}$ where $h = <h_1,...,h_k>$ is a sequence of relations between various domains of $M_1,...,M_n \in N$;

(v)   the collections N,M,R are set-theoretically definable; N and M satisfy appropriate closure conditions so that they can be defined in some logic.

Some comments are in order here :

(1) This notion of theory is of course more restricted (in various ways) than actual theories. It must be thought of as a "technical unit" which can be used for various metatheoretical purposes.

(2) The notions of similarity type and model are to be understood in a broad sense. For instance, a model may be thought of as a many-sorted structure in the sense of Feferman (1974), or as a Kripke model, etc.

(3) R can be generalized in many ways; it is only a technical matter. For instance, the elements of some $R \in R$ could contain infinitely many M_i's and h_i's. But the finite case takes care, e.g., of symmetry transformations h: $M_1 \rightarrow M_2$; and this ia a very important special case.

(4) Any sequence $<M_1,...,h>$ can be construed as a model of an appropriate type. This type is an expansion of τ.

Even though our notion of theory is structural, we consider the *role of logic* very important, even essential, here. By "a logic" we mean a logic in a *generalized sense* (as in abstract logic, or even more broadly). We do not fix any logic in advance by requiring that some given logic is to be applied to all theories, or to all theories under consideration. Instead, we even allow different logics to be applied to the same theory, even at the same time, so to speak. Which logic is chosen depends on mathematical and pragmatic considerations, perhaps even esthetic ones.

It follows from these methodological principles that logic no longer constrains metascientific study to the same extent as the traditional metascience. But it is still its function to give us an object language in which metatheoretical entities, perhaps even scientific entities themselves, can be precisely and explicitly described. Thus we are also generalizing the structuralist conception of theory (cf. Pearce and Rantala, 1983c).

We call any logic in which M and N are definable *adequate for* T. In applications, it may be natural to choose, if possible, an adequate logic which has some desirable properties (e.g., interpolation and definability, or compactness properties, and so on) or which has a clear-cut syntactic structure, or which is as weak as possible as to its expressive power. In general, "well-behaved" logics should be favoured. We may occasionally use other logics, too, besides adequate ones, for instance, for ontological reasons — to justify existence of some entities needed.

In terms of this theory concept, it is a rather straightforward task to define a correspondence relation so that it in a honest and abstract way generalizes this notion as it is used by physicists and philosophers of physics. At the same time it will generalize the notions of reduction and interpretation as they are used by logicians (see Enderton, 1972; Shoenfield, 1967; Szczerba, 1977).

If L is a logic, let $\mathrm{Sent}_L(\tau)$ be its class of sentences of type τ and let $\models_L$ denote its truth relation. Let $T = \langle \tau, N, M, R \rangle$ and $T' = \langle \tau', N', M', R' \rangle$ be theories. Let L and L' be logics which are adequate for T and T', respectively. Then a *correspondence of* T *to* T', *relative to* $\langle L, L' \rangle$, is a pair $\langle F, I \rangle$ of mappings :

(i) $F: K' \xrightarrow{\text{onto}} K$, where K and K' are non-empty subclasses of M and M', respectively,

(ii) $I: \mathrm{Sent}_L(\tau) \to \mathrm{Sent}_{L'}(\tau')$

such that the following conditions hold :

(2.1) K is definable in L and K' in L';

(2.2) for all $M \in K'$ and all $\varphi \in \mathrm{Sent}_L(\tau)$, $F(M) \models_L \varphi \Longleftrightarrow M \models_{L'} I(\varphi)$.

The mapping F is called the *structural correlation* and I the *translation* of the correspondence. In actual cases, the translation naturally reflects the formation of the structural correlation. The conditions (2.1) and (2.2) are necessary for continuity, for they guarantee that some relevant features *transfer* from one theory to the other. (2.2) states that *truth is preserved* by the mappings. If, in paticular, L' = L, we may require that F itself is definable in L, in a suitable sense.

A special case of correspondence, which is closer to the original sense of the word, is obtained by adding the condition that T is obtainable from T' as a limiting case. This means, intuitively, that the models in K are obtainable from the models in K' by some "limit" procedure; and similarly for the relations in R and R' (or rather, their appropriate restrictions). However, this limiting procedure can be replaced by an appropriate use of *non-standard topology,* generalizing more familiar methods of non-standard analysis (see Robinson, 1966; Machover and Hirschfeld, 1969). In its terms, the limiting case condition can be expressed as follows :

(2.3) for each $M \in K'$, $F(M)$ is a *standard approximation* of M; and analogously for the relations.

The notion of standard approximation used here is a straightforward generalization of a similar notion in the ordinary non-standard analysis. We cannot discuss it here, however (see Pearce and Rantala, 1983a).

From our general notion of correspondence we get, as a special case, a definition of *reduction* by stating that $K = M$, and that of *interpretation* by the condition $K' = M'$.

All these intertheory relations can be developed in several directions. For instance, a structural correlation can be defined more extensively; the definitions of the mappings can be refined; instead of considering single theories, one can define theory nets (like Balzer and Sneed, 1977) and consider relations between theories belonging to the same net or different nets. We shall not discuss these elaborations here (but see Pearce and Rantala, 1983b, 1983d).

3. Continuity in Correspondence

Let T and T' be theories as above such that there obtains a correspondence $\langle F, I \rangle$ of T to T', as defined above. To simplify our discussion, let us assume that the classes in question are axiomatised as follows :

$$M = \mathrm{Mod}_L(\Theta) \qquad\qquad M' = \mathrm{Mod}_{L'}(\Theta')$$
$$K = \mathrm{Mod}_L(\Theta) \cap \mathrm{Mod}_L(\sigma) \qquad K' = \mathrm{Mod}_{L'}(\Theta') \cap \mathrm{Mod}_{L'}(\sigma')$$
$$= \mathrm{Mod}_L(\{\Theta, \sigma\}) \qquad\qquad = \mathrm{Mod}_{L'}(\{\Theta', \sigma'\})$$

where Θ, $\sigma \in \mathrm{Sent}_L(\tau)$ and Θ', $\sigma' \in \mathrm{Sent}_{L'}(\tau')$ (cf. (2.1), above). Since $K \vDash_L \Theta$, it follows from (2.2) (by (ii)) that $K' \vDash_{L'} I(\Theta)$, whence

(3.1) $\{\Theta', \sigma'\} \vDash_{L'} I(\Theta)$.

Thus in a case of correspondence, the supplanting theory T' *explains* the supplanted theory T in a very clear-cut sense: The *translation* of the axiom of T is implied by the axiom of T' together with an additional (consistent) hypothesis.

Assuming that the models in K represent phenomena, physical systems, or the like, with respect to which T has proved "successful", we can even say that T' *explains this success* in the following sense: Given any $\varphi \in \text{Sent}_L(\tau)$ such that $\{\Theta, \sigma\} \vDash_L \varphi$, it follows from our conditions that

(3.2) $\{\Theta', \sigma'\} \vDash_{L'} I(\varphi)$.

In view of (3.1) and (3.2), we are entitled to say that there exists some amount of continuity in the transition from T to T'. How good the explanations (3.1) and (3.2) are depends, of course, on many factors, as, e.g., how natural is the hypothesis σ', how workable is the logic L', how effective is the translation I, and so on. It seems, however, that the logical features of our reconstructed notion of correspondence are in conformity with the informal discussion of Section 1.

We consider next symmetries more closely. Thus we assume that R contains relations which can be construed as symmetries. That is, if $R = \{<M_1, M_2; h>,...\}$ is such a relation, then $M_1, M_2 \in M$ and $h{:}M_1 \to M_2$ is a symmetry transformation. As we have argued elsewhere (Pearce and Rantala, 1983e), such a symmetry can be construed as a *category* M whose objects are all the models and morphisms all the symmetry transformations occurring in R. Given M, we consider its full subcategory K which is determined by K. Similarly we consider symmetry categories M', of T' and their full subcategories K' determined by K'. It is very natural to ask now how such categories determined by K and K' can be related in the correspondence. It may then appear that the structural correlation F is extendable to a mapping $\overline{F}$ such that the categorial structure of relevant symmetries, say K, K', is preserved under $\overline{F}$; that is, $\overline{F}$ will be a functor from K' to K. As we maintained in Pearce and Rantala (1983e), this seems to be a natural construal of the idea that relevant symmetries are somehow preserved in a scientific change represented by a correspondence. Thus it means that it is their abstract *algebraic* (categorial) *structure* which is preserved, rather than those symmetries themselves. This feature provides another important measure of continuity in scientific change, but on a different level than the continuity of laws.

We shall not discuss here how the structure of other "metarelations", i.e., relations in R, R', could be related to each other. But the role of symmetries seems to be more important in actual scientific changes.

REFERENCES

BALZER, W., and SNEED, J.D., "Generalized Net Structures of Empirical

Theories I", *Studia Logica* 36 (1977), 195–211.

EISELE, J.A., *Modern Quantum Mechanics with Applications to Elementary Particle Physics,* John Wiley & Sons, New York-London, 1969.

ENDERTON, H.B., *A Mathematical Introduction to Logic,* Academic Press, New York-London, 1972.

PEFERMAN, S., "Two Notes on Abstract Model Theory I", *Fundamenta Mathematica* 82 (1974), 153–165.

KRAJEWSKI, w., *Correspondence Principle and Growth of Science,* D. Reidel, Dordrecht, 1977.

MACHOVER, M., and HIRSCHFELD, J., *Lectures on Non-Standard Analysis,* Lecture Notes in Mathematics 94, Springer-Verlag, Berlin-Heidelberg-New York, 1969.

NICKLES, T., "Introductory Essay: Scientific Discovery and the Future of Philosophy of Science", in T. Nickles (ed.), *Scientific Discovery, Logic, and Rationality,* D. Reidel, Dordrecht, 1980, pp. 1–59.

PEARCE, D. and RANTALA, V., "A Logical Study of the Correspondence Relation", forthcoming (1983a).

PEARCE, D. and RANTALA, V., "Logical Aspects of Scientific Reduction", *Proceedings of the Seventh International Wittgenstein Symposium,* forthcoming (1983b).

PEARCE, R. and RANTALA, V., "New Foundations for Metascience", *Synthese,* forthcoming (1983c).

PEARCE, D. and RANTALA, V., "Constructing a General Model of Theory Dynamics", *Studia Logica,* forthcoming (1983d).

PEARCE, R. and RANTALA, V., "The Logical Study of Symmetries in Scientific Change", *Proceedings of the Seventh International Wittgenstein Symposium,* forthcoming (1983e).

POST, H. R., "Correspondence,Invariance and Heuristics: In Praise of Conservative Induction", *Studies in History and Philosophy of Science* 2 (1971),

213–255.

REDHEAD, M.L.G., "Symmetry in Intertheory Relations", *Synthese* 32 (1975), 77–112.

ROBINSON, A., *Non-Standard Analysis,* North-Holland, Amsterdam, 1966.

SHOENFIELD, J.R., *Mathematical Logic,* Addison-Wesley, Reading, Mass., 1967.

SZCZERBA, L.W., "Interpretability of Elementary Theories", in R. E. Butts and J. Hintikka (eds), *Logic, Foundations of Mathematics, and Computability Theory,* D. Reidel, Dordrecht, 1977.

WIGNER, E.P., *Symmetries and Reflections,* Indiana University Press, Bloomington-London, 1967.

SEPARATING PROBLEMS FROM THEIR BACKGROUNDS:
A QUESTION—THEORETIC PROPOSAL*

Matti Sintonen
University of Helsinki

1. Introduction

According to what may be called 'the received view', scientific problems can easily be distinguished from the theoretical background from which they arise. The best proponent of this view is Karl Popper: problems are identified as non-theoretically perceived phenomena (such as the problem of the planets), and they have a life independent from the background theories and other assumptions which scientists may have when they attempt to solve them. The latter belong to the problem situation, not to the problem itself (Popper, 1972, pp. 172–173). Problems thus are conceptually shallow. Only background theories, putative solutions, can be conceptually (and historically) deep.

Recent studies by the 'friends of discovery' (e.g. Gary Gutting, Thomas Nickles, J.N. Hattiangadi, and to a lesser degree Larry Laudan) have made the received view suspect. The emerging rival view holds that problems themselves have conceptual depth. In its most extreme version it maintains that problems cannot be separated from their backgrounds at all: all constraints imposed by background theories are in fact constitutive of the problem.

No one has in all seriousness held the extreme view, for it has unpalatable or even absurd consequences. For instance, it implies that problems can have no history. The intuitive view that Ptolemy, Copernicus and Galilei dealt with *the same* problem of the planets turns out to be an illusion. Since they worked in quite different intellectual atmospheres, their problems were quite different. It cannot even be said that one investigator attempts to solve a problem at different times, if that investigator alters his theoretical beliefs. Every time there is even a minor change in his web of belief, he has a new problem.

The friends of discovery have acknowledged the difficulty (see e.g. Nickles, 1981, p. 98), but the specific proposals for its elimination leave room for further development. In this essay I sketch a question-theoretic proposal which, I argue, provides a promising setting for these developments. First, problems are identified as various types of questions. This allows us to use erotetic logic to explicate scientific problems (see, e.g., Hintikka, 1981, and Niiniluoto, 1976). Secondly, I want to 'embed' questions so defined into pragmatic problem- and knowledge-situations. More specifically, scientific problems arise within scientific communities which hold a Kuhn-theory. The presuppositions which structure problems come from the various elements of Kuhn-theories. Furthermore, there are constraints on solutions not constitutive of the problems themselves. These constraints come from the fundamental metaphysical assumptions and values associated with a Kuhnian theory.

As a result of this enriched question-theoretic model we can get workable criteria of identity for scientific problems. First, problems can be identified as the *illocutionary contents* of the speech acts performed by investigators belonging to various scientific communities. Secondly, they can be identified in a more fine-grained fashion as complete questions which arise for holders of a Kuhn-theory. The content of the complete question, to be discussed in § 5, includes salient presuppositions derived from the various theory-elements.

2. Theories

A principled solution to the problem of the identity of scientific problems presupposes a more detailed notion of theory. The specific proposal I give in this section owes much to what has been called the Sneed-Stegmüller account of theories. Its main virtues, for our present purposes, are, first, that it allows us to distinguish between problems for a theory and problems for a scientist. Problems and theories in the former sense are Popperian third world entities. Problems in the latter sense are problems for an inquirer who holds a theory. The structuralist account of theories thus enables us to give a pragmatic characterization of problems and *Problemdynamik*. Secondly, the Sneed-Stegmüller notion of a theory is a *structured* one. Consequently, it gives a promise of identifying the various kinds of problems as conflicts between various theory elements and extra- and intra-theoretical beliefs. This is precisely what we need: we need to identify the presuppositions of questions and constraints on answers raised and answered in particular scientific communities arising from a structured theory (or more generally, from elements of a 'research tradition'). Third, it contains a pragmatic explicate for the domain of responsibility of a theory. This constitutes a tremendous advance in our understanding of the notion of a problem, I argue. Finally, the theory provides a criterion of identity for problems and solutions which steers between those of Popper and Nickles.

To solve the various problems in the notion of a problem we must spell out the Sneed-Stegmüller account, also called a structuralist or non-statement view, in some detail. Let us start with Sneed's suggestion according to which a theory-element T is an ordered pair $\langle K,I \rangle$ in which the core K and the set I of (classes of) intended applications is understood as follows (Sneed, 1976). The core K is an ordered quadruple $\langle M_{pp}, M_p, M, C \rangle$ where M_p is the set of all possible models, called potential models, for the full apparatus of the theory, and M_{pp} (potential partial models) the set of all models obtained by 'lopping-off' the theoretical components of M_p. M is a subset of M_p such that it picks out from the set of all potential models those which satisfy certain laws, the fundamental laws of the theory. C is a set of constraints on M_p, and they rule out certain combinations of theoretical function-values of the common core functions in different applications. Thus the core allows us to distinguish between what is excluded by the fundamental laws of the theory and what is excluded by constraints on the application of the core in different classes of intended applications[1].

The set I of intended applications of T is a non-empty subset of the power set of M_{pp}, roughly what the theory-elements are about. The claim of a theory-element, then, is that the set of intended applications I is a member of the set of possible non-theoretical applications A(K) of $\langle K,I \rangle$, where A(K) is obtained from M_{pp} by a certain selection rule. According to this rule a subset of M_{pp} is in A(K) if and only if each element of the subset can be enriched by theoretical functions so that it satisfies the theoretical laws (i.e. each element is a subset of the set M of the models of the theory) and the constraints C are met.

Next we need some (informally presented) notions for discussing inter-theoretical relations, viz. specialization, theoretization and reduction (see Balzer and Sneed, 1977). Suppose we have cores K and K' such that they have identical potential and partial potential models, i.e. $M_p = M'_p$ and $M_{pp} = M'_{pp}$. However, if $M' \subset M$ and $C' \in C$, i.e. if the set of models and constraints of T' are subsets of those of T, T' 'says more' about some potential and partial potential models than T. If K' is a specialization of K in the above sense, and if $I' \subset I$, T' is a specialization of T, symbolized by T'σT.

Specialization T does not add new concepts to T. But if we add to the potential models M_p new theoretical elements and require that all elements of M'_p are models of T' only if all elements of M_p are models of T, T' is a theoretization of T, that is T'τ T. If there is a (many-one) relation R from the partial potential models M'_{pp} of T' to the class M_{pp} of T, if the intended applications of T' are correlated with those of T, and if all that T' says about the intended applications I is entailed by what T says about the set I', T' is a reduction of T.

To complete this informal exposition of the structure of theories we need the notion of a *theory net* N. A theory net N is a set of finite theory elements partially ordered by the specialization relation such that for all ⟨ K,I ⟩, ⟨ K',I' ⟩ belonging to the set of theory-elements, K=K' if and only if I=I'. The most useful theory net contains a single basic theory element ⟨ K,I ⟩ such that all theory elements are specializations of it. Intuitively speaking basic theory elements generate more specific theory elements which say more about some potential models than the initial basic theory elements. That is, if N is a theory net, ⟨ K,I ⟩ and ⟨ K',I'⟩ are members of the set of theory elements, and T'σT, then A(K)⊂A(K') and I ⊂I'. Associated with the theory-nets there are core-nets N* and application-nets A(N*). I shall assume familiarity with them (see Balzer and Sneed, 1977).

The notion of theory-net enables us to say more about the claims made by a theory (or by those who hold a theory). For suppose there is a basic theory-element ⟨ K,I ⟩. Then the claim made by T is that there is some theory-net N* based on ⟨ K,I ⟩ such that I∈A(N*). One may look at the claim that I∈A(N*) as an array of claims of the form I'∈A(K') where I'∈Pot(I) and K' is obtained from a T'σT (Sneed, 1976, p. 129)[2]. The theory T can then be used for making claims about some applications by using special laws and constraints.

3. An Enriched Logic of Questions

To be able to solve the mentioned puzzles in the notion of a scientific problem we need two amendments. First, we need to be able to use erotetic logic to explicate the logical form of the questions underlying these problems. Here we face two options. Some writers, e.g. Nickles (1981) and Dacey (1981) treat with problems as conceptual structures, rather than linguistic entities. This is in line with Sneed's and Stegmüller's non-statement view. However, this choice has its difficulties, both with respect to theories and problems. One of these is that according to it theories and problems have no syntactic or semantic structure.

The alternative line is opened by writers such as Niiniluoto, Tuomela, Rantala and Pearce who have shown that the contrast between the non-statement and statement views has been overestimated.[3] We can in fact translate the structuralist proposals into a statement view. I choose this proposal, not because it is the only viable one, but because it best suits the intuition that problems are literally *questions.*[4] (For this reason also I adopt the statement view for *theories:* theories must be linguistically formulated because we want (the presuppositions of) theories to make logical contact with certain presuppositions of questions.)

Another amendment of, or addition to, the basic structuralist ideas is needed, to meet the demands for a pragmatic characterization of problems. Acts of explaining occur in particular contexts and paradigms, and there is no mention in the theory-elements of contexts, paradigms, or members of scientific communities. One can introduce the factors either by starting from an independent characterization of a scientific community and by then stipulating that a paradigmatic theory is what a scientific community so characterized accepts (cf. Achinstein, 1968). Or one can first define a notion of a theory and then introduce a notion of a scientific community as a community of scientists who hold such a theory. The latter option is chosen here. The pragmatization of Sneedian theory-elements is due to Ulysses Moulines, 1979; (the notation used here is due to Niiniluoto, 1980a). Suppose we have a theory-element $\langle K,I \rangle$ and a scientific community SC at time t. Then we can denote by $I_{SC,t}(K)$ the set of non-theoretical structures of the power-set of M_{pp} to which SC intends to apply K at t. Although the claim of SC is that all intended applications I belong to A(K), it may be (and characteristically is) the case that only some of the (classes of) applications at t have by that time been found to be members of A(K). Let us label these confirmed applications by $C_{SC,t}(K)$. Thus SC believes (accepts that) $C_{SC,t}(K) \in A(K)$ but claims also that $I_{SC,t}(K) \in A(K)$ and $I \in A(K)$.[5]

How are the non-theoretical structures in $I_{SC,t}(K)$ chosen ? I shall assume that they are determined intensionally through certain paradigmatic exemplars. $I_{SC,t}(K)$ is characteristically *clustered* and consists of separate (though possibly overlapping) domains of application. Any non-theoretical structure which is sufficiently similar to some paradigm examples belongs to a subset, an intended application, of the theory-element.[6]

Let us symbolize the pragmatically enriched theory-element (p.e. theory-element) of a scientific community SC at t by $\langle K, I_{SC,t}(K) \rangle$.[7] Analogously, we can pragmatize theory-nets. They are finite sets of pragmatically enriched theory-elements such that for each $\langle K_i, I^i_{SC,t}(K_i) \rangle$ connected by the specialization relation the scientific community and the time are identical.

Although the concept is pragmatic, it gives a static picture of the specializations of the basic theory-element at a given time. To be able to represent theory dynamics (and eventually problem dynamics), we need the notion of a theory-evolution. A theory-evolution E is a finite sequence of p.e. nets such that for each N^i the immediate successor p.e. theory-net N^{i+1} contains at least one theory-element obtained from a theory-element in N^i by specialization. This notion of theory-evolution does not rule out the possibility that the number of theory-elements decreases, nor that the basic theory-element remains the same. A theory evolution in which the latter condition holds is called Kuhnian: there is an initial core K_o (created by the founder) and a class $I_{SC,t}(K_O)$ of pragmatically chosen (intensionally circumscribed) intended applications which both remain fixed in the evolution.

This notion of a Kuhnian theory-evolution is still too weak for the realistic representation of some theory-evolutions. According to Kuhn a paradigm (a constellation of group commitments) contains symbolic generalizations, metaphysical (e.g. ontological) assumptions, values (such as simplicity, fruitfulness, etc.), and exemplars (textbook examples of successful applications). While we can identify K_O with the symbolic generalizations and exemplars with the I_O of the basic theory-element (Niiniluoto, 1980a, p. 32), we need to be able to represent values and metaphysical principles. These too create essential tension between tradition and innovation. This can be obtained by defining a stronger p.e. concept of a theory, called a Kuhn-theory. (See Balzer and Sneed, 1977, and Niiniluoto, 1980a.)

Assume that we have a paradigmatic basic theory-element $\langle K_O, I_p \rangle$ and its Kuhnian evolutionary stage at t. Then there is a Kuhnian $\langle K_O, t_p \rangle$-based theory-evolution E_t whose last theory net N_p contains all specialized theory-element-cores which SC intends to apply at t to the various subsets $I_o \subset I_p$. N_p is called the paradigmatic theory net. Assume then that the values and metaphysical assumptions of the members of SC have laid down certain constraints on the application of K_O to the subsets of I_p (the evolutionary stage at t may or may not be the initial stage).[8] The net N_p is not the only possible $\langle K_O, I_p \rangle$-based net. Then assuming that the metaphysical beliefs and values which have lead to the choice of $\langle K_O, I_p \rangle$ are constitutive of SC, they are shared by its members also at t. Then the quadruple $\langle K_O, I_p, N_p, N \rangle$ is a Kuhn-theory, where N is a set of theory-nets N such that all members of N are expansions of N_p having some $\langle K_O, I_o \rangle$ $(I_o \supset I_p)$ as their basic theory element (Balzer and Sneed, 1977). A Kuhn-theory thus consists of a basic conceptual apparatus, a set of classes of (non-theoretical) structures to which SC thinks K_O is applicable, a paradigmatic theory net which indicates how K_O has been applied to the various structures in I_p, and a restriction to the future development of the theory: N defines the set of (specialization) theory-nets admissible in attempts to apply K_O to other intended applications, and in attempts to say more about the members of I. The evolution of a Kuhn-theory can thus be represented as a sequence of theory nets N^t where $N^t \in N$ for all t.

4. Problems-for-a-Theory vs. Problems-for-a-Scientist

Suppose we have a scientific community SC who holds a Kuhn-theory $\langle K_O, I_p, N_p, N \rangle$ at time t. What is it to 'hold' a theory? It is, first and foremost, to believe that the certain confirmed intended applications $C_{SC,t}(K_O)$ are models of K_o and that they satisfy certain constraints. Secondly, it is to believe that the so far unexamined intended applications $I_{SC,t}(I_o)$ are its models.

Now it may be (and characteristically is) that the claim $C_{SC,t}(I_o) \in A(K_o)$ contains various types of problems. There are *clarification problems* having to do with obscurities in e.g. some special laws and constraints. There are problems of *precisizing* specialized cores to meet certain standards of accuracy laid down by the values (included in N) of the Kuhn-theory. There are problems of determining values for non-theoretical functions and of deriving predictions from specialized theory-elements and initial assumptions. Finally, there may be problems requiring explanations as solutions. E.g. if some theory-element $\langle K_1, I_1 \rangle \in N_p$ yields wrong empirical predictions for a $z \in I_1$ these predictions give rise to why-questions of the form "Why does z behave in a manner O (instead of O') ?" The existence of such normal-scientific problems is possible also within z's which are members of confirmed applications.

Another set of problems arose with respect to the claim $I_{SC,t}(K_o) \in A(K_o)$. There may be specialized theory-elements which already are in trouble at t. For instance, if a sufficient amount of empirical predictions have turned out false, these predictions based on a $\langle K_2, I_2 \rangle \in N$ constitute anomalies for $\langle K_2, I_2 \rangle$. The problem then is to alter the core K_2 (by tinkering with the special laws or constraints) in such manner that the why-questions which result from these false predictions can be answered.[9] Secondly, there may be some members $z \in I_{SC,t}(K_o)$ for which no specialized theory-elements exist. Then there is no inconsistency between theory and observation. Rather, the problem is to find an expansion N'_p of N_p which contains the missing theory-elements. Here the paradigmatic net N_p and N provides guidance by suggesting formal analogies (derived e.g. from other specialized theory-elements) and by suggesting what potential expansions are e.g. simple, consilient, non-ad-hoc or in consonance with the metaphysical assumptions constitutive of a paradigm.

To the extent the structuralist theory elements can be translated into a statement view the various theory-elements can be given linguistic formulations. It follows that the various types of problems can be given literal sense as questions which arise for these theory elements. For there can be, in an obvious way, contradictions between empirical claims and e.g. observation statements.

Furthermore, we can easily distinguish between queries that arise for theories and queries that arise *for scientists*. In a quite natural sense a scientist, say H, who holds a Kuhn-theory presupposes the basic theory-elements as well as the specialized elements at t, and these presuppositions provide the background for his questions in any problem contexts.[10]

The various types of problems can be construed as questions uttered in problem contexts. Like in ordinary discourse, there is, to adapt a phrase from Norwood Russell Hanson, more to a querier's question than meets the addressee's ear. First, there is the question sentence which we can put into its logical form. Secondly, there are the shortlived (roughly, perceptual) and long-lived (paradigmatic) contextual beliefs which further determine precisely what the querier's question is. Scientific discourse, including problem solving understood as a process of posing and answering questions, thus has the structure of ordinary discourse.

Let us see how a question-theoretic proposal can be used to illuminate various types of problems. In standard erotetic logic the notion of a presupposition is defined as follows: a proposition p is a presupposition of a question q if and only if the truth of p is necessary for the question to have a (direct) answer (cf. Belnap and Steel, 1976, p. 113). The presupposition of a question thus rules out as inappropriate all responses which violate the presupposition. If, for instance, the presupposition (2) fails, the question (1) has no direct answer:

(1)　(?p) Planets occasionally interrupt their westward movement and move backwards with respect to other stars because p.

(2)　Planets occasionally interrupt their westward movement and move backwards with respect to other stars.

I shall call (2) the (complete) logical presupposition$_1$ of question (1). This notion of presuppositionhood is however too weak for our purposes. What more is needed is suggested by Belnap and Steel. According to them a question characteristically contains further restrictions on answerhood, notably number and completeness specifications. For instance a querier may indicate – or it may be contextually obvious – how specific an answer must be.

Belnap's and Steel's suggestion works well for well-defined questions, such as yes-no, who, where-, and other wh-questions. Scientific questions, especially those which await explanations for answers, are often ill-defined. There is no antecedently fixed pool of potential answers from which the selection of the answer can be made.[11]

The proposal I make is that theories provide looser *speaker presuppositions*$_2$ which restrict the set of admissible answers. These restrictions can be found in the structured notion of a theory. In uttering a question sentence (1) a planetary astronomer presupposes a host of contextual assumptions which narrow down admissible answers. These assumptions have the status of mutual belief in the scientific community SC and therefore need not (indeed, cannot) be included in the interrogative sentence uttered by the astronomer. But a querier in SC assumes, and is normally entitled to assume, that his addressee is able to identify them. This is how there can be more to a querier's question than meets the explainee's ear.[12]

5. Individuation of Problems

Let us see how this proposal helps us to understand the problem of the identity of questions. In one obvious sense two scientists with entirely different background theories can deal with the same problem. Ptolemy, Copernicus and Kepler all dealt with the problem of the planets because they tried to answer (1). This notion of a problem is akin to that of Popper and Laudan, and it is rather unhelpful.[13]

A more fine-grained principle of individuation for problems is obtained by identifying problems not with the illocutionary content of the interrogative utterance, but with its underlying complete question understood as an ordered triple $Q = \langle (?p)q(p),r,s \rangle$. Here the first element is the logical form of the question sentence, the second the set of relevant presuppositions$_2$, and the third the set of type- or category restrictions. As an example of the latter we have the requirements, say, to give an answer in terms of proximate (contra distant) causes of an event.[14]

This much is, I think, uncontroversial. What remains to be examined is how much of the relevant background knowledge is included in the complete underlying question. This brings us back to the dispute between the Popperians and the friends of discovery. Should *all* constraints on the solutions of a problem be included in the problem? Is there any principled way of distinguishing between a problem and the background? According to Nickles (1981, p. 109) "a problem consists of *all* the conditions or *constraints* on the solution plus the demand that the solution (an object satisfying the constraints) can be found". Constraints here have a sense which differs from the technical notion in the above theory construction. Their role is obvious: like the presuppositions$_1$ of questions they rule out some solutions as inadequate and therefore determine what counts as a solution.

The important difficulty with this model is the vagueness of this notion of constraint. Nickles (1978, p. 139) observes that they vary in generality and importance, ranging from highly general and deep-rooted principles, such as symmetry principles in physics, to well established singular laws or "facts". But surely not *all* that a scientist holds true is constitutive of a problem. Certainly a solution which violates a well-established neighbouring theory or a fact no way related to a field is *prima facie* inadmissible. But it hardly is part of the problem. Similarly, there are, within any field of investigation, established facts which do not have the status of a constraint in the sense of erotetic logic.

Nickles notes the difficulty (1981, p. 114) and admits that his model must more directly address the individuation issue. He also expects help from discussion of theories. Now the structured notion of a theory given above meets the demand. The example of planetary astronomy is not the best available, for the notion of a theory given is designed for more mature sciences.

But even the Ptolemaic research tradition fits the model to some degree. There was a fundamental law or basic theory-core. Although there was no one single solution to the problem of the planets, all specific theories contained a system of earth-centered circles and major epicycles. Evolution within the tradition consisted of various specific epicycle-deferent-equant systems designed to explain minor irregularities (see Kuhn, 1966) that resulted from the core. There were also cosmological and physical background assumptions as well as values which narrowed down the ranges of admissible potential answers to the detailed questions arising from these minor problems. We can consider these specific proposals as specialized theory elements. A Ptolemaic astronomer thus presupposed the core, the Aristotelean physics and cosmology, the values, as well as the theory-net specialization at hand.

There is no context-independent way to specify how much is included in the specific question, and what is relegated to the background. The most natural line of division is between the basic core and its specializations. The cosmological and physical background assumptions as well as values can best be viewed as constraints on answers, not presuppositions of the questions. Things are clearer still with respect to more mature physical theories. The presuppositions$_2$ of a querier H who belongs to SC and holds a Kuhn-theory include the core K_O, the classes of paradigmatic intended applications I_p, and the paradigmatic theory-net N_p. There may for instance be a *subschool* among the holders of a Kuhn-theory the members of which disagree about some theoretical or nontheoretical claims concerning the promising expansions of N^t. To the extent it succeeds at time $t+1$ in finding a new theory-element, the formulation of that element may provide presuppositions$_2$ for further questions. Members of the subschool then "presuppose" N^{t+1}, and any solution to *their* problem-situation must be an answer not just to the question-sentence but must be in accordance with their presuppositions$_2$ in uttering the question sentence[15].

To the extent we can actually identify the basic theory element and the extant theory specializations we can distinguish the *"relevant portions of the background"* which constitute a problem in Nickles's sense. The question (1) thus may put different complete questions: Ptolemy and Copernicus had different problems because they held different basic theory elements. Two Ptolemaic astronomers, e.g. Ptolemy and Hipparchus, also had different problems in this sense: although they shared a common core-element, they held different specialized cores. Therefore their complete questions were different.

At the same time we can avoid the difficulties of the inclusion thesis. By restricting the "relevant portion of the background" to include the ingredients of a Kuhn-theory we can see that there may be, first, individual differences among holders of a theory or a subtheory, and secondly well-established facts and theories accepted by the school or subschool which are not constitutive of the problems. The proposal presented here thus steers between Nickles's and Popper's views: we need not assume that all constraints (in Nickles' sense) on answers are constitutive of the questions. Yet problems can have depth. The depth of a problem is measured by the length of the specialization branch to which it belongs, as well as by the form and width of the whole theory-net.

6. Genealogy of Problems

We can thus throw light on what can be called the genealogy of problems. Toulmin (1972) describes how problems evolve historically. Although the details of problem settings — and hence the problems *for the scientists* — change even radically, there are ancestral relationships between problem formulations. He specifically shows how problems can be structured on the basis of, say, the mathematical form or even content of another problem. So described, *Problemdynamik* poses problems of degrees of similarity and distance between, e.g. Ptolemy's and Copernicus's problems. Shapere (1980, p. 68), has also paid attention to such relationships. Although what counts as a legitimate theory or problem may radically change from one period to another, "there is often a chain of developments connecting the two different sets of criteria, a chain through which a 'rational evolution' can be traced between the two".

The notion of a theory-net which allows not just specialization relations but also theoretization and reduction relations offers a tool for the study of synchronic similarity and analogy relations between problems. The notion of a theory-evolution as a sequence of theory-nets provides a criterion of identity for problems. The complete questions of Eudoxus and Callippus (concerning Saturn, say) are closer to each other than those of, say, Eudoxus and Hipparchus, for Callippus was Eudoxus's successor and shared with him the same specialized theory-element. The complete questions of Eudoxus and Copernicus were further apart because they held different basic theory-cores. To the extent we can give the linguistic formulations of specific theory-elements in some suitable formal language as well as the questions which arise for these theory-elements, we can perhaps measure quantitatively kinship relations of problems as the distances of the complete questions from each other. I am not here proposing new techniques for historians of science, for there may be little point in carrying out such tasks. Rather, I want to point out the possibility of treating questions of the genealogy of problems by some rather well-studied logical tools[16]. Theory-nets and -evolutions provide precisely what Shapere looks for: chains of development.

Theory nets and evolutions also explain how we can speak of successively *sharper reformulations* of one and the same problem. Nickles (1981, p. 99) writes that a process of inquiry brings forth new constraints on the solution of a problem. As long as these constraints are already implicit in the relevant corpus of thought and practice they do not, Nickles thinks, constitute such radical departures from previous problem settings as to alter the problems. The notion of a theory evolution gives to this idea precise content. The core K_o, the set I_o, and the paradigmatic net N_p contain restrictions on admissible theory-net expansions, i.e. on new theory-elements. There may be a vague formulation (in K_o-nontheoretical terms, say) of a phenomenon prior to an attempt to apply K_o to it. When a Kuhn-theory is introduced any solution to the problem must accord with the presuppositions provided by it. Furthermore, the evolution of a Kuhn-theory brings forth new constraints in this sense: any solution to a problem for a specialized element $\langle K_o^t, I_o^t \rangle$ must accord with the special laws (and constraints) of its predecessor elements. This observation is a direct consequence of the definition of a theory evolution. In question-theoretic terms this is: a querier who holds ("works with") $\langle K_o^t, I_o^t \rangle$ presupposes$_2$ the predecessor elements.

We can now see why the structuralist theory concept is a decisive step forward in our understanding of *Problemdynamik*. It shows, namely, how initially very broad or inarticulate questions are refined to sets of more specific questions. Thus assume that the hunch about the identity of deep problems is essentially correct. Then a complete question of a scientist H holding a Kuhn theory at t and working on $\langle I_1^t, I_o \rangle$ has the form $Q = \langle (?p)q(p), \langle K_1^t, I_1^t \rangle, s \rangle$. Although the logical form of the question, the first element, may remain the same throughout theory evolution or even revolution, the second element, as well as the elements presupposed by it, are different. The same applies of course to the type of category specifications s.

This has several immediate consequences. What is crucial for a logic of discovery is the possibility of limiting the set of specific questions that arise in a problem context. The intended applications of a Kuhnian theory element as well as the evolved constraints, i.e. special laws and Sneedian constraints, have precisely that role. Such specific questions are often also in a form which Nature can understand, so to speak. They are no longer unmanageably broad why- or how-questions but e.g. yes-no or wh-questions. Moreover, the theory-elements provide ever more restricted heuristic guidance: an investigator who works on a new intended application follows Quine's maxim of conservatism: he keeps the background theory net fixed or at least makes minimum alterations in it. An elegant solution to a local problem, that of constructing a new special law, causes a minimum of changes elsewhere in the net.

We can also solve an apparent inconsistency in Laudan's problem-solving model. According to Laudan (1977) problems are what are *felt* to be problems — and these are finite in number. This contention has occasioned criticisms. Jarvie (1979, p. 494) understands Laudan to hold that theories (or research traditions) are to be assessed solely with respect to their capacity to solve a set of pre-existing problems. And he rightly points out that of course new problems arise during theory-evolution. Lugg (1979, p. 469) criticizes Laudan for holding the contrary view that new problems do arise. According to Lugg theories *should* be assessed only with respect to antecedently existing problems.

Laudan (1980, p. 279) rightly points out that Jarvie and Lugg cannot be both right about his view. According to Laudan there are pre-existing problems which a theory must solve at least if they have been solved by some prior theory. But he also admits that new hitherto unknown facts will emerge. What Laudan fails to make clear is what counts as a pre-existing and what a new problem. Lugg's criticism is based on the partial autodetermination of theories with respect to their problems. Part of this autodetermination is the waxing and waning of problems. Part of it is emergence of new constraints on a problem solution. Laudan's research tradition is a useful concept but needs even more structure: once we conceive it as (roughly) a Kuhnian theory-evolution we get a better grip over how a theory can be assessed with respect to pre-existing problems. For a scientist who holds a Kuhn-theory core K_o^t refines both his tool and finds new questions which are, in a very broad sense, implicit in the initial core K_o. They are of course not 'given', for there are alternative possible K_o-based theory nets and the actual net is a result of human creativity.

Next, we can solve a dispute about the structure of problems. Some writers have held that scientific problems are characteristically inconsistencies, arising e.g. from observations which clash with background beliefs. Recently e.g. Hattiangadi (1979) has argued that all problems have that structure. This view has been denied by Laudan (1977), Lugg (1979), Leplin (1980) and Nickles (1981). According to Laudan a mere logical compatibility between a theory and a description of a phenomenon may be a problem if there is a "premium" of solving it. Similarly Nickles writes that if there is a phenomenon $\emptyset$ in the domain of responsibility of a theory, the demand that $\emptyset$ be explained remains even if there is no incompatibility between $\emptyset$ and the theory.

Leplin (1980) talks of a broader notion of inconsistency or incompatibility in connection of unrelated phenomena. But all this is vague: surely we live in an ocean of unrelated phenomena, and we need an account of why some but not all those phenomena are felt to be problematic at all. When is there a premium for solving a problem ? The account given here does precisely this, for it gives an account of the domain of responsibility of various theory-elements: any $\emptyset$ (a structure) which bears a suitable (not necessarily non-theoretic) similarity relation to paradigm examples of intended applications is a potential problem. A holder of a Kuhn-theory believes not just that $C_{SC,t} \in$ A(K) but also that $I_{SC,t} \in A(K)$ and $I \in A(K)$. As long as there is a subset $I_0 \subset I_{SC,T}$ or $I_0 \subset A(K)$ for which no specialized theory-element exists, there is a *cognitive conflict* between these beliefs and the recognized achievements. Such cognitive conflicts are not outright inconsistencies, for the empirical claim of a Kuhn-theory is that *there are* suitable theory-elements. Such cognitive conflicts are Kuhnian challenges to ingenuity.

I think the structuralist concept thus explicates problems with inconsistent constraints (Lugg's, 1978, overdetermined problems, see also Nickles, 1980c) as well as problems which consist of well-defined "gaps" (Nickles, 1980a, p. 37). Nickles describes the latter as problems in which there is "the absence of a suitable connection between basic principles and some other law or phenomenon". This description fits precisely the absence of a specialized core for some intended applications. The constraints are provided by the already available theory-net.

It seems in fact that we have derived the two basic categories of scientific problems; Popperian and Kuhnian. Popperian problems are shallow empirical or deep conceptual inconsistencies, while Kuhnian ones are demands to fill in a detail in a theory-element or theory-net. Such a demand may be more or less difficult to meet, depending on the degree of normal-scientificness of the problem.[17]

7. Further Results

We can now clarify the notion of the weight of a problem and that of the value of a solution. The weight of a problem seems to involve centrality and importance. Clearly, empirical or conceptual problems which challenge the basic core are more central for SC than those which threaten a special core. Moreover, importance of a problem depends on whether it arises for an empirical claim concerning a paradigmatic application of the basic theory element $z \in I_0 \subset I_p$ or whether it arises for a specialized theory-element. Recall that the classes of intended applications are formed intensionally though paradigmatic exemplars. There are then two types of less serious problems. On one hand there may be a $z \in I_0 \subset I_p$ whose similarity with the paradigm structures of I_0 is looser. On the other hand there are new classes of intended applications which have emerged through net expansions.

The cognitive worth of a solution (answer) reflects the centrality and importance of the problem (question) as well as the extent to which it meets the values of the Kuhn-theory. This worth may be local, i.e. increase in the likelihood of an explanandum, within a specialized theory-element, or global, such as increase in consilience through a theory-net expansion.[18]

The notion of a theory-net also gives a precise solution to how Nickles's constraints are graded with respect to importance. Apart from the symbolic generalizations in K_o there are also the metaphysical assumptions and values which limit admissible expansions of N_p. Presumably these are already reflected in the choice of K_o, but their constraining force remains throughout the evolution of N_p^t to later nets N_p^{t+n}. These constraints seem to be highest up in the hierarchy of importance: any potential solution which violates a fundamental metaphysical assumption is deemed unacceptable. It does not follow from this that they are absolutely unalterable, of course.

But the most important distinction is provided by that between the basic theory-element and the specialized ones. Nickles does not accept the extreme inclusion thesis according to which tinkering with *any* constraint, however insignificant, alters the problem. Only *substantial* tinkering does. He argues against Lugg (1979) to the effect that "a significant change of setting" destroys the identity of a problem and creates a replacement problem. The notion of theory sketched here gives clues as to how settings are identified. Clearly rejection of the basic core is substantial tinkering (although not all changes in a core are always felt to be revolutionary; cf. Moulines, 1979). Similarly, tinkering with the special laws of a theory-element presupposed by a subschool is significant for that subschool, though not necessarily for the whole SC. How much normal-scientific leeway there is is highly contextual, and depends on the specific problems addressed as well as the values which rate alternative problem solutions, understood as solutions whose expected cognitive weights (promises!) are different.[19]

The structuralist account also explains what the so-called correspondence principle amounts to. Roughly, the principle says that a successor theory T_2 entails its predecessor theory T_1 as a special case. Although T_1 and T_2 are logically incompatible, the predictions of T_2 tend towards predictions of T_1 when the values of certain parameters of T_2 tend asymptomically towards extreme values (see Krajewski, 1977). The correspondence principle seems to have played an enormous heuristic role in physical sciences. In problem-solving terms we can explain this as follows. The predecessor theory serves as a constraint on further theorizing: any potential theory T_n must have its predecessor theories T_{n-1} etc. as limit cases. This does not mean of course that the predecessor theories are true, for the needed assumptions concerning the values of the parameters are characteristically idealizations.

This treatment of theory evolution fits both evolution and revolution. What is important to see is that such constraints are precisely what Nickles (1978, p. 137) has called *limit constraints*. Furthermore, we have provided limit constraints a natural home. The notion of a theory-net allows various kinds of intertheory relations in which a theory-element T_2 can have a predecessor theory-element as a limit constraint. The visual image of a theory-net branch explains in a concrete way how a scientist who holds a Kuhn-theory must pay heed to limit constraints.

8. We can now draw some general conclusions concerning the problem-solving model of scientific inquiry. One of these concerns the pragmatic aspects of inquiry. There has been, so to speak, a social order for an explicitly pragmatic treatment of *Theoriendynamik* and *Problemdynamik* : We can now see how the structuralist notion of theories automatically *is* also a representation of *Problemdynamik.* The question-theoretic proposal put forth here only makes explicit the local types of inquiries which are implicit in a Sneed-Stegmüller-type account. Its virtue, from the point of view of discourse analysis, is that it allows for a nice explication for the much discussed phenomenon of talking past one another. There are, e.g., conversational failures which result from a failure to address a querier's complete underlying question.

Another conclusion is this. Many writers on the topic have proposed that the problem-solving model reveals that, *pace* positivism and the dominant trend, problems and not theories are the fundamental logical units of philosophy of science. Nickles ((1980a), sect. VI) makes this view admirably clear. He says that the theory-oriented bias has obscured several issues and hampered development in philosophy of science. He stresses, e.g., that fruitful research begins with the selection of a good problem. Indeed, the theory-oriented bias leads us to think that inquiry does not begin from problems but from theories already in hand. It is part and parcel of this contrast to argue that just as we have previously been occupied by questions of the structure and dynamics of theories, the central problem now is the structure and dynamics of problems.

One of the potential lines of development which the theory-biased meta-theory of science has suppressed, in view of the friends of discovery, is the logic of discovery. They have argued that problems *are* structures of constraints and therefore provide heuristic guides for research. A problem itself points the way to its solution. Once the obsession with finished theories is overcome, it seems even that the positivist distinction between contexts of discovery and of justification breaks down (see Nickles, 1980a, Achinstein, 1980, Curd, 1980, as well as other essays in Nickles, 1980b).

Thirdly, it has been argued that problem-solving, not truth, is the central aim of science. Laudan (1977, 1979) has argued that the aim of a true theory is unattainable and that there is no notion of truthlikeness which would allow us to give comparative or quantitative judgements about nearness to truth.

I think my discussion shows that the first two points mentioned are based on a false contrast, made possible by the ill-developed notion of theory with which the friends of discovery have worked. The structure of the constraints for a solution of a problem is laid down by the *theory* for which the problem is a problem. The problem of individuating problems is largely the problem of individuating theories. Moreover, the concept of theory needed is something akin to the structuralist account, for any candidate concept must give an account of the domain of the theory and provide a criterion of identity for problems which has enough content for us to be able to identify it during theory-evolution. This is no place to argue for it, but I think e.g. Shapere's (1974, 1980) notion of a 'domain' as well as Darden's (1976) notion of a 'field' would get more precise content if translated to the structuralist account.

It seems that the false contrast theory vs. problem derives from two sources. First, problem-solving, unlike theory-construction, is local rather than global. This does not apply to Laudan who takes there to be two units of analysis, problems and research traditions. His concept of the problem-solving effectiveness of a research tradition nicely brings out the global features of inquiry, but it applies to many other friends of discovery. Secondly, the view that problems are logically primary fits such local inquiries in which non-cognitive, e.g., practical, values have a crucial role. But it does not fit basic theoretical sciences.

The importance of this latter distinction should not be underestimated. It is natural to think that in e.g. applied sciences where theories are not the goal but the means for achieving practical goals problems are *the* central unit. Roughly, an investigator with a practical problem is entitled to use any theory he pleases. Therefore problems are the umbrellas under which facts and theories are gathered.But it does not follow from this that problems have that role in theoretical science. On the contrary, as I have argued, theories retain their primacy and are needed as umbrellas under which problems are gathered.

There is something odd about the following argument. Nickles (1980, p. 35) agrees with Hempel's (1966, Chapter 2) criticism of induction as a method of discovery. Hempel's point is that one cannot start the inquiry from facts, not even from a problem, because without a specific hypothesis (a putative solution) one cannot know what facts are relevant for the problem. The specific hypothesis comes from a theory. Therefore, thinks Nickles, there can in Hempel's view be no genuine methodology for finding problem solutions, but only for testing already formulated theories. But, writes Nickles, once we recognize the heuristic role of problem constraints, we can see how a *structured* problem is a starting point in inquiry.

But this is an optical illusion created by a one-sidedly local point of view. The deep structure of problems is inherited from theories. Indeed, the structure of these problems reflects the structure of the specialized theory-element and the theory-net of which it is an offspring. To say that problems and not theories are a starting point of inquiry is to introduce a false contrast. Clearly there is a more or less well-structured theory and a problem for it: both are needed. Even a cursory glance at the slogan "Fruitful research begins with the selection of a problem" should show that the problem can be a problem only with respect to a theory. For how is one to select a problem, if not on the basis of available theories ?

Analogous remarks apply to discovery. Theories have a degree of auto-determination with respect to their problems. It is all-right to suggest that the constraints on a problem guide the search for solutions (Nickles, 1980a, p. 16), if it is admitted that these constraints are derived from theories. A more globalist picture is more adequate here also: the theory-elements, values and metaphysical assumptions determine the range of problems as well as the set of admissible solutions.

Notice that the claim that the presuppositions of theories or constraints on problems give guidance must *not* be understood as implying that the distinction between a context of discovery and a context of justification breaks down. It is true, as Nickles (1980a, p. 13) says, that the rational reconstruction of the argument from constraints to a solution will justify the solution "at least in a preliminary sort of way". But of course that justification is only preliminary. The traditional emphasis on the need for novel predictions and explanations can be seen as a requirement of further arguments. The right view is Nickles's and Gutting's (1980): the context of discovery is part of the context of justification and *vice versa*. Note specifically that heuristic constraints bring together the two ingredients of essential tension: they may equally well point towards incorrect solutions. The question-theoretic model can handle this aspect too: corrective answers may point to false presuppositions in theories.

NOTES

(*) While writing this paper I have enjoyed a grant from the Eemil Aaltonen Foundation.

(1) I shall omit the formal definitions of the core-elements, as they are of lesser importance for the purposes at hand. For these see Sneed, 1976, Stegmüller, 1976 and 1979, Balzer and Sneed, 1977, and Niiniluoto, 1980a.

(2) Niiniluoto, 1980a, argues that the intended applications of a theory also should include potential models. On his proposal, then, there would be along with non-theoretical claims of the form $I' \in A(K')$ also theoretical claims of the form $J(K) \in AT(K)$. I cannot go into this controversy here,

however.

(3) For discussion, see Tuomela, 1978, Rantala, 1978, Rantala and Pearce, 1981, and Niiniluoto, 1980a.

(4) It seems to me that conceptually the most satisfactory analysis of scientific discourse construes questions and answers as contents of illocutionary (and perlocutionary) acts of scientists belonging to a research tradition. Speech act theory allows us to better explicate pragmatic aspects of scientific discourse than its rival model according to which scientific inquiry consists of questions put to nature. The main reason is precisely that the phrase 'questions to nature', just as the phrase 'reading the book of nature', is *metaphorical.* I cannot go into this here, however.

(5) Analogously with beliefs concerning membership in the class of non-theoretical applications there are also theoretical beliefs of the form $J(K) \in AT(K)$. For now I shall not discuss this complication at all.

(6) This clustered notion of I as a set of classes of intended applications is due to Moulines, 1979. See also Stegmüller, 1979, p. 27, note 4.

(7) The phrase 'pragmatically enriched theory-element' is due to Stegmüller, 1979. Stegmüller's definitions are somewhat different, for according to him a p.e. theory-element is a quadruple $\langle T,SC,h,F \rangle$ in which T is a theory-element, SC a scientific community, h a time-interval (and not an instance of time) and F a subset of I. These differences do not matter here, however.

(8) Niiniluoto, 1980a, p. 34, refers to the possibility of including values in K_o. The reason is that the formal definition of the fundamental law of K_o does not exclude axiological assumptions. I think it natural, and faithful to Kuhn, to distinguish between symbolic generalizations and values, where the choice of symbolic generalizations K_o *reflects* these values, if only because values have to do with choices between possible theory-elements and -nets. Moreover, we are hard put to express these values in propositional forms.

(9) I shall assume, contra Lakatos 1970, and in agreement with e.g. Nickles 1981, Niiniluoto 1980a, Laudan 1977 and 1979, that there is no unalterable hard core to a research programme which is entirely immune to modification. The same applies to the set of intended — even paradigmatic

— applications.

(10) I want to emphasize that a problem-for-a-scientist need not be, although it can be, idiosyncratic. P.e. theory-elements and -nets are pragmatic, but characteristically involve reference to a subcommunity. Such a subcommunity might be a solitary figure, but we should separate idiosyncratic whims from well-crystallized group commitments.

(11) For this, see Bromberger, 1965 and 1966, Belnap and Steel, 1976, p. 86, Hintikka, 1976, p. 31, Tuomela, 1980, and Dacey, 1981.

(12) One of the attractions of using speech act theory to explicate questions is that it can nicely be embedded into a wider setting of linguistic communicating. Bach and Harnish, 1979, show how, according to a speech act theory, speakers and hearers employ certain linguistic and communicative presumptions as well as contextual background knowledge to interpret each other's utterances. As I have demonstrated in Sintonen (1984) this model explains in an orderly fashion certain pragmatic failures of scientific communication, such as failure to respond to an *addressee's* precise problem (here: to answer *his complete* question).

(13) For criticism of this notion, see especially Nickles, 1981.

(14) One good illustration of the force of such presuppositions is provided by the theory of evolution. Ernst Mayer, 1980, has noted the confusions which resulted in biology from the failure to distinguish between proximate and ultimate causes of a phenomenon. On the one hand there were the experimentalists with their allegedly superior standards of objectivity. On the other hand there were the evolutionists with their more sketchy ultimate explanations. Mayr nicely illustrates how the opponents literally talked past each other even when they dealt with the same phenomenon, for their *questions* were different. There were *two* sets of questions about, say, sexual dimorphism, requests for answers at functional and evolutionary levels.

(15) Notice how well the speech act-theoretical notion of a presupposition suits the purposes of the structuralists. Balzer and Sneed, 1977, talk of presuppositions-relation between theories: underlying the classical particle mechanics there was a classical space-time theory. Although holders of the former were perhaps not aware of it, they presupposed the latter. See also Stegmüller, 1979, p. 49.

(16) An analogous remark concerns the use of formal explicates of explanatory power, empirical content, degrees of truthlikeness, etc. Such formal explicates are not intended as tools which historians of science can use in record-keeping.

(17) I want to deny, explicitly, the primacy of one type of problem over the other. A contradiction as well as the non-existence of a theory-element (special law) can constitute an anomaly. Needless to say, all types of pragmatic factors of the type mentioned by Laudan, 1977, contribute towards the importance of the problem.

(18) Theories which have high explanatory power can be regarded as answers to quite general questions. These answers split into answers to more specific (local) explanation-seeking and other questions.

(19) For some remarks on centrality or importance by a structuralist, see Stegmüller, 1979, p. 48 and p. 54.

REFERENCES

ACHINSTEIN, Peter (1968), *Concepts of Science*. Johns Hopkins Press, Baltimore.

ACHINSTEIN, Peter (1980). "Discovery and Rule-Books", in Nickles (1980b), pp. 117–137.

BACH, Kent and HARNISH, Robert M. (1979), *Linguistic Communication and Speech Acts*. The MIT Press. Cambridge, Massachusetts, and London, England.

BALZER, Wolfgang and SNEED, Joseph D. (1977), "Generalized Net Structures of Empirical Theories", I, *Studia Logica* 36, pp. 195–211.

BELNAP, Nuel D. and STEEL, Thomas B., Jr. (1976), *The Logic of Questions and Answers*. New Haven and London, Yale University Press.

BROMBERGER, Sylvain (1965), "An Approach to Explanation", in R. J. Butler (ed.), *Analytical Philosophy,* 2nd Series, Basil Blackwell, Oxford, pp. 72–103.

BROMBERGER, Sylvain (1966), "Why-Questions", in R. Colodny (ed.), *Mind and Cosmos,* Pittsburgh University Press, Pittsburgh, pp. 86–111.

CURD, Martin (1980b), "The Logic of Discovery: An Analysis of three Approaches", in Nickles (1980b), pp. 201–219.

DACEY, Raymond (1981), "An Interrogative Account of the Dialectical Inquiring System Based upon the Economic Theory of Information", *Synthese* 47, pp. 43–55.

DARDEN, Lindley (1976), "Reasoning in Scientific Change: Charles Darwin, Hugo de Vries, and the Discovery of Segregation", *Studies in the History and Philosophy of Science* 7, pp. 127–169.

GUTTING, Gary (1980), "Science as Discovery", *Revue International de Philosophie",* No 131–132, pp. 49–89.

HATTIANGADI, J.N. (1978, 1979), "The structure of problems", Parts I and II. *Philosophy of the Social Sciences.*

HEMPEL, Carl G. (1966), *Philosophy of the Natural Science.* Prentice-Hall, New Jersey.

HINTIKKA, K. Jaakko J. (1976), *The Semantics of Questions and the Questions of Semantics.* Acta Philosophica Fennica, Vol. 28, No 4.

HINTIKKA, K. Jaakko J. (1981), "On the Logic of an Interrogative Model of Scientific Inquiry", *Synthese* 47, pp. 69–83.

JARVIE, I.C. (1979), "Laudan's Problematic Progress and the Social Sciences", *Philosophy of the Social Sciences,* Vol. 9, No 4, pp. 484–497.

KUHN, Thomas (1966), *The Copernican Revolution. Planetary Astronomy in the Development of Western Thought,* Harvard University Press, Cambridge, Massachusetts.

KRAJEWSKI, Wladyslaw (1977), *Correspondence Principle and Growth of Science,* D. Reidel, Dordrecht.

LAKATOS, Imre (1970), "Falsification and the Methodology of Scientific Research Programmes", in I. Lakatos and A. Musgrave (eds.), *Criticism and the Growth of Knowledge.* Cambridge University Press, pp. 91–196.

LAUDAN, Larry (1977), *Progress and Its Problems.* University of California Press. Berkeley, California.

LAUDAN, Larry (1979), "Historical Methodologies: An Overview and Manifesto", in P. Asquith and H. Kyburg (eds.), *Current Research in Philosophy of Science. Proceedings of the P.S.A. Critical Research Problems Conference,* East Lansing, Michigan.

LAUDAN, Larry (1980), "Views of Progress: Separating the Pilgrims from the Rakes". *Philosophy of the Social Sciences* 10, pp. 273–286.

LEPLIN, Jarrett (1980), "The Role of Models in Theory Constructions", in T. Nickles (ed.), *Scientific Discovery, Logic, and Rationality.* D. Reidel, Dordrecht.

LUGG, Andrew (1978), "Overdetermined Problems in Science", *Studies in History and Philosophy of Science* 9, p. 1–18.

LUGG, Andrew (1980), "Laudan and the Problem-Solving Approach to Scientific Progress and Rationality", *Philosophy of the Social Sciences* 9, pp. 466–474.

MAYR, Ernst (1980), "Prologue: Some Thoughts on the History of the Evolutionary Synthesis", in E. Mayr and W.B. Provine (eds.), *The Evolutionary Synthesis. Perspectives on the Unification of Biology.* Harvard University Press.

MEYER, Michel (1980), "Science as a Questioning-Process: A Prospect for a New Type of Rationality", *Revue International de Philosophie,* No. 131–132, pp. 49–89.

MOULINES, C. Ulises (1979), "Theory-Nets and the Evolution of Theories: The Example of Newtonian Mechanics". *Synthese* 41, pp. 417–439.

NICKLES, Thomas (1978), "Scientific Problems and Constraints", *PSA 1978,* Vol. 1, pp. 134–148.

NICKLES, Thomas (1980a), "Introductory Essay", in Nickles (1980b), pp. 1–59.

NICKLES, Thomas (1980b), *Scientific Discovery, Logic, and Rationality*. Boston Studies in the Philosophy of Science, Vol. 56, D. Reidel, Dordrecht.

NICKLES, Thomas (1980c), "Can Scientific Constraints Be Violated Rationally", in Nickles (1980b), pp. 285–315.

NICKLES, Thomas (1981), "What is a Problem that We May Solve It ?", *Synthese* 47, pp. 85–118.

NIINILUOTO, Ilkka (1976), "Inquiries, Problems, and Questions: Remarks on Local Induction", in R.J. Bogdan (ed.), *Local Induction,* D. Reidel.

NIINILUOTO, Ilkka (1980a), "The Growth of Theories: Comments on the Structuralist Approach", in J. Hintikka, D. Gruender, and E. Agazzi (eds.), *Pisa Conference Proceedings,* Vol. I, pp. 3–47.

NIINILUOTO, Ilkka (1980b), "Scientific Progress", *Synthese* 45, pp. 427–462.

PEARCE, David and RANTALA, Veikko (1981), *On a New Approach to Metascience.* Reports from the Department of Philosophy, University of Helsinki, No 1, 1981.

POPPER, Karl (1972), *Objective Knowledge,* Clarendon Press, Oxford.

RANTALA, Veikko (1978), "The Old and the New Logic of Metascience", *Synthese* 39, pp. 233–247.

SHAPERE, Dudley (1974), "Scientific Theories and Their Domains", in F. Suppe (ed.), *The Structure of Scientific Theories,* University of Illinois Press.

SHAPERE, Dudley, (1980), "The Character of Scientific Change", in Nickles (1980b), pp. 61–101.

SINTONEN, Matti, (1984), *The Pragmatics of Scientific Explanation.* Acta Philosophica Fennica, Vol. 37.

SNEED, Joseph (1976), "Philosophical Problems in the Empirical Science of Science: A Formal Approach", *Erkenntnis* 10, pp. 115–146.

STEGMUELLER, Wolfgang (1976), *The Structure and Dynamics of Theories.* Springer-Verlag, New York, Heidelberg and Berlin.

STEGMUELLER, Wolfgang (1979), *The Structuralist View of Theories. A Possible Analogue of the Bourbaki Programme in Physical Science.* Springer-Verlag, Berlin, Heidelberg and New York.

TOULMIN, Stephen (1972), *Human Understanding,* Vol. 1. Princeton University Press, Princeton.

TUOMELA, Raimo (1978), "On the Structuralist Approach to the Structure and Dynamics of Theories", *Synthese* 39, pp. 211–231.

TUOMELA, Raimo (1980), "Explaining Explaining", *Erkenntnis* 15, pp. 211–243.

LOGIC, DISCOURSE, DISCOVERY
AN AVERROISTIC REGISTER APPROACH

F. Vandamme

I. Historical background of the discovery problem

A. Hanson

It is mainly Hanson — we believe — who has renewed the interest and belief in the use and possibility of the logic of discovery. Herewith he was in direct conflict with the dominating methodology of science which argued that discovery was a problem outside the realm of logic and relevant only for the fields of psychology and sociology (1). In his final version Hanson introduces and interprets the logic of discovery as a logic for justifying the suggestion of a hypothesis (or in another terminology as a logic for justifying the plausibility of a hypothesis). He opposes such a logic to a logic of justifying the acceptance of a hypothesis. Much discussion then is going on, on the question if really these two activities, that is a) justifying the plausibility or b) justifying the acceptance of a hypothesis, really differ from each other, and if both activities can be organised in a logic. As opponents to his views, Hanson mentions Bacon, Locke, Hume, Mill, Reichenbach on the one side because they wrongly suppose that induction can do the job of discovery. On the other side, as opponents of the differentiation altogether, Hanson indicates Lensen, Braithwaite and Reichenbach. As forerunners of his ideas, Hanson points at Schiller, C.S. (Hanson 1958, p. 1073), but also at Aristotle, Pierce and Wittgenstein (Hanson, 1958, p. 1080). For many of the arguments for his case, Hanson searches in the scientific development of sixteenth and seventeenth century astronomy (Copernicus, Kepler, etc.).

That he does so, is not by accident, we believe, because if we look at the development of early modern science, we see that at that time there was very much awareness about these problems. We find this for instance in the work of Galileo too. The strong Averroistic influence in the development of modern science is responsible for this. We think here more particularly of the role of the University of Padua in the development of medicine and astronomy. The presence there of people like Galileo, Cusanus, Purbach, Regio Montanus, Copernicus, Vesalius, Harvey, etc. illustrates this. The Averroistic tradition culminated in this university. Its influecne on the development of scientific methodology in general and on the astronomy and physician school of Padua, has been widely discussed and illustrated. Therefore it seems to us interesting to pay some attention to the way that in Averroism the discovery problem was introduced. The work of Randall is rather illuminating here (Randall, 1940, 1961, etc.).

But, in order to do this it seems useful to pay attention to the earlier development of modern science. The roots of seventeenth-century scientific work go back, so it is argued more and more, through and beyond twelfth-century European learning (cf. Duhem, Randall, Renan).

Randall gives the following description of this development in a nutshell (2) :

There were two main critical movements during the later middle ages. The Ockhamites began in Oxford in the thirteenth century, and while persisting there found a new stronghold during the next hundred years in the Faculty of Arts at Paris. The Latin Averroists began in Paris in the thirteenth century, and shifted their seat to Padua early in the fourteenth. Both set out by expressing a secular and anti-clerical spirit, and by undertaking a destructive criticism of Thomism and Scotism, the thirteenth-century syntheses of science and religion. But both soon advanced beyond mere criticism to the constructive elaboration of natural science: they became the two great scientific schools of the later middle ages. The original work of the Ockhamites belongs to the fourteenth century, that of the Paduans, to the fifteenth and sixteenth. The former was done in dynamics, kinematics, and the logic of continuity and intensity; the latter, in methdology and in the further development of dynamics. Both turned from the earlier religious syntheses to the purely natural philosophy of Aristotle himself; and both developed primarily by a constructive criticism of the Aristotelian texts and doctrines. The Ockhamites were at first the more "progressive" and "modern"; they were interested in the free devlopment of Aristotelian physics, and their works take the form of questions and problems suggested by Aristotle's analyses. The Averroists, though much more secular and anti-clerical, were originally more conservative in their attitude towards Aristotle and his interpreter Averroes: their works are characteristically commentaries on the texts. From 1300 on, however, they knew and taught all the Ockhamite departures from Aristotelian doctrine: Paul of Venice (*1429) is remarkably up-to-date, and his *Summa Naturalis* contains an exposition of all the ideas of the dynamics of the Paris Ockhamites and the Oxford Logicians. The works of these fourteenth-century thinkers were printed in many editions as soon as the press reached Italy, all of them by 1490; and in the sixteenth century it was primarily the Italians who advanced by successive stages to the formulations of Galileo.

About 1400, therefore, the interest in the development of scientific ideas shifts from Ockhamite Paris to the Padua Averroists. From the time of Paul of Venice to Cremonini (*1631) Aristotelian physics and a nascent "Galilean" physics were in definite and conscious opposition at Padua, and this critical conflict contributed greatly to the working out of the latter. (Randall, 1940, pp. 180–181).

B. Randall's view of the discovery approach in the Paduan school (Randall, 1940).

The Paduan Averroists were concerned very much with method, and more peculiarly with the method for discovery and use of "principles" in science. They understood principium as Aristotle understood $\alpha\rho\chi\eta$, as being that from which a thing proceeds and has its origin in any way whatever. (In science a principium is that which is in any way a source of understanding.)

With Randall we can say that it is the achievement of the Paduan theory of science to have made a transformation of the demonstrative proof of causes into a method of discovery. So for instance Pietry d'Abano in his "Conciliator differentiarum philosophorum, et praecipue medicorum (1310)" makes a central distinction between two kinds of science and demonstration in terms of the theory of science developed in the Posterior Analytics. Science is defined as a demonstrative knowledge of things through their causes; its instrument is the demonstrative syllogism, which establishes the relations between causes and their effects. The problem of forming such syllogisms is the problem of discovering causes and defining them in such a way that they can serve as the middle terms of demonstrations. Pietro is thus distinguishing between two kinds of proof: that of effects through causes, and that of causes through effects (Randall, 1940, p. 186).

Pietro in his Tegni (Techne) or Art of medicine of Galen differentiates three doctrinae or ways of teaching medical science: by resolution, by composition and by definition. He is hereby strongly influenced by Averroes' threefold distinction in the Prohemium to his commentary on Aristotle's Physica. He differentiates a) demonstration simpliciter (or of cause and being), in which, as in mathematics, the causes are first both for us and for the order of Nature; b) demonstration propter quid, or of cause, in which, as in natural science, we start with what is first in nature but not first for us; and c) demonstration of being, or of sign, in which we start with effects to arrive at causes.

The differentiation between the procedure from effects to causes, and from causes to effects is Aristotelian. The terms resolutive and compositive to indicate them, came from Galen, Cicero and Boethius. It is however interesting to note that Averroes differentiates the procedure of mathematics from the a priori method or compositive method. It is also interesting to know that Averroes and many of his followers will call the resolutive method the method of sign.

It is also good to note what Galen says about the resolutive method (dissolutio): "in it you set up in your mind the thing at which you are aiming, and of which you are seeking a scientific knowledge, as the end to be satisfied. Then you examine what lies nearest to it, and nearest to that without which the thing cannot exist; nor are you finished till you arrive at the principle which satisfies it ...".

Jacopo da Forli (1413) who occupied alternately the chair of medicine and the chair of natural philosophy in Padua elaborates the method of resolution. He writes the following :

"Resolution is twofold, natural or real, and logical. Real resolution, though taken improperly in many senses, is strictly the separation and division of a thing into its component parts. Logical resolution is so called metaphorically. The metaphor is derived in this fashion: just as when something composite is revolved, the parts are separated from each other so that each is left by itself in its simple being, so also when a logical resolution is made, a thing at first understood confusedly is understood distinctly, so that the parts and causes touching its essence are distinctly grasped. Thus if when you have a fever you first grasp the concept of fever, you understand the fever in general and confusedly. You then resolve the fever into its causes, since any fever comes either from the heating of the humor or of the spirits or of the members, and again the heating of the humor is either of the blood or of the phlegm, etc.; until you arrive at the specific and distinct cause and knowledge of that fever." (Jacopo da Forli in Jacobi de Forlivio super Tegni Galeni, Padua, 1475).

Important here is that the resolution, contrary to the Galeni view, is looked at in a physical natural way, as well as in a logical way. The logical resolution is said to be metaphoric. It is anyway a search for causes.

Hugo of Sienna (1439, teacher of Medicine at Padua) remarks that in a complete science like physics or medicine, it is impossible to use only one method; both, the resolutive and the composite method or in modern terms, the discovery and the justification are required. He explains this as follows :

"In the discovery of the middle term or cause we proceed from effect to cause... Such a way of acquiring knowledge we call resolutive, because in that discovery we proceed from an effect, which is commonly more composite, to a cause which is simpler; and because by this discovery of the cause we certify the effect through the cause, we say that demonstration propter quid and of cause is the foundation of resolutive knowledge...". (Randall, 1940, p. 190). Here we get an idea of a criterion for a cause. A cause is commonly simpler than an effect which is more composite.

This idea of a double process in science is directly derived from Averroes and already exposed by Urban the Averroist in his large commentary on the Physics in 1334. Against Aristotle it is argued by for instance Paul of Venice (1429) that the double procedure in physical demonstrations is not a circular proof.

"Scientific knowledge of the cause depends on a knowledge of the effect, just as scientific knowledge of the effect depends on a knowledge of the cause, since we know the cause through the effect before we know the effect through the cause. This is the principal rule in all investigation, that a scientific knowledge of natural effects demands a prior knowledge of their causes and principles — This is not a circle, however: — in scientific procedure there are three kinds of knowledge. The first is of the effect without any reasoning, called quia, that it is. The second is of the cause through knowledge of that effect; it is likewise called quia. The third is of the effect through the cause; it is called propter quia. But the knowledge of why (proter quia) the effect is, is not the knowledge that (quia) is in an effect. Therefore the knowledge of the effect does not depend on itself, but upon something else." (Summa philosophiae naturalis magistri Pauli Veneti, Venice, 1503).

During the fifteenth century attention was increasingly focused on this "double procedure" involved in scientific method. It came to be known by the Averroistic term "regress": meaning the dependency of all strict demonstration on the prior investigation and establishment of the appropriate principles. Such methods for discovery were carefully examined for instance in Cajetan of Thiene's comment on the Physics. (cf. Gaietani de Thienis, Recollecte super octo libros Physicorum Aristotelis, Venice, 1496). This search for the cause is also sometimes explicit, called the procedure of discovering the cause (cf. Augustini Niphi philosophi seussani expositio ... de Physico auditu, Venice, 1552).

It would be interesting to analyse the details of his suggested discovery method in order to see how relevant they still are for the construction of a modern logic of discovery. The quotation of Randall permits already the determination of certain interesting features. So Nifo accentuates the´importance of the knowledge of the truth of the effects for such a discovery. This knowledge comes from the senses. Other relevant knowledge is knowledge why (remark a question) an effect is so and this is knowledge known to us through the discovery (inventio) of the cause. Nifo also adds: "That something is a cause can never be so certain as that an effect exists; for the existence of an effect is known to the senses. That it is the cause remains conjectural, even if that conjectural existence is better known than the effect itself in the order of knowledge propter quid. For if the discovery of the cause is assumed, the reason why the effect is so is always known. Hence in the Meteors Aristotle grants that he is not setting forth the true causes of natural effects, but only in so far as was possible for him, and in conjectural or hypothetical fashion." (Augustini Niphi philosophi suessani expositio ... de Physico auditu, Venice, 1552).

With Randall (1940, p. 194) we like to remark that at no time, the Averroistic Paduan medical Aristotelians attribute, unlike Thomas and Duns Scotus, to the intellectus the power to recognize the truth of principles. The method by which principles are arrived at is rather the guarantee of their validity; they are dependent on that method, and it is the "cause" of their explanatory power. Nifo makes explicit what was implicit in the Averroistic medical tradition in Padua.

Using the terminology of Hanson we could even say that the justification of the acceptance of a hypothesis (the deductive approach) is dependent on a justification of the plausibility of a hypothesis: that it is dependent on the logic of discovery.

The justification of acceptance, or the procedure from causes to effects, is called by Zimara the procedure of order. It is the procedure of teaching and exposition of the subject-matter. The other procedure is the method, concerned with the discovery and demonstration of its principles and properties. Zimara too like many others, accepts Averroes' "regress" as the procedure to be followed in physics: first there is the way of discovery, by which alone principles are learned from the investigation of experience; then the way of science and judgment by which we explain that experience.

Bernardinus Tomitanus (1576) repeats this but he accentuates the importance of particulars in the discovery process. He accentuates Averroes' notion of signs, which are, in Bernardinus' view, particular effects. His student Zabarella regards logic purely as an instrument: it is a tool, sought not for its own sake but for its utility in furthering science. Sciences are nothing other than logical methods put to use.

The whole treatment of logic is about second notions, but these are our own work, and by our will can either be or not be ... Logic is an instrumental discipline created by philosophers from the practice of philosophy, which constructs second notions in the concepts of things, and makes them into instruments by which in all things the true may be known and distinguished from the false ...

We have the impression that Averroes' stress on the "signs", with its association with language (cf. Zabarella's comparison between logic and grammar) brings us to a development rather near the sophist Protagoras, to a certain degree, and, we believe, towards the kernel of modern science.

Interesting also is that Zabarella differentiates between two ways of discovery:

"The one is demonstration from effects, which in the performance of its function is exceedingly efficacious; and we employ it for the discovery of those things that are very obscure and hidden. The other is induction, which is a much weaker form of resolution, and is employed for the discovery of only those things which are hardly unknown, but need only to be made a little clearer."

By induction we discover only those principles that are "known secundum naturam," that is, that are sensible, in that their instances or singulars are perceived by sense. By demonstration a signo we can discover those principles that are "unknown secundum naturam," that is, the instances of which are not sensible, and hence can only be inferred from their effects, like first matter or the prime mover. Zabarella is here following his teacher Tomitanus in making "induction" a form of the method of resolution. His distinction between the two kinds of resolution in terms of the two kinds of principle discovered is that of between arriving at a formal and at an explanatory principle; it is analogous to that made in the next century between the laws of motion and the forces causing acceleration, between the mathematical principles of natural philosophy and the forces of inertia and gravitation – both of which Newton likewise "deduced from phenomena".

Here already we met the Hanson-Reichenbach discussion on induction. The terminology and method defended by Zabarella we find in the procedure and terms used by Galileo (Randall, p. 199). Zabarella also stresses that in our way of discovery we are following the order of knowledge and not that of things. The regress viz. the combination of the dissolution and the composition, Zabarella describes therefore as follows:

"First we observe the particular effect. Secondly, we resolve the complex fact into its component parts and conditions. Thirdly, we examine this supposed or hypothetical cause by a "mental consideration" to clarify it and to find its essential elements. Finally, we demonstrate the effect from that cause".

With the Paduans we have a clearer differentiation between the theory of proof and the theory of discovery. Zabarella differs from Nifo in that he did not follow up the suggestion of Nifo that all natural science remains conjectural and hypothetical. This was so because he believed that an examination of particular instances would reveal an intelligible structure present in them. And it's precisely that faith, claims Randall, which inspired seventeenth-century science.

A claim which is Averroistic, but which is open to a wide variety of interpretations. Some of these are compatible with a Protagorean point of view, but others are antagonistic with it, an ambiguity which is still present in science today.

In summary, we argue that in the Averroistic tradition, and via this tradition, in the 16th and 17th century science up to Newton, there existed a clearcut differentiation between the logic of proof and the logic of discovery. The combination of both, being necessary in natural science, is called regress. Important in the logic of discovery is the separation and division of a thing into its components, this in the strict sense and metaphorically. The search for the more simple against the more composite in this process is guiding. The treatment in the Averroistic tradition of effects as signs, as particulars, and the comparison of discovery logic with language, with grammar is striking. Both logic and grammar are instruments constructed by the actor for realizing his purposes (Zabarella). Such a point of view is very suggestive for a modern logic of discovery. But a logic of discovery, which is also neatly related to a logic of discourse: the combination, the production and analysis of signs. And so we touch on the second part of our paper: the discourse and the logic of discourse. But also if we study the approach to discovery of Hanson and his proponents, we remark that in their description of the logic of discovery they too pay much attention to processes, features which seem strongly language- and discourse-dependent. So Hanson (1958) indicates as important factors in the logic for justifying the suggestion for a hypothesis: analogy (Hanson, 1958, p. 1077), symmetry (Hanson 1958, p. 1078) and authority (Hanson 1958, p. 1079). In his 1962 paper, he adds to this series, elegance (Hanson 1962, p. 185). Kordig (1978) suggest the addition of simplicity and explanatory fertility (Kordig, 1978, p. 113). And as Sheffer (1978) has argued rather convincingly, both are strongly language dependent.

All this strongly motivates us to turn to the logic of discourse, in order to approach better equipped the logic of discovery.

II. Discourse and discovery

A. Introduction

The strong relation between discovery and discourse comes in the open rather easily if you look at the etymological and philosophical meaning of discourse. The term "discourse" is derived from the latin "discurrere" and "discursus". This is a combination of the prefix "dis" (indicating an analysis, disruption in several directions) and the verb of movement "currere" (to run). Against this background we understand better the definition of the french "discours", as introduced in Lalandes. Lalandes differentiates between a general and a more specific interpretation. The general one he relates to the english "discourse" and the concrete one with the english "speech". So we read :

"A: Opération intellectuelle qui s'effectue par une suite d'opérations

élémentaires partielles et successives: "Discursus est transitus cogitantis a senten-
tia ad sententiam ordine quadam, sive consequentiarum, sive alio, ut in
methodo" (Leibniz, Opuscules et fragments inédits, ed. Couturat 459).

B: Spécialement, expression et développement de la pensée par une suite de
mots ou de propositions qui s'enchaînent."

So the more general interpretation is the meaning which is better known in
the use of its adjectival derivation "discursif". It means an intellectual operation
which is realized by means of a sequence of partial and successive elementary
operations. It is as such in direct opposition with intuition, which refers to a
direct intellectual operation without intermediate steps.

The more specific interpretation of discourse is an operation based on the
use of utterances, ultimately producing a construction of a set of utterances
connected and related to each other, with a strong cohesion in terms of a topic.
A logic of discovery related to the scientific discovery (as we have exposed it)
and a logic of discourse have at least in common their interest in and their dependency on the complexity and structure of their material. For both analyse
complex symbolic structures. In discovery, at least in the Averroistic tradition,
the search for more simple components in the observed data was crucial, in
other words the analysis with the intention to find or to create features is what
it is all about in the logic of discovery, at least in an early stage. As far as the
analysis of discourse is concerned, we find an analogy and correspondence with
primary discovery. It too is a search for elementary components and their
structure of interrelations. In the production of discourse, what is important is
the production of complexity on the basis of more simple elements. But for the
development and production of knowledge too, what is important is "regress".
This is the analysis and consequently the production of structures. For
discourse, the same is true. Taking the symmetry and analogy between regress
and discourse into account and the cognitive dimension of discourse, does it
not seem interesting to relate the method of regress, that is the combination
of discovery and proof, with the logic of discourse ? Could it even not be useful
and clarifying to consider "regress" as a special form of discourse ? In such a
perspective the study of discourse and its logic is crucial for a better understanding of logic of regress: the logic of discovery and the logic of proof. The
handling by Averroes of effects as signs (effects, the starting points of discovery)
is certainly a pointer in this direction. But if we proceed in this direction,
and thus believe that the study of discourse is relevant for the study of
regress in general and discovery in particular, how to approach discourse ?

B. Discourse and dialogue

Grize J.B. (1981) in his approach to the study of discourse argues that a discourse only can be understood as the result of a dialogue (une activité dialogique). But he remarks that a dialogue is for him not a mixture of two speeches. It is rather the production of a speech by two actors A and B, A being the speaker and B being the listener. Grize also remarks that in most speeches the actor B is only virtually present. That means that the actor A makes his speech taking into account his representation of the listener B, anticipating the incomprehensions and refusals of the listener.

Evidently we also can introduce the other type of discourse which is the result of two actors who are alternatively speaker and listener. Such a "discourse" also embodies a kind of cohesion and is also a product of discursive thought and symbolisation. It is also a construct of sequences of partial more elementary operations, transformations. So from the dialogue point of view, we can differentiate the discourse-dialogues in monologues (a), dialogues (b), trilogues (c), in function of the number of speakers which play actively a part in the discourse, neglecting in this classification the important role of listeners.

C. Disciourse production and discourse analysis

When we study or use symbols we have to differentiate two levels. The components of this dualism has been called by de Saussure: "langue" and "parole". Today we see that some authors use the labels "performance" and "competence" to indicate the same dualism. We also accept such a dualism, but in an Averroistic mode, we would rather speak here of a regress. This means that the langue, the competence, is constructed, discovered, invented on the basis of the parole, the performance. But once constructed, invented, discovered "langue", "competence" explains "parole", "performance". However, we must also take into account the dynamism in the performance, the "parole", motivated by the change of the context and the actors, and therefore causing adaptation of the "parole" to the changing and developing context and actors. A changing parole implies inevitably a changing competence ! The competence functions as a more stable structure of symbolisation interrelations, which are socially sanctioned. The performance level rather exemplifies attempts to construct symbolisation structures adapted to particular purposes of the actors in a specific situation. Taking into account the priority of the performance level as the basis of the regress, and taking into account the importance of purposes, and therefore of actions, on that level, we think it is important to organise the sets of symbols and symbolisation structures in both levels following criteria based on activities (performance level) and types of activities (competence level). A set of symbols related to a particular action or action type we call a register. A concrete register in the former case, an abstract register in the latter case. When we try to elaborate and describe registers exemplified in natural texts, we find it rather comfortable to differentiate between registers, subregisters and superregisters. Let us explain.

In a certain text one may be talking about food, in another text or part thereof about love and in a third one about familyduties. Each of these topics we characterise by a set of actions related to a specific set of symbols. Such a topic-description we call a register. So we get respectively a food register, a love register, a family register, etc... However, it is sometimes useful to differentiate a particular register in subregisters. For instance as far as food is concerned, one can produce them, prepare them, eat them, etc. So we can differentiate and define corresponding subregisters. But what is more, there are activities which transgress peculiar registers, even if a certain register they become idiomatic. We think here about praising, evaluating, communicating, etc.. The symbolic organization of those activities which transgress particular registers we call superregister. So we get the following overall picture:

R_1 .... R_n : superregisters — r_1 .... r_n : registers — r_{ia} .... r_{iz} : subregisters

We can construct however a field of such registers on the competence level or on the performance level. In the former case we call it the abstract field of registers, A, in the latter case the concrete field of registers, C. Discourse production and analysis then will be dependent on one or more particular concrete fields of registers C. Several procedures for discourse production and discourse analysis are possible. Several techniques, rules and features for such procedures have been discussed and elaborated in literature (Grize, Foucault, Hintikka, Halliday, Davey, etc.). We don't want to go into further detail on this. For our purposes in this paper, it is sufficient to introduce registers, that is the arguments of discourse production and analysis procedures. It is possible to define syntax, semantics and pragmatics in relation to these registers, but we don't want to go into this matter here (cf. Vandamme 1979).

For the perspective of relating discourse and discovery, we think it however fruitful to elaborate somewhat more on the C-field of registers. The C-field of registers is adapted to the context and actors of discourse. The relevant symbols here can be external. That is, they can be brought in on the basis of observation, or by intermediate inputs from the actors present in the situation. Some symbols however may be internal, that is they can be borrowed from the A-field of registers (4).

D. Discourse operating and dialogue

Above we have already differentiated between two types of dialogues. In one type (I) we have one speaker who produces his dialogue in view of a virtual listener or listeners. The other case (II) is the dialogue which is the result of the verbal interaction between several actors (2 or more eventually in nature) who are in turn listener and speaker.

We are convinced that these different types of dialogues are making use in a different way of the A- and C-field of registers and of the discourse production procedures (DPP) and the discourse analysis procedures (DAP). In the former case (dialogue type I) we can say that the data in the C-field of registers are borrowed mainly from the A-field. This is most and for all true about data on the virtual opponent. In the latter case (a genuine dialogue) most data in the C-registers are introduced from observation of the situation (symbolisation of the observations) and certainly many data are present which are the direct output of the opponent, more peculiarly their contribution to the dualogue. So we see an important asymmetry between dialogue type I and dialogue type II as far as their C-field is concerned on the basis of which the dialogue is produced. The asymmetry is even stronger if we take into account that in discourse production of type II, we need not only make use of DPP (discourse production procedures) but also of DAP (discourse analysis procedures). DAP is needed for the reason that speaker A needs to analyse the output of B, to be able to react to this output, for his contribution to the dialogue in view of the necessary cohesion. It is important to note that we didn't talk about coherence but about cohesion. This means that type II dialogue is far more complex than type I: a more complex C-field and an integration of DAP and DPP is needed.

E. Discourse and proof.

Proof production is discourse production of type I. It is a production of discourse realised by an actor in function of a virtual listener. It is abstract in the sense that new data of the situation and the concrete listener is in principle irrelevant. Scientific proof production furthermore requires certain restrictions on the DPP, for instance use of deduction, definitions, etc.

F. Discourse and discovery

Production of discovery, of invention, is a type II dialogue, a dialogue in which the data from the situation, the observations, are very important, including the reactions of the opponents. Such a discourse is an attempt to create relations in order to structure the observations, the new data. It is a discourse which requires much of creativity and originality. The data from the A-field can be useful in this matter, but in many cases, deviations from it are needed. Deviations which can be so successful sometimes that they not only permit the construction of specific registers or subregisters in the C-field, but even lead towards a fundamental restructuring of the A-field. In its turn, this change will lead to a new kind of type I dialogues. In this way we get the whole regress. By discovery a change in the A-field is realised by intermediation of the C-field and the discovery discourse. Once this change in the A-field is realised, we get a different discourse of proof.

Discovery procedures in general and the scientific discovery procedures in particular have certain specific characteristics. Metaphor, analogy, symmetry, simplicity, etc. can all be fruitful means in the search for a structure or a new structure in the C-field. A new structure which later on one must be able to justify in a proof discourse (I dialogue). How the metaphor, analogy, etc. can be used in the C-field is something which can and has been studied in terms of the DAP and DPP procedures for the II-dialogues. We will however not go into this matter here.

G. Logic and discourse

Logic is a tool for organising and so is discourse in its abstract sense. Or rather, in the Leibnizian sense, discourse is the intellectual operation, the activity, which has to be realised in order to get an organisation. Logic is then rather the procedure itself, the system which is exemplified in a discourse. If we take logic in this large meaning, it is a system of organisation. It is clear that in this case there exists a large variety of procedures and therefore a large variety of logics. Some of these procedures are developed in genuine systems, others are not. Some are to a high degree widely accepted in a certain group, a culture; other such procedures (eventually systems) are rather idiosyncratic. Certain social groups have even identified themselves so strongly with a certain logic, that the acceptance and use of it becomes a sine qua non for belonging to the group. The acceptance and use of a particular logic functions sometimes as a status symbol too.

All this suggests that efficiency is an important criterion for the evaluation of the development of logic (in the broad sense). The efficiency can be, however, very disparate. We can have social, economic, technical, persuasive, emotional, epistemic, etc. efficiency. The social efficiency of a logic will be dependent on the integration in a society it permits, and the degree of progress and adaptation of this society it stimulates. The persuasive efficiency of a logic will depend on the degree of persuasion of the listeners it results in. Epistemic efficiency will perhaps depend on the degree of explication and prediction it produces. Evidently sometimes, and even most of the time, the logic used can be efficient in more than one perspective (social and epistemic efficiency for instance).

But can and do we have to make a differentiation between the logics used in I-dialogues and the logics used in II-dualogues ?

The logics in I-dialogues are mostly socially normative logics; we call them I-logics. In II-dialogues the I-logics or parts thereof are rather frequently used too, but one shifts more readily from one system or procedure of logic to another one, in perspective of a peculiar efficiency or purpose one is looking to maximize. Also for the reason that the talk in the II-discourse is mostly less general, the logic used is also more informal, this means less standard. Consequently many of the procedures used for organising are not elaborated into strict systems, which is rather the case in the I-discourse. The more formal the talk, the more the logic used is standardised !

In the logic of II-dialogues (II-logics) analogy, metaphor, authority, esthetic elements and so on can easier be taken into account, for the reason that pressure in behalf of the normalisation is much weaker. So it is easier to sacrifice normalisation and standardisation in favour of elegance, metaphor, analogy, etc.

We already argued that the logic of proof is a logic of I-dialogues. On the contrary in our view, the logic of discovery is a logic of the II-dialogue. Taking this into account and the comment on the differentiation between type I-logics and type II-logics, do we not expect that the logic of discovery will be a logic much less standardised and normalised than the logic of proof ? This weaker standardisation is even — one could agree — the explication of and the guarantee for the stronger creativity and the higher heuristical value of the logic of discovery.

II. Conclusion

Finally we want to conclude with the statement that the Averroistic regress, the way from effects to the explanatory principles and vice versa is the center of the scientific method. This seems to be confirmed if we look into the history of modern science, giving attention to its earlier developments as well as to present-day results of scientists. This is true only on condition that we study not only the official published reports, but study also the lab-activities, the preparations of scientists for their publications etc.

This regress method can better be understood, we believe, if one studies it as a discourse, a dialogue. In this perspective it is possible to differentiate a logic of proof and a logic of discovery; both together are necessary for the regress. We think it's important and necessary to study intensively both types of logics of dialogues. Therefore this paper is finally a plea for better descriptive dialogue logics and for more intensive study of systems of dialogue logics.

NOTES

(1)   The following articles of Hanson are here crucial : Hanson 1958, 1961, 1960. Interesting reactions to Hanson's 1958 paper, which have caused elaborations of his views, come from Schon 1959. Relevant comments are also in Kording 1978.

(2)   We want also to attract attention : a) to the important controversy initiated in Padua by Cajetan of Thiene (1465) on a mathematical versus a qualitative physics; b) to the Tractatus de proportionibus of a Milanese physician, Johannes Marlianus (Pavia 1482) which brings experimental proof to bear on the quantitative side, describing the rolling of balls down an inclined plane to measure their velocity and acceleration, and narrating experiments with pendulums; c) the discussion in Padua in favour of "cause" as a mathematically-formulated formal cause (Randall 1940, pp. 181–182).

(3)   It is also interesting to note what Galenus, following a comment of the Arab Hali, says about the resolutive method : "in it you set up in your

mind the thing at which you are aiming, and of which you are seeking a scientific knowledge, as the end to be satisfied. Then you examine what lies nearest to it, and nearest to that without which the thing cannot exist; nor are you finished till you arrive at the principle which satisfies it." (Galieni principia medicorum Microtegni cum commento Hali, 1479).

(4)   A certain C-register, if it is very successful, can motivate the change of the corresponding A-register, and vice versa.

REFERENCES

DUHEM, P., 1906–1913. *Etudes sur Léonard de Vinci.* Paris (3 vols.)

DUHEM, P., 1905–6. *Origines de la Statique.* Paris (2 vols.)

GRIZE, J., 1981, Pour aborder l'étude des structures du discours quotidien, in: Bouacha A.A. & Portine H., *Langue Française,* mai, Laruousse, pp. 7–19.

HANSON, N.R., 1958, The Logic of Discovery, *Journal of Philosophy,* Vol. IV, pp. 1073–1089.

HANSON, N.R., 1960, More on "the logic of Discovery", *Journal of Philosophy,* Vol. LVI, pp. 182–188.

HANSON, N.R., 1961, A budget of cross-type inferences or invention is the mother of necessity, *Journal of Philosophy,* Vol. LVIII, 17, pp. 449–470.

KORDIG, C.R., 1978, Discovery and justification. *Philosophy of Science,* 45, pp. 110–111.

RANDALL, J.H., 1940, Scientific method in the school of Padua. *Journal of the History of Ideas,* Vol. 12, pp. 177–206.

RANDALL, J.H., 1961, *The school of Padua and the emergence of modern science,* Padua.

RENAN, E., 1861, *Averroes et l'averroïsme. Essai historique.* (2e ed.), Paris.

SCHEFFER, I., 1964, *The anatomy of inquiry,* Routledge & Kegan Paul, London.

SCHON, D., 1959, Comment on Mr. Hanson's "The logic of discovery", *The Journal of Philosophy,* Vol. LVI, 21, pp. 500–503.

VANDAMME, F., 1979. *Aspekten van pragmatiek. Een inleiding in register-pragmatiek.* Communication & Cognition, Gent.

2

THE DEVELOPMENT OF A LOGIC

AND/OR A

GENERAL THEORY OF DISCOURSE

DIFFERENT USES OF THE DEFINITE ARTICLE*

Jaakko Hintikka & Jack Kulas

1. Towards a pragmatic theory of the other uses of the definite article

In an earlier paper (Hintikka and Kulas (1982), we have developed within the framework of game-theoretical semantics (for it, see (Saarinen 1979: Hintikka 1982) a theory of *the*-phrases in their anaphoric use. This theory will now be extended in order to yield a treatment of several of the other main uses of *the*-phrases in English. They include (i) the Russellian use, (ii) what might be called the contextual or ostensive use (the phrase *the X* refers to a contextually conspicuous X), (iii) the generic use, and (iv) a number of the less prominent uses. (Certain other, *prima facie* separate uses, e.g., the epithetic one, have already been treated.) The extensions considered in the present paper are pragmatic rather than semantical. That is, instead of showing that the different uses to be treated all fall under suitable semantical rules, it will be argued that contextual and other pragmatic factors frequently distort the basic semantical rules so as to yield certain other uses as a natural consequence.

The basic use we shall start from is the anaphoric one. This procedure is not obvious and needs a few words of explanation. For one thing, it might seem tempting to formulate a more general rule (G. *the*) for the English definite article which is like (G. anaphoric *the*) (see below) except that the set *I* is left open, and is to be filled by further specifications. Then we could obtain, on the one hand, (G. anaphoric *the*) and, on the other hand, the game rules governing various others uses as so many special cases. For instance, we obtain (G. Russellian *the*) as a special case by choosing *I* to be the whole universe of discourse (or, rather the subdomain determined in the way indicated in (Hintikka 1983)).

More explicitly, on this treatment we would start from the following general rule :

(G. *the*)   When the game has reached a sentence of the form

(*) $\qquad$ $[X - [\text{the Y}]_{NP} [\text{who Z}]_S - W]_S$

then an individual, say b, is chosen by Myself from a certain set I of individuals, whereupon Nature chooses a different individual, say d, from the same set I. The game is then continued with respect to

(**) $\qquad$ $[[X - b - W]_S, [b \text{ is } [\text{a Y}]]_{NP}]_S, [b \ Z]_S,$ but

$[d \text{ is not } [\text{a Y}]_{NP} [\text{who Z}]_S]_S.$

Then the Russellian treatment results by choosing I = the whole domain (or, rather, the appropriate subdomain or "category", as indicated in (Hintikka 1983). The anaphoric use results from choosing I so that it contains:

(i) $\quad$ The individuals chosen by the players so far in the same subgame.
(ii) $\quad$ The individuals referred to by proper names in the input sentence of the game.

Additionally, I is the smallest set which contains (i)–(ii) and which is closed with respect to all the functions "remembered" from earlier subgames. (Certain further qualifications and explanations are needed here, but they are not relevant to our present purposes.)

The rule (G. *the*) as formulated is to be thought of as a special case of a more general rule, as in the case of our other quantifier rules. It is subject to the same restrictions as the special cases of our other quantifier rules formulated in other treatments of game-theoretical semantics.

There is no blatant mistake in this course of action, i.e., in starting from (G. *the*) and in considering the different uses of phrases containing *the* as being obtained from it through different pragmatically guided choices of the set I. Indeed, it offers a useful framework for studying different uses of the definite article. However, it does not yield the best overall theory here. Not only does it leave the choice of I completely unexplained. What is more, it does not specify which use of the definite article (which choice of I) is to be considered as the fundamental one, i.e., the one in the light of which the others are to be understood. What we shall do is to consider (G. anaphoric *the*) as the fundamental rule, and we shall try to explain the other subcases of (G. *the*) as pragmatically determined variants of (G. anaphoric *the*). In this explanation, important use will be made of the so-called principle of charity.

This procedure is also supported by the following observation. It seems to us that when the anaphoric interpretation of *the*-phrases is possible (i.e., when the set I is not empty), the anaphoric reading excludes the Russellian one.

The following might perhaps be examples :

> (1)   All fifteen of Bob's schoolmates were interested in chess. They all admired the best chess player.

> (2)   You want to see Mr. Lowell ? Well, today the president is down in Washington conferring with Mr. Roosevelt.

(Reputedly said by a Harvard secretary in the early thirties to a visitor who wanted to see Abbot Lawrence Lowell.)

2. The deictic and presupposing uses

Let us first point out two deviations from (G. anaphoric *the*) which are easily explainable pragmatically. First, we must normally admit into I more individuals than it has so far been allowed to contain. Over and above the individuals referred to by the proper names occurring in the initial sentence, we must also admit certain individuals given contextually. If an animal trainer in a circus is in trouble and I shout to him :

> (3)   Look out for the tiger !

the intended reference of the *the*-phrase is specified neither by an earlier proper name nor by the selection from individuals chosen earlier in a semantical game. What is involved in such uses ? At first sight, it might look as if we had to deal with a simple relativization to a contextually restricted domain of entities. There are some uses of *the*-phrases where this is the right diagnosis. Witness, e.g., the following :

> (4)   When driving through the town of Stone Mountain, John wanted to mail a postcard but could not find the post office.

However, mere relativization is not all that can happen. If we recall some of the famous Donnellan-type examples, we can see that in many cases apparent relativization really means letting one's quantifiers range over perceptually identified objects.

In order to see this, note how we can deal with examples like the following :

> (5)   The man with a martini glass is a famous economist.

The referential reading of (5) can be captured by taking (5) to mean

(6)   The man who I believe has a martini glass is a famous economist.

and then by giving the definite description in (6) the *de re* (wide scope) reading. But I can *believe* that others in the same context (at the same party) have martini glasses in their hands. Hence (6) does not capture the intended meaning of (5), unless it is assumed that the quantifiers implicit in (6) are restricted to perceptually identified individuals. In order for the utterance to make sense, these individuals must be among the perceptual objects of both the speaker and the hearer.

Here, then, we have a pragmatically conditioned extension of *I*. This extension consists of the set *I* of those entities that belong to the perceptually identified individuals of both the speaker and the hearer. (For the notion of a perceptual (perceptually identified) individual, see (Hintikka 1969, 1970, 1974).)

This procedure might seem to be motivated more epistemologically than linguistically. It has a striking etymological precedent, however, in that *the* is a descendant of the Old English demonstrative *se, seo*, another form of which has come down to us as the demonstrative *that*. As Russell already recognized, demonstratives are the archetypal ways of referring to an object of acquaintance. As we may put it, one can refer demonstratively in an utterance to an object and be understood if and only if the object referred to belongs to the perceptual objects of both the speaker and the hearer.

Our latest modification of (G. anaphoric *the*) opens the door for another extension. Above it was noted that by using certain anaphoric *the*-phrases we can attribute various properties to individuals chosen by players earlier in the game or referred to by proper names in relevant preceding sentences. This was what the epithetic use of *the*-phrases amounted to. It was likewise seen that by using anapohric *the*-phrases we can impose conditions on the individuals that are introduced by expressions dealt with earlier in the semantical game. The so-called epithetic use of *the*-phrases is a case in point.

Now it is equally natural for a speaker to use *the*-phrases to indicate which individuals he or she is including in the background set *I'* that we just introduced. When a cabinet minister in answering a parliamentary question addresses an M.P. as "my right honorable friend", he is not thereby branding all his other friends as "right dishonorable". He is indicating that at the time of utterance his selected set *I'* contains only one friend of his, that is, that he is temporarily restricting his attention to the one friend he is addressing.

3. The Russellian use

So far, we have not attempted a treatment of the Russellian use of *the*-phrases. Such a treatment — a pragmatic one — is nevertheless very easy. Suppose, as we propose, that the anaphoric use is the normative one and that it is governed by our rule (G. anaphoric *the*). All we have to do is to ask, How would one naturally interpret a *the*-phrase in circumstances (in a context) in which the anaphoric reading does not make any sense or in which it is clearly not what the speaker means ? Russellian uses of *the*-phrases are typically cases in point. Suppose someone says to us,

(7)   The author of *Waverly* is a Scot.

How am I to understand this utterance ? Here we can profitably borrow a leaf from Donald Davidson's book and resort to the crucial *principle of charity*. It seems to us that linguists and philosophers have not realized to what an extraordinary extent Davidson is right about the use of the principle of charity in the semantical interpretation of various utterances.

But how is the principle of charity supposed to guide us in understanding (7) ? The understanding of (7) by means of (G. anaphoric *the*) depends on the possibility of the two players of our semantical games making certain choices from a contextually given set I of individuals. But in the example (unless there is more to the context than we have mentioned) there is no such set available to the players. Yet the speaker is obviously trying to convey something to us.

What, in such circumstances, is more natural — more in keeping with the principle of charity — than to assume that the domain of choice I that the speaker intends is the domain of individuals which is given to us and to him and to all speakers of the language together with the normal interpretation of the English language ? Surely the natural thing is to take I to be the domain over which standard quantifiers of the same kind as are normally used in (7), e.g., 'someone' and 'everyone', range.

But, as was pointed out above, this results precisely in the Russellian treatment of *the*-phrases. Russell's "theory of definite descriptions" thus assumes a relatively modest niche as a special case of our treatment of 'the', which assigns the pride of place to anaphoric uses of the definite article. Russell's theory is, as it were, a special case of ours distorted by contextual, pragmatic pressures. From another perspective, however, the honors nevertheless belong to Russell, for our "anaphoric" theory was originally inspired by him. ·

It is thus possible to see in pragmatic terms how the Russellian use of *the*-phrases can be considered as a variant of the anaphoric use. Briefly, since there is no nonempty set I in the sense of (G. anaphoric *the*) available, the hearer interprets the *the*-phrase by making the next most obvious choice, that is, setting I equal to the whole domain of discourse (strictly speaking, to the relevant category). It is important to realize that such a reading is very much a reading by default. It is the best one can do in the absence of further relevant background information. When such information is available, other things may happen which, for instance, can lead us to the so-called generic uses of *the*-phrases.

It would be very interesting to ask whether the absolutistic character of Russell's theory of definite descriptions, reflected by the fact that Russell, as it were, sets I equal to the whole fixed domain of discourse, is based on Russell's belief in "language as the universal medium" in the sense of (Hintikka, 1981a, 1981b). (Cf. Hylton 1981; Goldfarb 1979). After all, one of the main corollaries to that belief is that the ranges of our quantifiers cannot be varied, that our universe of discourse is fixed once and for all. It is fairly clear that this in fact was the background of Russell's theory. However, the historical details are hard to pinpoint, and the question whether the corollary is really an inevitable one remains to be answered.

4. The generic use motivated

Our pragmatic account of the generic use of *the*-phrases will assume that the anaphoric use of *the*-phrases is the normal (and even normative) one. It can be dramatized in the form of an imaginary internal monologue which I can carry out when somebody addresses the following sentence to me :

(8)   The tiger is a dangerous animal.

"Is the speaker trying to warn me ?" I turn quickly and look around to see whether there is a situationally given big cat around which the speaker might be referring to (or, for that matter, any other individual around which the speaker might have mistaken for a tiger). (This usage of *the*-phrases is what the set I' discussed above was supposed to enable us to handle.) Seeing and hearing none, I continue : "The speaker is obviously serious, and is obviously trying to make a nontrivial remark." There is also no indication that he might be intending his words in a nonliteral sense. "Now what can he possibly mean ? There is no nonempty set I given in the sense of (G. anaphoric *the*); hence the speaker cannot be using the *the*-phrase anaphorically to make a nontrivial point. Moreover, he knows — and he knows that I know — that there is more than one tiger in existence. Hence, he cannot, by the same token, be using the *the*-phrase in a Russellian way either, for then the falsity of what he is saying would be patent. What, then, can he possibly mean by speaking of *the* tiger ? He is obviously presuming that the statement he made is true — or at least not obviously and trivially false. Now the use of the definite article presupposes uniqueness for the truth of (8). Hence the utterer must be envisaging an imaginary situation in which there is precisely one tiger in the set *I* of individuals which is to be considered. More generally, there presumably is (by parity of cases) one representative individual from each one of a range of species in the *I* which is being presupposed."

"How is this tiger to be selected, then ? The context gives me no information that would guide the choice. Moreover 'tiger' is a word for a biological species, and we know a biological species is fairly uniform. Therefore, the only reasonable prerequisite for the role of the single tiger to be considered is its representativeness. Hence the force of (8) will have to be an assertion of what is true of a species-typical tiger."

This, of course, is precisely what the force of (8) is. The line of thought just sketched can be generalized, and through this generalization we get a "transcendental deduction" (more accurately, "pragmatic deduction") of the force of generic *the*-phrases in ordinary discourse. A number of comments on this "pragmatic deduction" are in order, including further conclusions we can draw from it.

5. Conclusions from the "pragmatic deduction"

(a) First and foremost, the deduction shows that generic *the*-phrases serve to express species-characteristic properties. This seems to be the case. Notice that the precise force of "species characteristic" is important here. For instance, notwithstanding contrary claims, generic *the*-phrases do *not* express *per se* lawlike characteristics. This can be shown by means of a variety of examples. Even if some of the instances of this usage can perhaps be taken to express nomic connections, the following is a clear counterexample to the lawlikeness claim :

(9)   The kangaroo lives in Australia.

No nomic connection is required for the truth of (9). It is a geographical and geological accident that kangaroos are confined to Australia. If a herd of kangaroos should escape from a zoo, multiply, and fill South America, no natural laws would be violated. Yet (9) would become false.

(b) Generically used definite articles have a meaning closely related to comparable uses of the indefinite article. For instance, (8) says almost the same as

(10)   A tiger is a dangerous animal.

However, the mechanism through which this meaning comes about is quite different in the two cases. The indefinite article functions much more like the usual universal quantifier. This difference will sometimes show up in differences of meaning. The following examples illustrate a case in point :

(11)   The mammoth lived in Siberia during the ice age.
(12)   A mammoth lived in Siberia during the ice age.

Here (12), but not (11), easily prompts one to ask : Which mammoth are you talking about ? Or do you mean "A *species* of mammoths..." ?

(c) Should our "museum scenario" (our postulated situation in which precisely one representative from each of the number of kinds of individuals is present), which was used in the "deduction" of the semantical force of generic *the*-phrases, strike the reader as being unrealistic, Jespersen (1933, 166–167) reminds us that a class of generic uses of the definite article are, historically speaking, based on precisely this type of situation :

"The article in *to play the fool, act the lover,* etc., originates from the old character-plays.... Similarly with *look* :

I made shift look the happy lover.

This leads to the use of the definite article to denote 'the typical' whatever it is, chiefly in the predicative :

He is quite the gentleman.
She was the perfect girl, the perfect companion.
Mr. Lecky is always the historian, never the partisan (MacCarthy)."

The role of our "museum scenario" is here played by character plays, in which each of the players represents one character or type.

(d) Our "deduction" shows the different assumptions which the generic sense of the definite article depends on. Not only must the context rule out both the anaphoric and the Russellian uses of the definite article. More importantly, the range of entities from which the one representative is thought of as being chosen (say, all the Xs) must be uniform as far as typical speakers of the language are concerned. If that range is not as uniform as a biological species is, there may be a naturally designated individual which serves as *the* X. For instance, if, instead of the species *tiger,* we were considering a Highland clan, we would not find uniformity. Instead, there would be a natural candidate for the role of a distinguished individual, to wit, the head of the clan. Thus.

(13) The MacDonald

is to be expected to be, not a typical member of the clan, but *the* MacDonald, the head of the MacDonald clan. This expectation turns out to be correct. For instance, the sentence

(14) The Macleod is very frugal.

does not claim that frugality is a characteristic mark of the Macleods. It is a statement about *himself* (another Highland locution for the head of a clan), one particular man, the chief of the Macleods. (We are here grateful to Eve Clark for highly useful information.)

Hence we have reached, as a by-product of our general line of thought, an explanation of a rare but interesting use of *the*. This use of *the* may appear not only rare but exceedingly far-fetched. There is nevertheless a similar use which is quite common. Even though it is a plural use of *the* and therefore does not fall within our treatment, it is clearly essentially similar to the Highland usage. It is illustrated by examples like the following :

(15) We invited the Smiths over for dinner, but they could not find a babysitter.
(16) The Joneses are getting a divorce, but it has not been decided who will have the custody of their children.

In this usage, the phrase *the Xs,* where X is a family name, does not refer to all the members of the family, but to the two distinguished members of it, viz., the husband and the wife, rather in the same way as *the Macmillan* picks out the distinguished member of the clan, viz., its chief.

A closely related but more general type of usage is the one acknowledged in the *OED* where the phrase *the X* is used to refer to the preeminent X, the only one worth speaking of and hence, we can put it, the natural choice from the set of all Xs. Usually, this kind of *the* is emphasized. An example is

(17) Caesar was *the* general of Rome.

(e) Another usage which deserves a discussion is the Platonic one. It amounts to using the phrase *the X* to refer to the Form of X. This Form is best construed, it seems to us, as the paradigmatic instance of X-hood, imitated by the other, less perfect Xs. So conceived, the X is a particular entity, albeit an abstract one.

This Platonic usage has strong overtones of the generic use. On a purely historical level, it is an open question how strong an element of the generic usage there was in Plato's actual thinking. It is nevertheless clear that the Platonic usage, as we shall label it, differs from the generic one. The following are examples which are true on a generic construal of the definite article but false on the Platonic one :

(18) The tiger is found in many parts of Asia.
(19) The dodo is extinct.
(20) The shark is evolutionarily older than the whale.

How is the Platonic usage to be accounted for ? The following sketch will have to suffice here.

It has been argued by several linguists and psycholinguists that systematically the comparative is prior to the positive (see, e.g., (Fillmore 1971; Clark 1976)). If this was Plato's view, we could at once understand his problems with a thing which is, at the same time, both great and not great (namely, in relation to different objects of comparison). If we could also let Plato assume, as it has been argued that Aristotle did, that any sequence of comparisons will have to come to a unique end in a finite number of steps, then there is going to exist an absolute X for each adjective word X derived from the corresponding comparative (relational) term. Then the phrase *the X* is naturally taken to refer, when used absolutely, to this absolute X.

The difference between the generic and the Platonic uses of the phrase *the X* can be characterized by saying that in the generic use, the phrase *the X* is used to refer to a *typical* or *characteristic* X, whereas the phrase *the X* used Platonically is closely related to the Highland use of such phrases as *the Macleod* discussed above. What is characteristic of Plato's usage, in this interpretation, is that the field of a general term is assumed not to be uniform in the way which in our pragmatic deduction above necessitated the choice of a typical X as the reference of the phrase *the X*. Fields of Platonic general terms are no democracies. Each of them has a distinguished member, the preeminent X. It is thus no accident that Plato referred to the Form of X as *the* X and identified it with the *perfect* X. Even though this subject needs a great deal of further discussion, it can already be seen that our observations help to put Plato's views in a highly interesting systematic perspective.

REFERENCES

CLARK, Herbert H. 1976. *Semantics and Comprehension.* The Hague : Mouton.

FILLMORE, Charles. 1971. Entailment Rules in a Semantic Theory. In *Readings in the Philosophy of Language,* edited by Jay F. Rosenberg and Charles Travis, pp. 533–48. Englewood Cliffs, N.J. : Prentice Hall.

GOLDFARB, Warren D. 1979. Logic in the Twenties : The Nature of the Quantifier. *Journal of Symbolic Logic* 44 : 351–68.

HINTIKKA, Jaakko. 1969. On the Logic of Perception. In *Models for Modalities.* Dordrecht : D. Reidel.

HINTIKKA, Jaakko. 1970. Objects of Knowledge and Belief : Acquaintance and Public Figures. *Journal of Philosophy* 68 : 869–83.

HINTIKKA, Jaakko. 1974. Knowledge by Acquaintance — Individuation by Acquaintance. In *Knowledge and the Known.* Dordrecht : D. Reidel.

HINTIKKA, Jaakko. 1981a. Semantics : A Revolt against Frege. In *Contemporary Philosophy : A New Survey,* Vol. 1, *Philosophy of Language/ Philosophical Logic* edited by G. Floistad and G. H. von Wright, pp. 57–82. The Hague : Martinus Nijhoff.

HINTIKKA, Jaakko. 1981b. Wittgenstein's Semantical Kantianism. In *Ethics : Foundations, Problems, and Applications* (Proceedings of the 5th International Wittgenstein Symposium), edited by Edgar Morscher and Rudolf Stranzinger. Vienna : Hölder-Pichler-Tempsky.

HINTIKKA, Jaakko. 1982. Game-Theoretical Semantics : Insights and Prospects. *Notre Dame Journal of Formal Logic* 23 : 219–41.

HINTIKKA, Jaakko. 1983. Semantical Games, the Alleged Ambiguity of 'Is', and Aristotelian Categories. *Synthese* 54: 443–68.

HINTIKKA, Jaakko, and Jack KULAS, 1982. Russell Vindicated : Towards a General Theory of Definite Descriptions. *Journal of Semantics* I : 387–97.

HYLTON, Peter. 1980. Russell's Substitutional Theory. *Synthese* 45 : 1–32.

JESPERSEN, Otto. 1933. *Essentials of English Grammar.* New York : Holt, Reinehart and Winston.

SAARINEN, Esa, editor. 1979. *Game-Theoretical Semantics.* Dordrecht : D. Reidel.

FREGE'S CONTEXT PRINCIPLE

Leila Haaparanta

1. Introduction

Gottlob Frege has often been regarded as an originator of analytical philosophy and his thinking has been considered through the frames of the philosophy of language which was developed after him and which was also inspired by his ideas. That kind of approach prevails, for instance, in Dummett's notable work on Frege's philosophy of language. Frege has, undoubtedly, exerted a great influence on the analytical tradition. It is also true that he repeatedly stresses the importance of conceptual analysis in philosophy. He writes as follows :

> We can see from all this how easily we can be led by language to see things in the wrong perspective, and what value it must therefore have for philosophy to free ourselves from the dominion of language. If one makes the attempt to construct a system of signs on quite other founda- tions and with quite other means, as I have tried to do in creating my concept-script, we shall have, so to speak, our very noses rubbed into the false analogies in language. (NS, pp. 74–75; Long and White, p. 67).

Nevertheless, the view according to which Frege takes logic and philosophy of language to be almost the only branches of philosophical research is, to a great extent, mistaken.

In this paper I shall argue that even if Frege looks upon it as a philo- sopher's task to reveal the errors caused by natural language and to free our thinking from their power, it is, however, epistemology that is, for Frege, the starting-point of all philosophy. If Frege's philosophy is considered from this point of view, his semantic principles also turn out to be basically epistemo- logical principles.

As to Frege's semantic tenets, a similar approach has been suggested by Tyler Burge (1979) and Gregory Currie (1980). Frege's epistemological doctrines

83

have most carefully been scrutinized by Hans Sluga (1976, 1980). It is true he lays special emphasis on Frege's role as the first true analytical philosopher, but instead of paying attention to what became of Frege's ideas when analytical philosophy took up the themes which Frege introduced, he focuses on considering Frege's German background, thereby trying to reassess the roots of the analytical tradition itself. In his book entitled *Gottlob Frege* (pp. 59–60) Sluga concludes that Frege was an opponent of naturalism and radical empiricist epistemology, which prevailed in Germany in the late 19th century, and that he joined the tradition of German idealism, especially Kantianism. What I shall claim in this paper goes partly on the same lines as Sluga's interpretations of Frege's philosophy.

In the sequel, I shall try to give an interpretation of one of Frege's much debated semantic doctrines, namely, the so called context principle, which Frege formulates in the introduction of *Die Grundlagen der Arithmetik* (1884). The principle runs as follows :

Nach der Bedeutung der Wörter muss im Satzzusammenhange, nicht in ihrer Vereinzelung gefragt werden. (GLA, Vorwort, p. X.)
(J.L. Austin's translation :
Never to ask for the meaning of a word in isolation, but only in the context of a proposition.)

In addition, Frege states in the *Grundlagen* that if the principle is ignored, we are almost forced to take as the *Bedeutungen* of words mental pictures or acts of the individual mind, and so to offend against another principle, according to which we should always sharply separate the psychological from the logical, or the subjective from the objective.

In the *Grundlagen* we can also find many other closely similar formulations of the context principle like, for instance, the following :

Man muss aber immer einen vollständigen Satz ins Auge fassen. Nur in ihm haben die Wörter eigentlich eine Bedeutung. ... Es genügt wenn der Satz als Ganzes einen Sinn hat; dadurch erhalten auch seine Theile ihren Inhalt. (GLA, § 60).
(J. L. Austin's translation :
But we ought always to keep before our eyes a complete proposition. Only in a proposition have the words really a meaning. ... It is enough if the proposition taken as a whole has a sense; it is this that confers on its parts also their content.)

2. What is the Bedeutung of the Grundlagen ?

Frege scholars have argued for and against the claim that the context principle was maintained by Frege throughout his philosophy. Except for some hints, there is no clear reference to the principle in Frege's later writings. There is no mentioning of the rejection of the principle, either.

Interpretations for the context principle have been suggested by Ignacio Angelelli (1967), Gregory Currie (1980), Michael Dummett (1973, 1981), Michael D. Resnik (1967, 1976, 1980), and Hans Sluga (1980). According to Angelelli, the principle formulated in the *Grundlagen* plays no important part elsewhere in Frege's texts (Angelelli, 1967, pp. 73—75). He assumes that, on the one hand, Frege just gives advice to mathematicians on how to deal with numbers, i.e., objects which are neither subjective nor perceptible, and, on the other, Frege forbids us to look for a spiritual designatum of numerals, because he himself does not want to be accused of mathematical mysticism.

In his book on Frege's philosophy of language (1973) Michael Dummett argues that since Frege did not formulate the distinction between *Sinn* (sense) and *Bedeutung* (reference) until 1892, it is quite possible and perhaps even more advisable to interpret the *Bedeutung* of the context principle as the *Sinn* of Frege's later writings (p. 193). More generally, Dummett takes the principle to stress the role of sentences in language : we cannot do anything with a word but with sentences we can accomplish linguistic acts (*ibid.*, p. 194). He remarks that this was an important insight, to which Frege unfortunately never returned (*ibid.*, p. 196). In addition, Dummett takes it to be possible to construe the principle as a defence of contextual definitions (p. 495). In his book *The Interpretation of Frege's Philosophy* (1981) Dummett concludes that the *Bedeutung* of the *Grundlagen* can be rendered both as sense and as reference and that in the *Grundlagen* Frege's main concern is to apply the context principle to the references of numerals (p. 369). Interpreted this way, the principle says, according to Dummett, that if a sense has been fixed for all possible sentences in which an expression (a numeral) may occur, a reference is thereby conferred on that expression (*ibid.*, p. 380).

Michael Resnik also assumes that the principle applies both to the *Sinn* and to the *Bedeutung* of Frege's later philosophy (Resnik, 1967, pp. 357—358). According to Resnik, Frege takes psychologism to be mistaken both in asking for the reference of a word in isolation and in supposing that there are units of sense smaller than the senses of sentences. Resnik maintains that Frege gave up the context principle after the *Grundlagen*.

Unlike Dummett and Resnik, Sluga holds the view that Frege endorsed the context principle throughout his philosophy. He sees the principle as an expression of Kant's thesis according to which a judgement is prior to its constitutive concepts and claims that the doctrine reached Frege through Lotze's influence (Sluga, 1980, pp. 94–95).

An epistemological interpretation, closely similar to what I shall argue for in the sequel, is represented by Gregory Currie. He renders the context principle as the claim that knowledge of a thing is always knowledge of some proposition concerning that thing (Currie, 1980, p. 242).

Frege scholars have mostly puzzled over how to interpret the word *Bedeutung* in the principle formulated in the *Grundlagen.* In the article 'Ueber Begriff und Gegenstand' (1892) Frege himself states as follows :

> When I wrote my *Grundlagen der Arithmetik,* I had not yet made the distinction between sense and reference; and so, under the expression 'a possible content of judgment', I was combining what I now designate by the distinctive words 'thought' and 'truth-value'. (KS, p. 172; Geach and Black, p. 47).

However, in this connection Frege only refers to the distinction between the *Sinn* and the *Bedeutung* of a sentence. What the *Bedeutung* of a word is for Frege in the day of the *Grundlagen* is still in need of clarification.

In order to solve the problem, let us take a look at another term, namely, the term *Inhalt,* which is mentioned in the above quotation. It is used by Frege both in the *Begriffsschrift* (1879) and in the *Grundlagen* (1884). In the *Begriffsschrift* he remarks that in an identity statement the two symbols have the same *Inhalt,* but different *Bestimmungsweisen* (BS, § 8), while in 'Ueber Sinn und Bedeutung' (1892), where he makes the distinction between *Sinn* and *Bedeutung,* he claims that in an identity statement the two names have the same *Bedeutung* and different *Sinne,* or different *Bezeichnungsweisen* (KS, p. 143). Furthermore, in 'Funktion und Begriff' (1891), where he already refers to the distinction between *Sinn* and *Bedeutung* (see KS, p. 132, note 4), he identifies the *Inhalt* with the *Bedeutung* of a sign (KS, p. 126). The *Bedeutung* and the *Inhalt* of a word are also identified in the *Grundlagen* (§ 60). Therefore, I am inclined to argue that, as far as words are concerned, the *Bedeutung* of the *Grundlagen* is to be understood in the same way as Frege's later concept of *Bedeutung* : it is an object *(Gegenstand),* to which a proper name *(Eigenname),* i.e., a complete expression, refers, or a function *(Funktion),* to which a function-name *(Funktionsname),* i.e., an incomplete expression, refers. That statement must, however, be discussed in more detail.

In the *Grundlagen* Frege already distinguishes objects from concepts (Vorwort, p. X). Later he makes his distinction between objects and functions, in which concepts are included (GGA I, Vorwort, p. X). Respectively, Frege divides linguistic expressions into complete and incomplete (GGA I, pp. 43–44).

Complete expressions, or proper names, are *gesättigt,* i.e., they have no gaps in need of filling. Incomplete expressions, or function-names, are *ungesättigt,* i.e., they have gaps, which can be filled with other expressions. Function-names include concept-words, e.g., '( ) is a capital', which have one empty place, and relation-words, e.g., '( ) is the capital of ( )', which have two or more empty places. Besides concept-words and relation-words, there are function-names like, e.g., 'the capital of ( )', which do not turn into sentences when their gaps are filled with complete expressions. Proper names refer to objects like particular things and numbers, and sentences, which are also proper names, refer to truth-values, the True and the False. Function-names refer to functions: concept-words refer to concepts, relation-words to relations, and other function-names to other functions (GGA I, Vorwort, p. X; 'Ueber die Grundlagen der Geometrie I–III', KS, p. 285). Consequently, the *Bedeutungen* Frege is mainly interested in in formulating his context principle are, according to my interpretation, objects, on the one hand, and concepts, on the other.

3. The Interpretation of the Context Principle

As many scholars have maintained, Frege follows his context principle in the *Grundlagen* by considering how numerals are used in language. In § 46 he states that 'it should throw some light on the matter to consider number in the context of a judgement which brings out its basic use'. For instance, we can meaningfully say that if a tree has green leaves, then each of the leaves is green, but it does not make sense to say that if a tree has a thousand leaves, then each of the leaves is a thousand (GLA, § 22). That does not, however, exhaust the content of the context principle.

If the principle were restricted to concern function-names, its content would be obvious. We come to know the references of incomplete expressions only through sentential contexts, for incomplete expressions always occur in connection with complete expressions. Still, there is more to understanding the context principle even in the case of function-names. Hans Sluga has convincingly argued for his claim that the context principle has its origin in Kant's thesis, according to which a judgement is prior to its constitutive concepts. Sluga's interpretation also presupposes that the *Bedeutung* of the principle of the *Grundlagen* is the same as the *Bedeutung* of Frege's later works, since Sluga takes it to mean concepts. However, Sluga does not deal with the problem concerning the bearing of the context principle on proper names. If that question is answered, new connections will be detected between Frege's semantic principles and his epistemological standpoint.

Frege's semantic view concerning *Sinn* and *Bedeutung* is a form of anti-haecceitism, as David Kaplan, among others, has suggested (Kaplan, 1975,

p. 725). Frege does not regard it as possible to talk meaningfully of an object without referring to concepts or individual properties of that object. In 'Einleitung in die Logik' he writes :

> But we can't say that an object is part of a thought as a proper name is part of the corresponding sentence : all we can say is that to the object there corresponds, in a certain way that has yet to be considered, a part of the thought. (NS, pp. 203–204; Long and White, p. 187).

In 'Ausführungen über Sinn und Bedeutung' he remarks :

> Thus it is *via* a sense and only *via* a sense that a proper name is related to an object. (NS, p. 135; Long and White, p. 124.)

Thus, according to Frege, we do not know an object directly but only from some perspective or perspectives. Those very modes of presentation are the *Sinne* expressed by the name of the object. Frege argues that complete knowledge (*allseitige Erkenntnis*) of the reference would require us to be able to say immediately whether any given sense belongs to it but that to such knowledge we never attain ('Ueber Sinn und Bedeutung', KS, p. 144). If we, moreover, take into account that, according to Frege, we are able to express a thought only by means of a sentence (See GLA, § 26, and 'Der Gedanke', KS, pp. 357–359 and pp. 361–362), we can put forward the following simple inference :(1) I know an object only by knowing it *as* something. (2) "To know an object *as* something" is the same as "to know a thought concerning an object". (3) The thought is the *Sinn* of a sentence where the name of the object occurs. (4) Hence, we know the *Bedeutung* only through a sentential context. In other words, as far as proper names are concerned, the context principle is a consequence of antihaecceitism, provided that the *Bedeutung* of the principle is interpreted as an object, to which a proper name refers.

Interpreted this way, the context principle does not contradict Frege's compositionality principle, according to which the sense of a complete expression is compounded out of the senses of its constituents. The idea of compositionality appears in Frege's writings in the 1890s, and also later, e.g., in 'Einleitung in die Logik', (1906) he writes :

> As the proper name is part of the sentence, so its sense is part of the thought. ... As the thought is the sense of the whole sentence, so a part of the thought is the sense of part of the sentence. (NS, pp. 208–209; Long and White, pp. 191–192).

In 'Kurze Uebersicht meiner logischen Lehren' (1906) he points out :

> To the unsaturated part of the sentence there corresponds an unsaturated part of the thought and to the complete part of the sentence a complete part of the thought, and we can also speak here of saturating the unsaturated part of the thought with a complete part. A thought that is put together in this way is just what traditional logic calls a *singular* judgement. (NS, pp. 217–218; Long and White, p. 201).

Now, if Frege holds the view that in order to understand the sentence, we must understand the senses of the words it contains, he cannot demand that, in order to understand the senses of words, we must know the sentences in which the words occur. This problem, however, arises only if we suppose that the *Bedeutung* of the principle expressed in the *Grundlagen* is regarded as the same as *Sinn* in Frege's later writings.

What has been argued for becomes even more obvious if Frege's position is compared with that of Russell's. In his article 'The Philosophy of Logical Atomism' (1918) Russell writes :

> ... the logic that I should wish to combat maintains that in order thoroughly to know any one thing, you must know all its relations and its qualities, all the propositions in fact in which that thing is mentioned; ... . (*Logic and Knowledge,* p. 204).

The critique presented by Russell is directed against Hegelians, but it also hits Frege's theory of knowledge and, as Russell's mode of expression incontestably suggests, also his context principle. It is precisely Frege's view that we should have complete knowledge of the reference only if we knew all the thoughts of it, which, however, he regards as impossible for a finite human being.

If the context principle is interpreted in the proposed manner, Frege's conception of identity also turns out to be related to it. For Frege, identity is indefinable (see, e.g., 'Rezenzion von : E. G. Husserl, Philosophie der Arithmetik I', KS, p. 184), but still, he adopts Leibniz's law as his tool for understanding the identity relation. In the *Begriffsschrift* he states as follows :

> *Now let* $\vdash (A \equiv B)$
> mean : *the symbol A and the symbol B have the same conceptual content, so that we can always replace A by B and* vice versa (BS, § 8).

In the Grundlagen he writes :

Now Leibniz's definition is as follows :
"Things are the same as each other, of which one can be substituted for the other without loss of truth". ... Now, it is actually the case that in universal substitutability all the laws of identity are contained (GLA, § 65).

Thus, as an object is known to us only through its properties, likewise the identity of objects implies sameness of their properties and their substitutability in all contexts, in which they may occur.

4. Frege's Epistemology

Frege's view of the identity of objects seems to contradict the following passage taken from the article 'Was ist eine Funktion ?' (1904) :

If anything varies, we have in succession different properties, states, in the same object. If it were not the same one, we should have no subject of which we could predicate variation. (KS, p. 274; Geach and Black, p. 109).

In this passage Frege endorses the view that an object can remain the same although its properties change, which position undoubtedly deviates from what Frege claims about the concept of identity.

The contradiction can, however, be shown to be merely apparent. As we have already noted, Frege takes it to be impossible for us to know objects independently of concepts, or properties of objects. According to him, we know objects as bundles of properties, and, respectively, identity is sameness of the properties of objects, as far as our knowledge is concerned. Frege seems to adopt Leibniz's law as his epistemological account of identity, whereas the passage quoted above is most naturally construed as a statement concerning objects as non-qualitative carriers of properties, and, moreover, as being beyond the reach of our knowledge. An object is for us a bundle of properties, while an object as what it is in itself is transcendent.

The units that cannot be exhausted by our concepts Frege calls *logisch einfach* (logically simple). In 'Ueber Begriff und Gegenstand' he states :

What is simple cannot be decomposed and what is logically simple cannot have a proper definition. (KS, p. 167; Geach and Black, pp. 42–43).

In a letter to Hilbert in 1899, after discussing definitions and other sentences of mathematics, Frege points out :

One can also recognize a third kind of proposition, elucidatory propositions. ... They are similar to definitions in that they too are concerned with laying down the reference of a sign (or word). ... If in such a case the reference to be assigned is logically simple, then one cannot give a proper definition but must confine oneself to warding off the unwanted references among those that occur in linguistic usage and to pointing to the wanted one, and here one must of course rely on being met half-way by an intelligent guess. (BW, p. 63; Kaal, pp. 36—37).

The above considerations help us to see the context principle in a broader perspective. The thesis concerning *logisch einfach* can be regarded as a new formulation of the context principle, relating to both objects and concepts. Concepts can be decomposed into more primitive units, which are their characteristics. The most primitive concepts that we reach are the *Bedeutungen* of the concept-words which can no more be defined. Still, we can elucidate them by using them in judgements. That very idea is suggested by Frege in 'Ueber die Grundlagen der Geometrie I—III'(1906) (KS, pp. 288—289).

From the point of view of my present purposes, it is, however, more important to consider the relation between Frege's context principle and his conception of elucidatory propositions when objects are concerned. As also Jaakko Hintikka has pointed out, the context principle can be rendered by saying that the only use of primitive symbols is in sentences and that we cannot say what a primitive entity is, we cannot define it, we can only say what it is like, i.e., what properties it has. According to Frege, we are not able to know objects in themselves, but we can, however, fix them through the contexts in which we use their names.

That kind of interpretation serves to create a new connection between Frege's context principle and another principle formulated in the *Grundlagen* (Vorwort, p. X), which states that we should never lose sight of the distinction between concept and object. In the light of the proposed interpretation, the two principles amount to saying that an object is, by its nature, irreducible to concepts or to its properties, but still, it can be approached by means of our concepts.

If we follow the line of thought suggested above, we finally come to one of the basic doctrines of Frege's philosophy, which Hintikka (1981a, 1981b) calls the assumption of language as the universal medium. Frege himself states in his article 'Ueber den Zweck der Begriffsschrift' (1883) that he does not want to present, in Leibniz's terms, only a *calculus ratiocinator* like Boole but he attempts to create a *lingua characterica* (BS, 1964, p. 98). He uses the expression *lingua characterica* instead of *lingua characteristica*, which is used by Leibniz. Günther Patzig has proposed (see footnote 8 in Gottlob Frege, *Logische Untersuchungen*, edited by G. Patzig, p. 10) that Frege took the term from *Historische*

Beiträge zur Philosophie written by Adolf Trendelenburg. As Jean van Heije-noort (1967) and Jaakko Hintikka (1979, 1981a, 1981b) have pointed out, for Frege, the *Begriffsschrift* is a proper language, which must be learnt by suggestions and clues. Frege is committed to the doctrine that we are not able to step outside the limits of our language in our speaking and thinking. As far as my interpretation is correct, Frege's context principle proves to be an expression of the very idea that objects cannot be considered independently of our language, or our conceptual systems.

Still, for Frege it is not only the case that we cannot escape from our conceptual frameworks in our knowledge-seeking processes. In the article 'Der Gedanke' (1918) he states that things as we know them are produced by combining sensory qualities with non-sensory elements and that without the non-sensory elements we should remain locked into our own inner worlds (KS, p. 360). In the *Grundlagen* he also writes :

> It is this way that I understand objective to mean what is independent of our sensation, intuition and imagination, and of all construction of mental pictures out of memories of earlier sensations, but not what is independent of the reason — for what are things independent of the reason ? To answer that would be as much as to judge without judging, or to wash the fur without wetting it. (GLA, § 26).

Moreover, he remarks as follows :

> Now objectivity cannot, of course, be based on any sense-impression, which as an affection of our mind is entirely subjective, but only, so far as I can see, on the reason. (GLA, § 27).

As we have noticed, for Frege things cannot be known in themselves, i.e., independently of our ways of knowing them, but none the less, we are not, in his view, forced to support subjectivist epistemology. What we have still left are concepts, which, according to Frege, guarantee the objectivity of our knowledge. In the *Grundlagen* Frege discusses perception and knowledge and states :

> What is objective in it is what is subject to laws, what can be conceived and judged, what is expressible in words. What is purely intuitable is not communicable. (GLA, § 26).

According to Frege, the rejection of the context principle would lead to blurring the distinction between the subjective and the objective. If, namely, we gave up the context principle we should support the idea that we are able to know some objects directly without any propositional knowledge, or without *Sinne*. That amounts to saying that the *Bedeutungen* of names would then turn out to be our private ideas. In 'Rezension von : E. G. Husserl, Philosophie der Arithmetik I' (1894) Frege describes the position that he opposes in the following manner :

> The references of words are ideas. Objects are ideas. ... Everything is transformed into something subjective. But just because the boundary between the subjective and the objective is obliterated, what is subjective acquires in its turn the appearance of objectivity. People speak, e.g., of such-and-such a mental image, as if it could be in public view, detached from the imagining mind. (KS, pp. 181–182; Geach and Black, p. 79).

If the context principle is interpreted as an epistemological principle as I have suggested, it is most natural that the ideas of contextuality and objectivity are connected in Frege's philosophy. What is, however, more exciting here is how very close Frege's views really come to Kant's epistemological doctrines.

BIBLIOGRAPHY

FREGE, G., *Begriffsschrift, eine der arithmetischen nachgebildete Formelsprache des reinen Denkens,* Verlag von L. Nebert, Halle a.S., 1879; repr. in Frege (1964), pp. 1–88. (Referred to as BS.)

FREGE, G., *Die Grundlagen der Arithmetik : eine logisch mathematische Untersuchung über den Begriff der Zahl,* Verlag von W. Koebner, Breslau, 1884; repr. and transl. by J.L. Austin in *The Foundations of Arithmetic / Die Grundlagen der Arithmetik,* Basil Blackwell, Oxford, 1968. (Referred to as GLA.)

FREGE, G., *Grundgesetze der Arithmetik, begriffsschriftlich abgeleitet, I. Band,* Verlag von H. Pohle, Jena, 1893. (Referred to as GGA I.)

FREGE, G., *Grundgesetze der Arithmetik, begriffsschriftlich abgeleitet, II. Band,* Verlag von H. Pohle, Jena, 1903.

FREGE, G., *Translations from the Philosophical Writings of Gottlob Frege,* ed. by P. Geach and M. Black, Basil Blackwell, Oxford, 1952.

FREGE, G., *Begriffsschrift und andere Aufsätze,* ed. by I. Angelelli, Georg

Olms, Hildesheim, 1964.

FREGE, G., *The Basic Laws of Arithmetic, Exposition of the System,* transl. and ed. by M. Furth, University of California Press, Berkeley and Los Angeles, 1964.

FREGE, G., *Logische Untersuchungen,* ed. by G. Patzig, Vandenhoeck & Ruprecht, Göttingen, 1966.

FREGE, G., *Kleine Schriften,* ed. by I. Angelelli, Wissenschaftliche Buchgesellschaft, Darmstadt and Georg Olms, Hildesheim, 1967. (Referred to as KS.)

FREGE, G., *Nachgelassene Schriften,* ed. by H. Hermes, F. Kambartel, and F. Kaulbach, Felix Meiner Verlag, Hamburg, 1969. (Referred to as NS.)

FREGE, G., *Conceptual Notation and Related Articles,* transl. and ed. by T.W. Bynum, Clarendon Press, Oxford, 1972.

FREGE, G., *Wissenschaftliche Briefwechsel,* ed. by G. Gabriel, H. Hermes, F. Kambartel, C. Thiel, and A. Veraart, Felix Meiner Verlag, Hamburg, 1976. (Referred to as BW.)

FREGE, G., *Logical Investigations,* ed. by P. T. Geach, Basil Blackwell, Oxford, 1977.

FREGE, G., *Posthumous Writings,* transl. by P. Long and R. White, Basil Blackwell, Oxford, 1979.

FREGE, G., *Philosophical and Mathematical Correspondence,* abridged for the English edition by B. McGuinness and transl. by H. Kaal, Basil Blackwell, Oxford, 1980.

ANGELELLI, I., *Studies on Gottlob Frege and Traditional Philosophy,* D. Reidel, Dordrecht, 1967.

ANSCOMBE, G.E.M. and GEACH, P.T., *Three Philosophers,* Basil Blackwell, Oxford, 1961.

BURGE, T., 'Sinning Against Frege', *The Philosophical Review* 88 (1979), 398–432.

CURRIE, G., 'Frege on Thoughts', *Mind* 89 (1980), 234–248.

DUMMETT, M., *Frege : Philosophy of Language,* 2nd ed., Duckworth, London, 1981. (First published in 1973.)

DUMMETT, M., *The Interpretation of Frege's Philosophy,* Duckworth, London, 1981.

VAN HEIJENOORT, J., 'Logic as Calculus and Logic as Language', *Synthese* 17 (1967), 324–330.

HINTIKKA, J., 'Frege's Hidden Semantics', *Revue Internationale de Philosophie* 33 (1979), 716–722.

HINTIKKA, J., 'Theories of Truth and Learnable Languages', in S. Kanger and S. Öhman (eds.), *Philosophy and Grammar,* D. Reidel, Dordrecht, 1980, pp. 37–57.

HINTIKKA, J., 'Semantics : A Revolt Against Frege', in G. Fløistad (ed.), *Contemporary Philosophy,* vol. 1, Martinus Nijhoff, The Hague, 1981, pp. 57–82. (Referred to as Hintikka, 1981a).

HINTIKKA, J., 'Wittgenstein's Semantical Kantianism', in E. Morscher and R. Stranzinger (eds.), *Ethics, Proceedings of the Fifth International Wittgenstein Symposium,* Hölder-Pichler-Tempsky, Vienna, 1981, pp. 375–390. (Referred to as Hintikka, 1981b.)

KANT, I., *Kritik der reinen Vernunft,* 1781, 2nd ed., 1787, in *Kant's Gesammelte Schriften, Band III,* G. Reimer, Berlin, 1904; transl. by N. Kemp Smith, The Macmillan Press, London and Basingstoke, 1929.

KAPLAN, D., 'How to Russell a Frege-Church', *The Journal of Philosophy* 72 (1975), 716–729.

KITCHER, Ph., 'Frege's Epistemology', *The Philosophical Review* 88 (1979), 235–262.

RESNIK, M.D., 'The Role of the Context Principle in Frege's Philosophy', *Philosophy and Phenomenological Research* 27 (1967), 356–365.

RESNIK, M.D., 'Frege's Context Principle Revisited', in Schirn (1976), Band

III, pp. 35—49.

RESNIK, M.D., *Frege and the Philosophy of Mathematics,* Cornell University Press, Ithaca and London, 1980.

RUSSELL, B., 'The Philosophy of Logical Atomism', *The Monist* 28 (1918), 495—527; repr. in B. Russell, *Logic and Knowledge, Essays 1901—1950,* ed. by Ch. Marsh, George Allen & Unwin Ltd., London, 1956, pp. 175—281.

SCHIRN, M. (ed.), *Studien in Frege/Studies on Frege I—III,* Frommann-Holzboog, Stuttgart - Bad Cannstatt, 1976.

SLUGA, H.D., 'Frege as a Rationalist', in Schirn (1976), Band I, pp. 27—47.

SLUGA, H.D., *Gottlob Frege,* Routledge and Kegan Paul, London, Boston and Henley, 1980.

PARSING, MENTAL REPRESENTATION, AND DISCOURSE INTERACTION

László I. Komlósi
Dept. of English, Janus Pannonius University
Pécs, Hungary

0. Introductory Remarks.

The problems raised and discussed in the present paper were initiated by considerations bearing on *general linguistics*. One can formulate the basic idea like this : studying particular languages, one is inclined to assume a general type of structural relations which is realized in each language by distinguished structural positions. We call this general phenomenon of (human) languages the *"invariance of syntactic structure"*. However, different languages (or types of languages) make use of an invariant structure for different ends. In *Section 1.* a comparison is made between a much studied group of languages (Indo-European languages) and Hungarian, a non-Indo-European language to show that the invariant structure in Hungarian serves a strictly *communicative function,* facilitating *interactive discourse.* This function is fulfilled by *topic-focus articulation.* The few authors on this feature of Hungarian agree these days that models elaborated for Indo-European languages either in the traditional or in the transformational generative fashion have not succeeded in sufficiently accounting for the phenomena under consideration here. What linguistic theory could then do this job ? *Section 2.* sets out to answer this question. No final answer is intended to be and no satisfactory answer can be given, however, a partial answer suggested in the paper is believed to show a viable direction for further research. We claim that topic-focus articulation is contextual, i.e. of communicative nature which is determined by earlier semantic information in a particular structure of discourse. In order to capture this aspect of natural language, we need a linguistic theory which has, as its subtheory, a *psychologically real theory of parsing and processing.* Studies in psycholinguistics, drawing heavily on findings in cognitive psychology and artificial intelligence, have successfully attempted to give account of the human (sentence) parsing mechanism. We point at the methodological hesitation between the two basic research objectives of linguistic theory, namely, the *grammatical characterization problem* and the *grammatical realization problem.* It is argued that at the present state of the art it is the latter one that has come up with crucial claims concerning the construction of a psychological model to represent the processing mechanism at work in the cases of both kinds of languages compared in Section 1. A psychological model of sentence processing, making use of *on-line processing data* and referred to in the literature as the *Interactive-Parallel Theory of Sentence Processing* is discussed and considered as a candidate for a general psychological model of sentence processing and as the one to be hoped to influence our concepts of linguistic theory in an important way. *Section 3.* deals with what is very differently conceived of by different people and is referred to by the terms : syntactic representation, semantic representation, word and world representation, etc. We enter the discussion of these different concepts under the term *"mental representation".* The explication of the notion "mental representation" and the consequences of mental representation being in the centre of research is meant to show a possible convergence, very much looked for by many scholars in the field, between a psychological theory and a formal theory of language. *In Section 4.* a new model of discourse interaction is suggested, the visualization of which is facilitated by a diagram illustrating the relationship between the different components of linguistic theory within a broader frame of discourse interaction.

1. Structural Relations and Functions in Languages

The linguistic analysis of language of different language types suggests that a *general type of structural relations* is present in each language. Such structural relations are realized in the existence of *distinguished structural positions* which in turn allows us to sensibly talk about the existence of an *invariance of syntactic structure,* a very general phenomenon serving some important function in natural language. It would, however, be false to interpret the existence of an invariant syntactic structure as something serving the same purpose in each language. We argue that the distinguished structural positions in languages belonging to the Indo-European language family (and well-studied in the linguistics literature), like English and *especially* English, serve a function that can be called the *"parts-of-speech" function.* This is a subject-predicate dichotomy, in terms of subject, predicate, indirect object, direct object, etc. The same function in Hungarian, however, is fulfilled by a complex case structure which is indicated by a rich morphological system. On a closer analysis one finds (as shown, for example, in E. Kiss 1981 and Szabolcsi 1981) that Hungarian does have distinguished structural positions, thus putting the earlier view on the "freedom" of Hungarian word order, i.e. on Hungarian being a so-called non-configurational language, in a somewhat different perspective. As a result, such findings render Hungarian a language having an invariant syntactic structure. Also, this invariant syntactic structure has been found to be unrelated to the case frame of the language. The structural relations, then, must serve some different purpose. *The invariant structure in Hungarian serves a strictly communicative function facilitating interactive discourse.* The invariant structural relations, i.e. the syntactic rules on word order in Hungarian, are independently motivated by topic-focus articulation, a phenomenon which is influenced by both linguistic and extralinguistic context. A detailed description of topic-focus articulation in general and especially in Hungarian would be irrelevant here, however the reader is suggested to consult, for example, Kuno 1972, E. Kiss 1981, Szabolcsi 1981 for further reference.

Let it suffice to say here that the functional utilization of a sentence structure is specific to a particular language, or, at best, to a language type. The communicative function in English, for example is incorporated into the structural relations together with other functions. The "parts-of-speech" function in Hungarian, as mentioned above, is basically realized on the morphological level, thus leaving the "distinguished structural positions" level empty to be filled by another function of the language. We maintain that topic-focus articulation in Hungarian is a major contribution to the fulfillment of the communicative function of the language.

These considerations about the connection between structural relations and functions in languages in general raise the question of how we can give account of the language faculty of an individual to acquire and use, say, languages of different types (e.g. languages in the cases of which the utilization of structural relations is motivated by different functions) in the same time and on the same level of competence. (We assume that the very last statement of such a language faculty is tenable). In order to answer a question like this we have to turn to the discussion of psychological models of sentence processing, psychological theories of language production and comprehension and (psychological) theories of grammars.

2. Psychological Models of Sentence Parsing and Processing

In the discussion to follow we shall proceed as this : first, methodological considerations concerning the research objectives of linguistic theory for natural languages, then theoretical considerations concerning a general model of sentence processing will be made.

In Chomsky's Aspects (Chomsky 1965 : 9) one can read : "A reasonable model of language use will incorporate, as a basic component, the generative grammar that expresses the speaker -hearer's knowledge of language." This assumption bears directly on the two basic research objectives, namely, the *grammatical characterization problem* to represent the language user's knowledge of language and the *grammatical realization problem* to specify the reelationship between the grammar and the model of language use. As far as the grammatical characterization problem is concerned, there are many, sometimes radically different grammatical theories in the background; for example the Aspects-model, the Generative Semantics model, the Extended Standard Theory, the lexical-interpretive theory of transformational grammar, truth-conditional model-theoretic semantics, Generalized Phrase Structure Grammar, etc. The present ordering of the different theories listed, following a rough chronology in the same time, shows a tendency in linguistic theory to shortening the transformational derivation which, in turn, is compensated for by greatly enlarging the *role of non-transformational rules* — phrase structure rules, lexical rules (word-formation rules included), interpretive rules. The theoretical interest of these nontransformational solutions is that they express generalizations not adequately explained by transformations. Also, Fodor, Bever, and Garrett (1974) conclude that the experimental evidence tends to support the psychological reality of grammatical structures, but the evidence does not suggest the reality of grammatical transformations in speech perception and production. In light of such empirical findings the derivational theory of complexity, i.e. the theory that the number of transformations operating in the grammatical derivation of a sentence provides a measure of the psychological complexity in comprehending or producing a sentence, cannot be sustained.

The earlier picture suggested by the Aspects-model of TG that virtually the entire computational burden of relating meaning to surface form is borne by transformations has, on account of the introduction of nontransformational rules, changed to suggest the *cooperating interaction of separate information processing systems in speech production and perception.* The basic idea of this change is expressed in (Bresnan 1978 : 14) as follows : "As nontransformational relations are factored out of the transformational component, the transformational complexity of sentences is reduced, deep structures more closely resemble surface structures, and the grammar becomes more easily realized within an adequate model of language". This is exactly when and how one arrives from the grammatical characterization problem to the grammatical realization problem.

On the basis of some recent empirical evidence arrived at somewhat independently of the above referred to linguistic tradition by psycholinguists working on sentence processing problems, one has a strong conviction that, from a methodological point of view, there is no primacy of the characterization problem over the realization problem.

In our days, *psycholinguistics* has ceased to be subservient to theoretical linguistics (mostly to the TG-model advocated by Chomsky); the broadened methods and matured theory of psycholinguistics have become more independent, bringing about a discipline on its own. Contemporary psycholinguistic theory is out to pursue *three major objectives* (for reasons of simplicity put in form of questions) :

(a)   the first is of epistemological nature : what do we know when we know a language ?

(b)   the second is about language production and language comprehension : how do we use our knowledge when we produce or comprehend speech ?

(c)   the third is about language acquisition : how do we acquire the knowledge about language and the ability to use it ?

For the present purposes we engage ourselves in discussing the problems entered in clause b; problems which are to be dealt with in a *subtheory of parsing and processing.*

It is perhaps in order to note here that the methodological shift of emphasis in recent years on matters of psychological reality in language theory and the subsequent criticism from a psychological perspective bears a striking resemblance to what has also been happening to formal semantics since the mid-seventies. Formal semantic theories of formal rigor and explicitness have been criticized by a party of linguists, psycholinguists and cognitive psychologists for being too strong to realistically model human cognition by ignoring the psychological limitations of the human mind. (Only to mention some of the most recent criticisms, see Johnson-Laird 1982 and Partee 1982). The roots of criticism against both formal semantics and the theory of parsing and processing are intricately connected but it would be inappropriate to pursue this idea any further here and now. (For further discussion, see Komlósi 1982b and Komlósi 1982c).

It seems that some recent solutions to the realization problem have a great deal in common, especially as far as their basic assumptions are concerned. Partee argues for the possibility of our having to face two different kinds of human psychology : one is a hereditarily acquired, highly syntax specific mental structure that accounts for empirical findings supporting the existence of highly specific universals in syntax, like the transformational cycle, the generative processes, recursivity and the like; the other one involves properties of the human mind, such as "the ability to make inductive inferences, to solve open-ended problems, to develop notions of causation, action, time, will, freedom, etc.". (Partee, 1980 : 76).

A distinction of a similar nature is made in (Bresnan 1978 : 14) : "I assume that the syntactic and the semantic components of the grammar should correspond psychologically to an active, automatic processing system that makes use of a very limited short-term memory. I assume, in the same time, that the pragmatic procedures for producing and understanding language in context belong to an inferential system that makes use of a long-term memory and general knowledge."

The different models of sentence processing reflect and make use of the two or more distinguished processing systems in a very different way. The basic tenet of the so-called "serially ordered processing models" is the primacy of the syntactic analyses in comprehension. The two major representatives of such models are the Augmented Transition Networks and the Two-Stage Parsing Model advanced in Wanner and Maratsos 1978 and Frazier and Fodor 1978, respectively. (It might be of interest to the reader to consult the subsequent debate between these two models in Cognition). These models, in the same time, assume no cooperation between autonomous subcomponents, i.e. processing systems of different levels. A different kind of model, called the *Interactive-Parallel Theory of Sentence Processing,* allows for within-clause semantic processing and on-line interaction of the different components of the grammar. (See, especially, Marslen-Wilson 1975 and Tyler 1981). This theory assumes that the listener constructs a *multi-level representation of the speech input* as he hears it. On-line experiments suggest that the listener starts developing syntactic and semantic representations of the utterance he is hearing from the first word on. The representations continuously interact with each other and also with the prior context so that the listener arrives at a correct interpretation of the utterance.

In discourse, processing of the new input is determined by the semantic contextual constraints imposed by the prior sentences. We argue that *topic-focus articulation functions in discourse as semantic contextual constraints.* Processing analysis in a stretch of discourse pays attention to the type and amount of connections between context (prior utterances) and new input sentences, as to whether information in the latter is basically old or new.

In case of new information the complexity of structural processing increases which is probably due to the listener making links between prior referents and pronouns, building up the context for currently mentioned events, elaborating and updating his existing multi-level or higher-level representation. In contrast, *in case of old information* the complexity of structural processing does not increase. Processing old information primarily involves mapping the output onto an already existing representation of the information.

We can conclude from our discussion so far that the increase of the complexity of structural processing conceived of in a psychological model of parsing and processing, which assumes an interactive-parallel mechanism of multi-level representations, can find well-established conventions in a given language, as, for example, in Hungarian where topic-focus articulation motivates and results in an invariant syntactic structure.

3. Mental Representation

Psycholinguistics investigates linguistically relevant mental processes and structures which, in turn, makes it a branch of cognitive psychology. *Cognitive psychology* is the study of mental structures and processes relevant for the way "... people perceive, represent and use knowledge". (Norman and Rumelhart 1975 : 3). In Section 2, we overviewed the major objectives of psycholinguistics and argued that only one objective was engaged in answering problems raised by speech production and comprehension. It should, by no means, suggest that we need no joint efforts obtained from the different objectives pursued for answering some different kinds of questions. One such question is "mental representation". As we have indicated above, in the present discussion we introduce the notion "mental representation" as a general and cover term for representations of different levels, namely, syntactic, semantic, pragmatic (or extralinguistic) representations. What each represents is syntactic, semantic, pragmatic information, respectively. It should be clear that in the study of parsing strategies and comprehension processes we are to take into consideration the epistemological aspects of psychological research as well. This is why an interactive-parallel mechanism of multi-level representations basically assumes the cooperation of different knowledge sources making up a body of linguistic knowledge in a mental competence grammar.

If our psychological models are expected to be psychologically more real we must have a different picture of the organization of linguistic knowledge in a mental competence grammar as well as of the organization of the mental representation itself. It seems tenable and compelling to assume that there is *either* one single higher-level representation computed during processing as a result of cooperation between the syntactic, semantic and non-linguistic knowledge sources of a speaker/hearer, *or* a multi-level representation with continuous interaction of the representations of different levels. We think that it makes no crucial difference whether we accept the first or the second model. If we accept the first one, we assume either a direct access of the different knowledge sources to the single higher-level representation or an indirect access via partial representations that bear striking resemblance to syntactic, semantic and nonlinguistic representations. If we accept the second one, we assume a continuous interaction between separate syntactic, semantic and nonlinguistic rerpesentations feeding on different knowledge sources appropriately assigned to each. In either model, the mechanism bringing about "mental representation" must correspond to what we call comprehending a sentence or a stretch of discourse.

Thus, a somewhat complete and psychologically real model is expected to include the *cooperative contribution of different knowledge sources* a tentative list of which is suggested here (see a slightly different version of *a body of speaker/hearer's linguistic knowledge in Komlósi 1982a)* :

1. *structural rules the knowledge of which presupposes highly syntax-specific mental structures*
2. *syntactic* categories and semantic types
3. semantic relations
4. procedures for deductive and inductive inferences
5. preference ordering
6. rules of action : utility function, decision and cooperation maxims, adjustment and readjustment strategies, processing and reprocessing strategies, procedures for control and correction.
7. intensions, stereotypes, extensions (beliefs, intentions, motives, expectations, images, fears, etc.)
8. knowledge of the world.

4. Discourse Interaction

We have just argued that different knowledge sources are assigned to syntactic, semantic and pragmatic representations. But what are the criteria of drawing a line between these representations ? If there are any, which are the ones that are active and which are passive or automatic in speech production and comprehension to determine the structure of discourse ? Any attempt to describe the structure of discourse must encounter and take into consideration a common dichotomy in language theory; namely, a distinction advanced by Putnam and adopted by others (see, for example Putnam 1979, Dowty 1979) : *a theory of language understanding* (use theory) and *a theory of reference and truth.* According to the former theory, in Putnam's view, one can use one's language without having any sophisticated notion of truth at one's disposal. Understanding language is, by no means, equated with the knowledge of truth conditions. The latter one is about a correspondence between words and things, or sentences and states of affairs. The notion of truth and reference is of great importance in explaining the relation of language to the world. It should be noted, though, that such a separation is mainly of theoretical importance, since, after all, "talk of use and talk of reference are parts of the total story", as Putnam himself puts it. But in order to understand the actual working of language, i.e. the functioning of discourse in an endless variety of contexts, we should also propose an analysis of a special feature of discourse. In obtaining true information about the world (in other words : fixing intensions) it is not only the *language-to-world grounding* that is of crucial importance, but also the *language-to-language grounding.* (The distinction is adopted by Partee, see Partee 1980). In other words, a communicative interaction between speaker/hearer and speaker/hearer in different discourse situations turns on a specifically emphasized function of discourse interaction which naturally changes from time to time under different conditions of communication.

To make it more clear, we suggest a scheme explaining the complementary status of the theory of language understanding and the theory of reference together with a more general explanation of the interaction of the requirements a human semiotic system is subject to. We want to help the reader to visualize the suggested scheme in form of a diagram that incorporates Dowty's triangular diagram (see Dowty 1979) in a certain sense, although the relationship between the three, allegedly separate phenomena has, in our scheme, been put in a different perspective. Let us first recapitulate *Dowty's triangular diagram* :

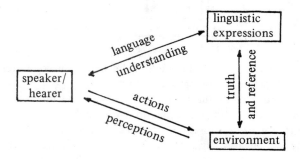

Instead of representing the relationship between the three, distinct fields (the theory of reference and truth, the theory of language understanding and the theory of action and perception) in a triangular way, we suggest that the two sides be collapsed onto the axis to represent the discourse interaction of speakers/hearers (the diagram is adopted from Komlósi 1982c) : (p. 104)

By doing this we want to place more emphasis on cognitive and perceptual processes underlying all three fields.

What is going on in this scheme ? In our view, linguistic expressions are not only *to exhibit some kind of correspondence* between language and environment (i.e. to make a link between extra-linguistic objects and linguistic expressions), but they are also *to reflect*

a) the nature and structure of environment,

b) the nature and structure of interaction between speakers/hearers and environment ("language-to-world grounding"),

106

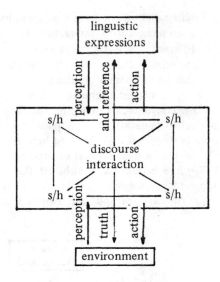

c) the nature and structure of interaction between speakers/hearers and speakers/hearers ("language-to-language grounding"),

d) the nature and structure of the mental activities of the mind, and also *to provide for* a short-cut direct interaction with environment by receiving true linguistic information from other speakers/hearers.

What this scheme should also suggest is, in our view, a greater proportion of pragmatic factors in discourse. We find our attempt to be worthwhile of comparison with what Vandamme considers to be comprised in the field of pragmatics today (see Vandamme 1981 : 110).

5. Conclusion

Some special features of structure and function in Hungarian lead to supporting the generalization that instead of the transformational account of grammatical derivations in speech production and comprehension a cooperating interaction of separate information processing systems should be assumed. The psycholinguistic model which allows for within-clause semantic processing and on-line interaction of the different knowledge sources resulting in multi-level representations of speech inputs is called the Interactive-Parallel Theory of Sentence Processing. To understand language faculty in a mental competence grammar we need to explicate the notion of mental representation. What we assume to make up mental representation is either one single higher-level representation computed during processing as a result of cooperation between the syntactic, semantic and pragmatic knowledge sources of a speaker/hearer or a multi-level representation with continuous interaction of the representations of different levels. It is assumed further that the dynamics of the interaction of representations has a direct effect on the dynamics of discourse. A discourse interaction scheme is proposed in which greater emphasis is laid on cognitive and perceptual processes together with a reevaluation of the proportion of pragmatic factors in discourse.

REFERENCES

BRESNAN, J. (1978) A Realistic Transformational Grammar. In : Halle, M., J. Bresnan and G.A. Miller (eds.) Linguistic Theory and Psychological Reality, MIT Press, Cambridge, Massachusetts, pp. 1–59.

CHOMSKY, N. (1965) Aspects of the Theory of Syntax, MIT Press, Cambridge.

DOWTY, D.R. (1979) Word Meaning and Montague Grammar, Reidel, Dordrecht.

FODOR, J. A., T. G. BEVER and M.F. GARRETT (1974) The Psychology of Language, McGraw-Hill, New York.

FRAZIER, L. & J.D. FODOR (1978). The Sausage Machine : A New Two-Stage Parsing Model, Cognition 6, 291–325.

JOHNSON–LAIRD, P.N. (1982) Formal Semantics and the Psychology of Meaning. In : Peters, S. and E. Saarinen (eds.), Processes, Beliefs, and Questions, Reidel, Dordrecht, pp. 1–68.

KISS, E.K. (1981) Structural Relations in Hungarian, a "Free" Word Order Language, Linguistic Inquiry 12, 2. pp. 185–213.

KOMLOSI, L.I. (1982a) A Formal Concept of Speaker/Hearer's Linguistic Knowledge, to appear in : Proceedings of the 7th International Wittgenstein Symposium, August 22–29, 1982, Kirchberg, Austria.

KOMLOSI, L.I. (1982b) Universals of the Linguist's Grammar : Pursuit of Psychological Reality in Semantic Theories, Ms., paper presented at the 15th SLE Meeting, September 8–11, 1982, Athens, Greece.

KOMLOSI, L.I., P. WEINGARTNER and H. CZERNIAK (eds.), Epistemology and Philosophy of Science, pp. 77—80.

KOMLOSI, L.I. (1982c) On What Linguists Know About Linguistic Knowledge, to appear in : Acta Linguistica Academiae Scientiarum Hungaricae.

KUNO, S. (1972) Functional Sentence Perspective, Linguistic Inquiry 3, pp. 269—320.

MARSLEN—WILSON, W.D. (1975) Sentence Perception as an Interactive Parallel Process, Science 189, 226—228.

NORMAN, D.A. and D.E. RUMELHART (1975) Explorations in Cognition, San Francisco : W. H. Freeman.

PARTEE, B.H. (1980) Montague Grammar, Mental Representations, And Reality. In : Kanger, S. and S. Ohman (eds.) Philosophy and Grammar, Reidel, Dordrecht.

PARTEE, B. H. (1982) Belief-Sentences and the Limits of Semantics. In : Peters, S. and E. Saarinen (eds.) Processes, Beliefs, and Questions. Reidel, Dordrecht, pp. 87—106.

PUTNAM, H. (1979) Reference and Understanding. In : Margalit, A. (ed.) Meaning and Use, Reidel, Dordrecht.

SZABOLCSI, A. (1981) The Semantics of Topic-Focus Articulation. In : Groenendijk, J.A.G., T.M.V. Janssen and M.B.J. Stokhof (eds.) Formal Methods in the Study of Language, Amsterdam, pp. 513—540.

TYLER, L.K. (1981) Serial and Interactive-Parallel Theories of Sentence Processing. Theoretical Linguistics, 1981, 29—65.

VANDAMME, F. (1981) Pragmatics and Adequacy, Philosophica 28, pp. 107—118.

WANNER, E. & M. MARATSOS (1978), an ATN Approach to Comprehension, In : Halle, M., J. Bresnan and G.A. Miller (eds.), Linguistic Theory and Psychological Reality, The .MIT Press, Cambridge, Massachusetts, pp. 118—161.

3

CASE STUDIES ON LOGIC OF

DISCOURSE

AND THE

LOGIC OF SCIENTIFIC DISCOVERY

SYMBOLIC ORDER IN KEPLER'S WORLD

F. Hallyn
R.U.G. – U.I.A.

Metaphor and symbol

Epistemology usually ascribes two functions to metaphor in scientific discourse : a pedagogical and a heuristic one. Metaphor can be used as a pedagogical tool, in order to make new descriptions or explanations understood by analogical reference to already well-known descriptions and explanations. As for the heuristic function, it can occur on two levels : first, in terminology, when metaphorical terms are introduced where no previous terms existed (catachresis); second, in theory-change and theory-constitution, when the metaphor becomes an instrument which leads to formulating new hypotheses by developing the potential analogies between one object and another. These functions of metaphor have been well studied, e.g. by Boyd (1979) – on the metaphorical relation between computer science and cognitive psychology – or by Marchal (1980) – on the development of paleontological theories in relation to geology and biology.

Metaphor occurs in other, more hidden ways, in scientific discourse, such as those studied by Bachelard. The "themes" of individual scientists, studied by G. Holton (1981), throw light on the influence of extra-scientific facts which often lead a scientist to a personal research program or research practice based on implicit metaphorical displacements. Holton's "theme" studies also point the way to another metaphorical involvement of scientific discourse, which leads to psychoanalytical or sociological approaches.

Kepler would undoubtedly offer an exemplary object for all the ways in which metaphor is present in science. As he often says to himself, he is "fond of analogies". But speaking of metaphorical aspects of Kepler's discourse, one should, first of all, avoid a danger of confusion. Are we really speaking about metaphors ? Or rather about symbols ? How are metaphor and symbol to be distinguished ? It seems impossible to make a satisfactory opposition on the level of semantics, for most of the definitions of this type can be applied to

111

both. What the *Vocabulaire* of Lalande, for instance, has to say on the symbol: "Ce qui représente autre chose en vertu d'une correspondance analogique", is valid for metaphor as well. The only satisfactory distinction is to be made on the level of reference : metaphor and symbol can be opposed in function of the language game that is being played or, in other words, in function of the reference attributed by the speaker or the hearer to the sequence or the discourse in which they appear.

In rhetoric, a metaphor is classified among the "figures of thought". To be more precise, one should say : the figures of *individual* thought. Aristotle, for example, says that metaphor is a figure which should never be borrowed from someone else, but always reflect the linguistic creativity of the speaking subject. Metaphor is a personal reordering of individual thought by a particular use of a sign. It does not affect reality or the intrinsic meaning of reality, but the individual relation to reality through signs. Metaphor exists only in a discourse, it is a consequence of a particular relation of the discourse to the system. It implies a new "language-game", with its own rules autonomously fixed by the actual speaker (or perceived as such by the hearer). Metaphor is always perceived as a game with signs as such : a change of the rules, of the possibilities of signs, but not of reality.

For the speaker or the hearer who accepts a symbol as such, the situation, is different. The meaning of a symbol is not primarily located on the level of discourse, but in an already existing language. The game and its efficiency are thought of differently. No individual language-user can propose a new symbol in a discourse, unless he proposes at the same time a new language. For a symbol does not affect merely the individual perception of the environing world through discourse, but implies a (supposed) original relation of the system to reality. It implies, more precisely, that the discourse is only a reflection of the fundamental language of reality itself. The word "tree" can only act as a symbol as long as the object "tree" is considered to be a symbol (but it can be metaphorical in many other circumstances). The belief in symbolism implies that an original language-game, the Game of games, is being played among things.

Naturally, it is not always possible to make a sharp opposition between metaphor and symbol on the grounds of the given distinction. The first reason for this lies, of course, in the fact that the distinction itself is made in this particular game which I am playing and which by no means can claim to transcend all the others : I can only make a distinction between games in a supplementary game which is already obeying the rules which it pretends to define. But there are other, more contingent reasons for not making the distinction between symbol and metaphor an absolute one.

In the first place, in spite of Aristotle's rule concerning the originality of metaphor, one has to admit that the same metaphors appear in many different discourses. This fact tends to give to certain metaphors a generally accepted "linguistic" status, to make them part of a language the possibilities of which individual users explore, like we do with a language of symbols. Metaphors can become so much a part of an accepted game (e.g. in the complete works of a given author or among the members of a literary school), that they seem to be, to certain users, the reflections of a game of reality — just as symbols do.

The distinction between metaphor and symbol can be blurred also by a different apprehension of signs by speaker and hearer. That which is symbolical for the speaker may seem metaphorical to the hearer. And when they confront their points of view, it is possible that the hearer stands by his opinion, accusing the speaker of metaphorical realism, or that the speaker suspects the hearer of nominalistic use of symbols. In connection with this, I want to say that when I speak of the metaphors of Kepler, it should be understood that I mean to stress the particular use he makes of certain signs which, to him, are not metaphors at all, but symbols rooted in a divine language. Those symbols, however, exert the same modelling power as metaphors. At the same time, they are inspired by an unspoken metaphorical shift : Kepler applies to God's cosmos a way of thinking about human art.

Geometrical symbolism and metaphorical shift

Kepler's world is still a symbolical world, in which every fact is related to a transcendental meaning. His "celestial physics", which should replace "the theology or the metaphysics of Aristotle", constitutes a basis on which cosmogonic and cosmologic speculations continue to be nourished. There is a fundamental metaphor in Kepler, which is none other than the metaphor of metaphor, telling us that the world is a sign which resembles the object it denotes.

It is interesting to remark that Kepler himself often uses the word "game" *(ludus, Spiel)* when he comments on his own speculations on the meaning of the world. Meaning and discourse are already language-games to him. It is evident, he says, that God has *played* in the creation of the world and that the particular object of his game was to form the world into an image of its creator : "For, in the formation of the world, God played by disposing the adorable image of his Trinity in it." (GW, II : 19). It is also clear for him that God has taught his creation to play in its own turn and, more precisely, to play the very game that he was playing himself : "Just as God, the Creator, has played, so He has taught Nature to play as his Image — and precisely the game He was demonstrating." (GW, IV : 243). This metaphor of the game expresses the original liberty of God : to let be or not to let be, this was indeed the question, but it was a question that God was free to ask or not and to answer or not. This game, though, once it was played, became immediately the most necessary of games.

According to the principle of sufficient reason (of which the importance in Kepler has often been underlined), a perfect God cannot but have made a perfect world. Now, since the only perfect model for a perfect world was God himself, the world has necessarily been created as an image of its Creator (GW, II : 19). The main question thus becomes : how to read the world as an image of God ?

In semiotic terms, Kepler's world is a *sign* related to an ultimate *object,* which is God, by means of an *interpretant.* Kepler rejects traditional interpretants such as numerology and kabbalistic anagrammatism or etymology. Neither numbers nor letters or words can help us to discover the meaning of the world, because they all lend themselves to numerous conflicting significations which, at the end, appear arbitrary. The only place to look for the clue to the interpretation of the world is *geometry.*

In his creation, God chose geometrical quantity as the *causa formalis* of the world. Geometry itself, as the signifying side of a semantic code, offers the basic opposition between curved and straight lines, which represents, on the level of the signified objects, the difference between Creator and creation : "God wanted quantity to exist before everything else, so that the Curved and the Straight could be compared. For this one fact, Nicolas of Cusa and others seem divine to me : for having attached so much importance to the reciprocal relation of the Straight and the Curved and for having dared to compare the Curved to God, the Straight to creation. For it is just as vain to compare the Creator to the creation, God to man, divine thoughts to human thoughts, as to try to equate the curved to the straight, the circle to the square". (GW, I, 23)

Kepler himself quotes Nicolas of Cusa as the most important source for the selection of his basic semantic opposition. Some important differences should be stated, however, because they are responsible for the specific action of the geometrical "theme" in Kepler :

- In Nicolas of Cusa, the geometrical forms receive their metaphorical importance from their extension to the infinite. The specific mode of his thinking consists in a continuous passing from the finite to the infinite, on the level of geometrical potentialities as well as on the level of the actual extension of the world. Kepler, on the other hand, postulates a finite world and organizes his hermeneutics in function of finite geometrical forms. Geometry serves a negative theology in one case, a positive cosmology in the other.

- The second difference concerns the selection of the principal geometrical form, which, for Nicolas of Cusa corresponds to the circle, and for Kepler to the sphere. Circle and sphere have in common the same potentialities for structural symbolism, but the sphere possesses also deductive symbolic potentialities which are absent from the circle.

The structural symbolism of circle and sphere is based on the fact that the relations between center, rays and circumference or surface can be thought of as the representation of the relations between the members of the Trinity. It is well known that, for Kepler, the center represents God the Father, the rays the Sun, and the Surface the Spirit. (A minor difference consists in the fact that for Cusanus the rays represent the Spirit and the circumference the *Sun.*) Kepler considers the structural relationships within the sphere to be the model according to which the general shape of the world was formed. As G. Holton has shown, the concept of a real and unique center located in the sun is especially overdetermined : the sun is at the same time the *mathematical* center of the world (for the calculation of the celestial movements), its *physical* center (the cause of the movements) and its *metaphysical* center (the tabernacle of God). The following sentences illustrate the overlapping of physical and metaphysical thought : "Now, since the sun stands in the middle of the wandering planets, at rest itself and nevertheless source of movement, it shows the image of God the Father, of the Creator. Because that which is creation in God, is movement in the sun." (GW, I : 19). We find here a clear illustration of metaphorical *interaction* or the process of reciprocal selection of predicates between different objects of thought. The basic reasons for Kepler's acceptance of the central position of the sun are, without any doubt, *mathematical* : they concern the coherence of the image of the world. But the central mathematical position of the sun gives the opportunity to reactivate, in the form of condensation, two traditional *metaphysical* themes : the sun as the image of God and the center as the archetype of a generating principle, the active, creating Father. The superimposition of the metaphysical themes on the mathematical model sustains, on its turn, the production of a new *physical* hypothesis : the sun being thought of as the image of the Father becomes an *active* center, so that one should not work with "fictional" circles, but rather postulate the real, physical action of the centre, a thought which will eventually lead to the discovery of the elliptical orbits. The metaphysical themes will not only affect the physical conception of the world, but will also renew the *mathematical* foundation on which they were based in the first place : it is the belief in the sun as the unique center of a finite world which leads ultimately to Kepler's search for harmony and to his third law : only the belief in such a center, whose symbolic dignity makes it the very point to which the mathematical harmony should be reported, provides a starting-point from which the new search for harmony can begin.

As far as harmony and the third law are concerned, the other, deductive symbolic potentialities of the sphere are just as important. Kepler considers the sphere to be the metaphysical Origin of all other geometrical forms. In the

Epitome, he opposes the "mechanical" generation of these forms, starting from the point, and their "metaphysical" generation, which starts from the sphere (GW, VII : 267). All geometrical shapes can be derived from the sphere, first by suppression, then by suppression and/or adjunction. The derivation creates a hierarchy which allows for classifying the forms in a descending order reflected in the order of their intervention as *somatopoïetic* and *cosmopoïetic* unities (GW, XIV : 65 sq.) :

- the world as a whole corresponds to a *sphere;*
- the sphere generates first rectilinear volumes, which inform the disposition of the *substances* of the world, i.e. the planets separated by the five platonic solids: these five regular polyhedra are the "somatopoïetic" forms of the cosmos;
- the volumes, in their turn, generate polygons, which correspond to the volumes as qualities to substances, so that they inform not the parts of the world, but their relations; the polygons can be classified according to their "scibilitas" or to their "congruentia" : the first order determines more specificly the astronomic movements, the second, the astrological aspects (*Harmonices Mundi;* GW, VI).

In this way, metaphysical geometry, descending from the sphere to the polygons, models the whole worldorder, from the general shape to the movements and aspects of its parts. This conception of the role of geometry helps to lead Kepler to his theory of harmony and, incidentally, to his third law.

Nowhere in earlier astronomy does one find any attempt to construct such a type of coherent, deductive system of somatopoïetic and cosmopoïetic forms. The reference to art theory is important here, not only because of Kepler's own sympathetic allusions to Dürer (GW, VI : 55, for instance), but also because art-theory was *the* place where, during the XVIth century, the study of the regular solids and of harmonic proportions of polygons had been developed. The most important works in this respect are, after Pacioli's *Divina proportione* (1509) and Piero della Francesca's *De quinque corporibus* (1492), Dürer's *Quatuor institutionum geometricarum libri* (1525), Jamnitzer's *Perspectiva corporum regularium* (1563), Stoer's *Geometria et Perspectiva* (1567) and Barbaro's *La pratica della perspettiva* (1569). In the light of books like these, Kepler's work clearly involves a metaphorical shift by which ways of thinking about human artists are applied to the divine artist of the world. But there are also striking differences between those Renaissance treatises and Kepler's mannerist enterprise. Neither Dürer nor the others offer the same type of deductive reasoning. Dürer starts from the point and continues with the lines, the polygons and the solids, offering a "mechanical" geometry, where there is no stringent exclusion, for example, of "unknowable" or irrational forms. The same lack and the same absence of an all-involving hierarchy characterize the other artistic treatises : they offer practical rules for the construction of geometrically acceptable representations and ask for coherence of the representation. Kepler, at the contrary, asks for the *a priori* principles which govern the manifestation of geometrical order in the world and from which astronomy can be deduced, just as mannerist art-theory asks for the ultimate truth from which art-practice itself can be deduced. This parallelism with mannerism can be explained.

In the words of Koyré (1973 : 56), Kepler is a "Janus bifrons". His astronomy, more than Copernicus's, sweeps away deeply rooted ideas, but he remains nevertheless "the last scientist of the Renaissance". Koyré (1973 : 213) even suggests that, because of the elliptical orbits, Kepler's astronomy may have appeared to his contemporaries as a "mannerist" astronomy. This suggestion can be developed, for not only are there strange internal analogies between Kepler and the mannerists, but — as we shall try to show here — Kepler's place in his own historical series (the history of astronomy) is analogous to the place of mannerist artists and writers in their own history.

In his *De stella nova* (1606), Kepler gives a long enumeration of the political, cultural and other transformations of the European society between 1450 and 1600. This fragment is important because it shows how he thinks of his own situation as an astronomer in the global context of what we call the *Renaissance* : the evolution of astronomy conforms itself to a general pattern. Kepler starts by quoting the often repeated image of the awakening of man after the long sleep of the Middle Ages. He describes the decline of civilisation since Antiquity and relates, in very minute detail, the accomplishments of the past century and a half. He ends by inserting astronomy in the general movement : "... today a new theology and a new jurisprudence have been created, the followers of Paracelsus have renewed the field of medicine, and the Copernicans have renewed astronomy..." (GW, I : 329–332).

But, if Copernicus has "restored" a form of ancient astronomy and thus participated in the task of "restoration" which is the Renaissance, his theory has not yet (at the moment when Kepler is writing) really replaced the traditional geocentric theory. If heliostatism introduced a greater coherence, it also posed new difficulties and new questions; even the simplification of calculation was doubtful. Copernicus did not offer a generally accepted and definite response to a "crisis" — for how many of his contemporaries did a crisis really exist ? — but in a sense he rather himself provoked a crisis : from the *De revolutionibus* on, astronomers not only had to find a solution for anomalies within an accepted framework, they had, first of all, to choose a framework. And very soon, a third choice would be available : Tycho Brahe's mixed system, so that, when Kepler appears on the scene, the first thing to do for an astronomer is not to work guided by a given theory, but to choose, by a problematical choice, his theory and his "manner" of posing questions. This was exactly the situation with which mannerist artists and writers were confronted, as has been stated by A. Hauser (1965) : with mannerism, more than ever before, the adherence to a school or tendency is a matter of conscious choice, of individual programme-setting, and becomes, therefore, problematical.

But, of course, the sole necessity of a choice does not suffice to define mannerism. In painting, there are, at the same moment, choices which we would not call mannerist. So it should be added that one does not only choose a theory or a framework, but also an attitude towards it, an angle from which to approach it, a series of preferential questions to be resolved by it. At this point, a differentiation can be introduced which gives a more precise meaning to the concept of scientific mannerism.

Generally speaking, Copernicus proposed a new world-*system,* a new conception of the organisation of the world, of the laws and the relations which governed its parts. On one important point at least, he added to his description a signifying function : the central place of the sun, the governor of the planets, was a representation of the dominating position of the Creator in his creation. In Rheticus' *Narratio prima,* other signifying functions are attributed to the system : e.g. the number of the planets — *six* — is related to the symbolical value of this perfect number.

These speculations show that it was possible to adopt two attitudes towards the system. One could study the internal relations *in* the system and try to make its representation as such more acceptable. This was to be, for example, the attitude adopted by Galileo, and Kepler was certainly also one of the greatest contributors to this type of search. But — and this fact is what deter-mines his *style* — he could not be satisfied by this practice alone and, instead of giving only, as Copernicus and Rheticus did, some indications on the signi-fying function of *some* facts, he tried to correlate the *whole* system to a signi-fying function. In other words, he tried to change the system into an elaborated *code.* As becomes clear already from the epigraph of this first work, the *Myste-rium cosmographicum,* the first questions are, for Kepler, questions of the sense of the whole and all of its parts : "Why the world ? What cause and what reason guided God in its creation ? From where the numbers ? What rule for such a whole ? Why six circles and what orb explains their intervals ? Why such a hiatus between Jupiter and Mars, which do not correspond to the first orbs ?" (GW, I : 4).

The fact of asking this type of question gives to Kepler's work a specula-tive aspect which is always present and which is also to be found in the theory of art of the mannerists. For, if Copernicus renders the relation of man to the order of the world problematical, the relation to the work of the artist had become just as problematical during the XVIth century. Because of the confir-mation of the difference between perception or observation and the representational canons of the High Renaissance, and because of the refusal to attribute this difference to merely subjective or psychological reasons, art theory comes to asking "the questions of representation as such". Panofsky (1968 : 83) uses words which can be literally applied to the situation of a post-Copernican astronomer : "... that which in the past has seemed unquestionable was thoroughly problematical : the relationship of the mind to reality as perceived by the senses." (p. 83). It is precisely a problematical situation of that kind which Kepler tries to transcend by transforming the Copernican system into a code. For reasons which are specific for each field, but on the same horizon of the Renaissance as a *total* phenomenon which created everywhere specific problems as a result of the general "restitution", art theory and astronomy are thus driven to ask similar questions and to follow a similar speculative path. In their speculations, Kepler and the mannerists also return to the same or to similar sources. For if Kepler makes a fundamental choice for Copernicus, to which should be added the demand for observational precision inherited from Tycho Brahe, his speculations are nourished by Pythagorean hermeticism, by the neoplatonism of Proclus, by Nicolas of Cusa — all sources identical or similar to the ones used by, say, Zuccari or Lomazzo. It is as if Kepler had followed in his own field the two ways proposed by Armenini to young artists in search of their own "manner" (Barocchi, II : 1584) : "There are two ways to learn 'la buona maniera' : one consists in copying often the works of several good workmen; the other in concentrating on one exquisite model." Copernicus is, beyond any doubt, Kepler's "one exquisite model"; but this fidelity does not prevent him from borrowing from many other workcraft, so that his work becomes a composite and overdetermined entiry.

Concluding remarks

The kind of thought described thus far may seem strange to us, not only in itself, but also because it is accompanied by a strong and perfectly lucid criticism of other conceptions of the world as a signifying object. This last fact illustrates Kepler's situation as a transitional figure in the history of epistemological constraints. He still cannot but imagine the world as a signifying object; yet he is so critical of most existing types of interpretation that he is forced to place the interpreting system in one very restricted field : geometry. The combination of three important qualities allow for distinguishing Kepler further from earlier readings of the world and announce already, within the limits of analogical thinking, properties of the "classical" apprehension of the world by XVIIth century science and philosophy.

1. Traditional readings of the world usually worked with qualitative similarities, even when geometry was concerned. The best example is probably

the platonic association of the five regular solids with the five elements : the cube presents an aspect of solidity, of firmness, through which it is associated with the earth. Kepler criticizes the arbitrariness of such associations and puts at the origin of the signification of the world another type of analogy : not intrinsic, qualitative similarities, but a structural similarity or, better, a similarity of structures, which provides an elementary axis of signification. The constitution of this axis is not ultimately based on similarity, but on *difference* : it is the irreductible difference between curved and straight, between creator and creation, it is this *similarity of differences* which makes signification and the subsequent play of other similarities possible.

2. Traditional readings of the world usually had the form of an open series. Their style was characterized by enumeration, parataxis, heterogenous inductions. This kind of reading lacks a real end as well as a real beginning : it explores possible relations between two levels of thought, but does not possess a stringent principle which would explain the internal order of the two levels or the order of the application of the one to the other. Kepler's style, on the contrary, is deductive and hypotactic, as I tried to show by referring to his "metaphysical geometry", which, starting from the sphere, provides a "proper" place for the successive interventions of the different "somatopoïetic" and "cosmopoïetic" forms.

3. Kepler develops a new conception of the relation between physical signs and their geometrical interpretants. The importance of metaphysical geometry is not accepted as long as it is not proved (eventually altered) by experience. He does not simply try to make the world-order correspond to preconceived forms, to a spiritual $\epsilon\iota\delta os$. The geometrical forms must not be imposed, but discovered and explained as the result of relations between material forces. Before Kepler, astronomy was a science of forms, after him it will be a science of forces. His own astronomy can be described as a conflict between the thought of form and the thought of force. One last analogy with mannerism should be mentioned in this context. For the mannerists also discover, after the idealizing, geometrical experience of the Renaissance, that forms in material objects do not reproduce a spiritual $\epsilon\iota\delta os$ of form, but are distorted by the dynamics of material movement, just as the orbits of the planets are distorted circles or ellipses produced by a conflict of forces. The $\epsilon\iota\delta os$ of forms and their material production should be kept separated (Danti in Barocchi, II : 1769) : "It is true that some ancients and moderns have written, with much diligence, on the representation of the human body; but this was clearly without use, because they wanted to formulate their rule by means of a determined quantitative measure; but this measure is not perfect in a human body because it is, from the beginning to the end, constantly in movement."

It would be greatly exaggerated of course, to say that his geometrical

symbolism lead Kepler directly to his discoveries, to the new *answers* he introduced in astronomy. But it is true that this symbolism was a factor which urged
him to ask the *questions* which ultimately would prove to lead to right answers.
A situation like this one might not be atypical.

BIBLIOGRAPHY

All references to Kepler's works are taken from the *Gesammelte Werke,* ed. M.
CASPAR & W. VON DYCK, München, Beck, 1938 — Abbreviation : GW.

BAROCCHI, Paola, *Scritti d'arte del Cinquecento.* Milan-Naples, Ricciardi,
    1971 sq., 3 vol.

BLUMENBERG, H., *Paradiami per una metaforologia.* Bologne, Il Mulino,
    1969.

BOYD, R., *Metaphor and Theory Change : What is "Metaphor" a Metaphor
    for ?,* in A. ORTONY (ed.), *Metaphor and Thought.* Cambridge (Mass.),
    Cambridge University Press, 1979, pp. 356—408.

HAUSER, A., *Mannerism. The Crisis of the Renaissance and the Origin of
    Modern Art.* New York, Kropf, 1965, 2 vol.

HOLTON, G.,*L'imagination scientifique.* Paris, Gallimard, 1981.

KOYRE, A., *Etudes d'histoire de la pensée scientifique.* Paris, Gallimard,
    1973.

LALANDE, R., *Vocabulaire technique et critique de la philosophie.* Paris,
    P.U.F., 1972.

MARCHAL, P., *Discours scientifique et déplacement métaphorique,* in : R.
    JONGEN (ed.), *La métaphore : approche pluridisciplinaire.* Bruxelles,
    Publications des Facultés Universitaires Saint-Louis, 1980, pp. 99—139.

NORMAND, C.,*Métaphore et concept.* Bruxelles, Ed. Complexe, 1976.

PANOFSKY, E., *Idea. A Concept in Art Theory.* New York, Icon Ed., 1968.

SOME REMARKS ON THE CONSTRUCTION OF DEFINITIONS IN THE DAY–TO–DAY WORKING OF A LABORATORY

Dirk Vervenne & Dani De Waele

1. Introduction

This project involves research into knowledge acquisition, representation and processing within several different contexts: a seminar and a laboratory at a university and various selected classes in secondary schools. Our approach to these different contexts is based on a register-pragmatic method: we differentiate knowledge-engineering actions into registers. We define them tentatively as clusters (sets and/or sequences) or symbols (verbal and/or non-verbal) that are related to individual and collective actions.[1]

In order to make this working hypothesis more solid, aiming for concrete tentative check-ups, we observed the different fields in an exploratory way during a preliminary period of six months. This resulted in around 1000 pages of observational data.

At the moment, the project is working on two interrelating levels which are developing simultaneously :

On one side we are classifying these data into several items that are clusters of actional symbols, grouped on the basis of their mutual dependency. Some of these items will be examined in depth during five months of re-observation. In focussing on some topics, we want to attain specific hypotheses on the construction and representation of knowledge; arguments useful for elaborating these hypotheses will arise from our other approach to the handling of the collected data; On the other side we are preparing, in cooperation with artificial intelligence researchers, investigations in simulating register-construction and representation with a computer, in order to have better insight into structural relationships between classes of actional symbols situated on different levels of abstraction. Simulating action-patterns with a computer can support our specific hypotheses on the manufacturing of knowledge and is also a powerful tool in forcing the programmer to make explicit hidden presuppositions[2].

123

2. Concerning pathways of observational discourse during an internal three-hour meeting of a sub-group in the lab.

2.1. Situation

We made observations within a genetic research lab. The lab has been functioning for eleven years, having been officially organized in 1974. I was a scientific member of the lab team while pursuing research on my doctorate. The team is composed now of about forty persons, all working on one general subject : analysis of the formation of plant tumours which are caused by a bacterium.

We made observations in this lab during a period of several months; this paper is confined to one specific part of our observation material, that part covering the dealings of some people in the lab who are working together very closely: their meetings with each other are very frequent or, rather, more organized. The work of this subgroup consists in the making of specific mutants of bacteria. They analyse the bacterium for those specific genes which are necessary for tumour formation on the plant. Therefore, they fabricate changes, "mutations", in genes in order to see, to make visible, the different function for which each gene is coded, to discover which functions are needed for producing a tumour. (A major rule in genetic and other scientific work is the method of "anlaysing by means of disturbing".)

So, they have fabricated bacterial mutants, analysed them as far as possible (mapping them in the genetic region responsible for tumour induction), and have infected different types of plants with different bacterial mutants. Twice, at different times, certain members of the group observed the effects of the mutants on the plants and registered their observations on paper. A third time, however, the whole group came together in the lab to observe, together, the plants, to discuss and register their observational conclusions, and to decide which plants they would analyse further by physico-chemical methods.

It was at one of these terminal observation meetings that we assisted and took notes. The meeting concerned the observation of 25 sets of plants and took thee hoors.

In the first, explanatory, phase of our project we used no tape recorder, but we were intensely attentive to verbal and non-verbal communications or actions. We took notes during the meeting and typed them out accurately (with some systematization) as soon as possible.

2.2. Approach

In order to analyse further our own interestingly complex observational

125

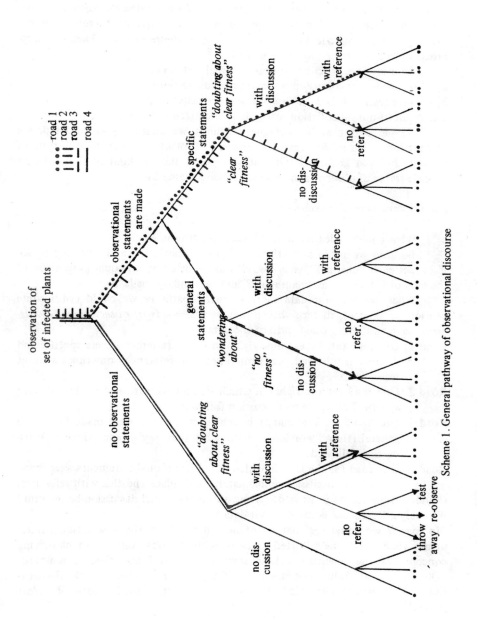

Scheme 1. General pathway of observational discourse

data, we tried to distill from them a *general pathway of observational discourse.*
Regarding each set of plants infected with one type of bacterial mutant,
discourse took place among the seven members of the meeting. Each discourse
process can be described by three phases :
1) Observations are articulated: observational statements;
2) Observations are discussed: observational discussions;
3) Further testing, based on observations, is discussed.
The result of our "distillation work" is schematized in Scheme 1.

Having arrived at this scheme of things, we then analysed each separate
observational discourse (regarding one set of plants exposed to one type of
mutant) in even greater detail, and composed another kind of frame, i.e., a
specific frame of observational discourse (see Scheme 2).

2.3. Observational discussion during discourse

What could we learn about this general pathway ?

Because we made a "pathway of possibilities", it was interesting to see
if in fact each "channel", each "way" was followed by an equal proportion of
the data or if there were "main roads" and "secondary roads".

When we put our data in this general pathway we could (with some
caution of course), discern *four discourse mainroads of observational discussions:* each containing one-fourth of the data:

Road 1: One read (at the extreme right) in which statements were specific and
discussion followed, was sometimes with reference, sometimes without
reference;

Road 2: One road (at the right) in which statements were also made and were
specific but where no discussion followed;

Road 3: One road (in the midst) in which statements were made but were
general (they "wondered about what they say"), and where NO discussion followed;

Road 4: One road (at the left) in which NO observational statements were made
but where discussion immediately took place and this with reference.

Could this branching in ways of having an observational discussion be relevant?
We analysed again the content of our data :
- In road 2 we could see that no discussion was held, the observational statements were clear, they "fitted" clearly with the observational or classifying
concepts of the scientists, whose remarks expressed also their satisfaction:
"Oh, that's really plus, just pumpkins!" or "very nice plus" or "clearly negative" or "splendid example". Therefore we call this road a road of *"clear
fitness".*

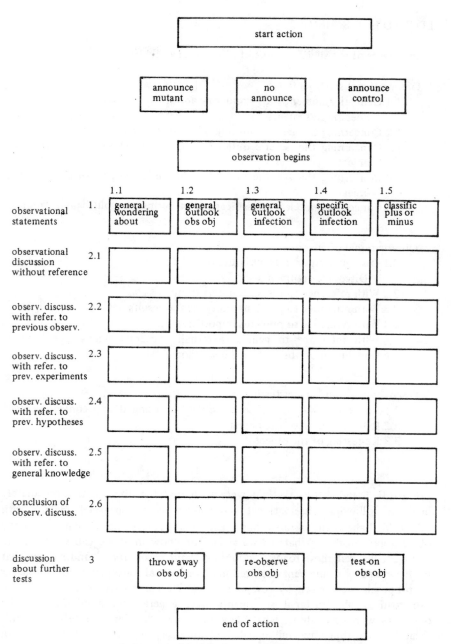

Scheme 2. Specific frame of observational discourse

LEGEND FOR SCHEME 2

Components of the specific frame of observational discourse.

1. Observational statements
    1.1 General statements of "wondering about"
        Specific statements :
    1.2 Concerning the general outlook of the observed object
    1.3 Concerning the general outlook of the infected part of the observed object
    1.4 Concerning the specific outlook of the infected part of the observed object
    1.5 Concerning a clear classification in terms of "plus" and "minus"

2. Observational discussions
    2.1 Discourse arguments without reference
        Discourse arguments
    2.2 With reference to previous observations
    2.3 With reference to previous experimental results
    2.4 With reference to previous hypotheses
    2.5 With reference to general externally accepted knowledge (papers)
    2.6 Conclusion of observational discussion

3. Discussions about further testing
    3.1 Throwing away the observed object or using it as a control element
    3.2 Re-observation of the object
    3.3 Re-testing of the object

- In roads 1 and 4, observations were such that the discussions (immediately held or following observational statements) were concerned mainly with "doubting" about the observations themselves or about the terminology of the observations made: "What are we seeing" or "how must we call what we are seeing?". We call these roads : *"doubting about clear fitness"* and we saw that in these roads a refinement occurred in observational concepts: creative remarks or proposals were given by several persons. We come back to this in part 3.
- In road 3 observational statements were general and non-indicative; the observers wondered about what they saw, they "couldn't place", "couldn't locate" what they saw and decided in all cases, without further discussion

(which would have been highly hypothetical), to analyse further. We can say that the set of references they were using, i.e., clear fitness or doubting about clear fitness, could not furnish them with possible explications. Therefore, we call this road one of *"no fitness"*. In the examples we had, they always called what they saw "strange" or "not understandable". These were cases where different results were obtained on a same set of plants or even on a same plant, after infection with one type of mutant. (In biology, at least, obtaining different results within a same experiment on apparently identical objects, is indeed strange). Our group did not discard the object but decided to analyse first (and then discuss).

So, to summarize: we have four mainroads and three possible items: clear fitness (everything is OK), doubting about clear fitness (refinement and/or testing) and no fitness (testing!).

SEQUENCE OF EVENTS IN DISCOURSE

	obser-vation	observational statement		discussion		- throwing away - re-observe - re-test	items
		general	specific	no ref.	refer.		
road 1	▮→	→	▮→	▮	→ ▮	→ ▮	doubtful fitness
road 2	▮	→	▮	→	→	→ ▮	clearly fitness
road 3	▮	▮→	→	→	→	→ ▮	no fitness
road 4	▮	→	→	→	▮→	→ ▮	doubtful fitness

A proposal for further investigation is :
1. Do discussions during observational discourse indeed branch into ways of reasoning and do they change in the course of further experiments?
2. Are these ways correlated with a specific type of discourse, or are they quite general for most observational discussions?
A comparison with observations done in other labs or in other disciplines could be interesting.

2.4. The actors in discourse

A part from this analysis, we were interested in the contributions of the diferent members in this observational discussion and in a more subtle analysis of their different kinds of statements.

In this meeting seven persons were present (an eighth person missed the meeting because of a misunderstanding): one male student; five scientific members of the lab — three without a Ph.D. (one Dutch woman and two men, about the same age) and two with Ph.D. (two Americans, male and female); an one technical engineer, a woman who has been in the lab since its early beginnings.

For each plant discussion, we checked who said what and noted this on our specific frames (see Scheme 3). For this detailed analysis and those which follow, this working method proved to be very useful. Most of the individual statements were "observational statements" and "statements concerning discussion without reference". We could see that four of the seven persons made mostof the statements and that the contributions of the other three were obviously less in number (the student, the American woman with Ph.D. and the Dutch woman without Ph.D.).

There was some task division within this subgroup so that it is evident that, e.g., the person had the plants under his eyes would and did most frequently make observational statements, and that the person whose task it was to analyse the plants further made a great many of the statements on the level of: "conclusions of the observational discussion and discussion about testing or not".

Apart from these evident correlations, we found it interesting that, e.g. one person made more statements than the others did in the discussion *without* reference, and another one made more statements in the discussion *with* reference. Or that the female technician was explicitly active on each level of the observational discourse, this in sharp contrast to the other two women.

Of course, further analysis with more data are needed to see, e.g., if this division and if these differences are significant or not, and, a more interesting question, upon what this division could be based.

Without giving now more details, or conclusions which are preliminary, we can say that different aspects were playing a role in the contributions of different persons to the discussions: task division within the experiment; different kinds of knowledge (knowing much about various lab results, or knowing much about general literature, or knowing much about know-how); having a Ph.D. or not (which at the least will mean having more or less experience); being a man or a woman.

We also analysed the occurrence of what we called *"hidden messages"* or even *"hidden norms"*. "Hidden" because it was not always the meanings explicit to the content of what was said which were informative to us. Very often things were said, the meanings of which were implicit, or "meta-messages" were given, both verbal and non-verbal.[3]

In our data, e.g., somebody said, after observation of the plant, "I would not say there is much difference", and said this with alook of inquiry at one person. He had made an observational statement, *but* it was also a "prudent proposal": he asked for "consultation" and made an appeal to an "authority". Or, when somebody made a decision, e.g., to throw away a plant, another asked, "Yeah ??" and so played a role of "prudent control".

Most of the time, these "hidden messages" can be called "hidden norms" because they can tell an outsider something about "how to do good science", but, as we said, seldom explicitly.

For me, as I myself had been a scientist, it was almost a delight to discover (or re-discover) these hidden norms in the mass of our observations and to bring them to light, to make them more visible. "Methodical rules", e.g., are very important, and are frequently pointed or applied. They concern topics such as "treachery" (which is strictly forbidden of course, yet flutters permanently like a little devil above the heads — or in the heads — of each scientist), "reproduceability", "consistency" and others.

So, again for our observational discourse, we made a listing of the several "hidden messages" and located them on the different levels of our specific frame (see Scheme 2).

We see that "hidden messages" occurred on each level. When we look to the kinds of "hidden messages" most used, we see that "methodical rules" occur remarkably on each level; that in the observational statements there is the addition of "prudent-control"; in the discussion without reference, of "prudent proposal" and "consultation"; and in the conclusion of discussion an addition of "proposals".

But to stay with the "methodical rules" used on each level: in the announcements of kind of mutant used to infect a set of plants, at first, until the discussion with reference, "methodical rules" were used with a laugh. However, when references were introduced in the discussion, "methodical rules" were used seriously, and concerned "consistency", e.g. "when you call the other thing B, you must call this B". In the conclusions of observational discussion, methodical rules treated mainly of conditions for observation.

We cannot go into more detail here, but we want to stress the important function of these "messages", which most of the time are *"hidden messages"* or even *"hidden norms"*.

In fact they function as a permanent control on the observational process, and this seriously or humorously (humourously in this lab). Some persons were even "specialists" in the use of specific norms, as was, e.g., the woman technician with "prudent control" and the male Dutch scientist with "consistency" (It was also this last one who incited most of the important consultations with the whole group.)

When tentative statements are made or decisions are taken, this kind of unorganized but permanently alive scepticism becomes activated by one or another person, and then often consultations within the group take place. To end, we can say that the group discusses mainly about three themes or about three important questions:

1) are we observing precisely?

2) do we give a correct name for what we observe?

3) shall we analyse further?

3. Register analysis of a discourse dialogue

In this part we want to analyse one particular extract from our lab observations, which illustrates the way discourse and discovery are intertwined and how a register approach can support an adequate description.

3.1. Extract from some observations made during laboratory action 140 (sub-actions 1—24).

1. *Group* observes the next plant infected with pathogenic bacteria X.

2. Nestor: "X makes shoots".

3. Roger to Nestor: "When you call the other thing shoot, you must also call this shoots,

4. even three shoots".

5. Side talk during which Roger quotes the term "teratoma", then:

6. Roger in English to Nestor: "Do they call this a teratoma?"

7. Roger to Ingrid: "What do they call a teratoma?"

8. Ingrid: "A shoot is one or two structures, teratoma is many structures.

9. There are shoots coming from the stem and shoots coming from the top".

10. They conclude that this plant is not a good plant for seeing what is called a shoot and what is called a teratoma.

11. Karel: "The only way to see it is to analyse the shoots".

12. Roger asks for the definition of teratoma.

13. Roger: "Finally, we are not sure if it is a teratoma or a shoot,

14. so let's call it shoots".

15. Nestor: "O.K."

16. Everybody agrees.

17. Before observing the following plant, Roger recalls the question in a side talk, then:

18. Nestor: "How call they in medicine a teratoma?"

19. Roger recalls a paper of Braun on plant pathology that says: "Each formation of tissue is a teratoma".

20. Ingrid (with others): "The definition of teratoma is: many types of tissue coming from one structure".

21. Karel: "Let's speak about transformed shoots and untransformed shoots".
22. Everybody agrees.
23. Nestor: "Yeah, that is a good idea. It simplifies the terminology and it is more precise".
24. Everybody agrees again.

What is the story about in action 140 ? The members of the lab discuss the results of an infection on a plant with a pathogenic (control) bacterium X. So we have:

BEFORE:

Bacteria X is a control bacteria because in the past they had analysed that same bacteria; so they have strong reasons to believe that the result of this test in action 140 should be "really plus". This means a tumor should appear as the result of the infection.
So we have:

THEY EXPECTED TO SEE:

and they should classify this result as "plus" (1.5 in Scheme 2).

The problem in action 140 is that they actually see as a result of the infection something like:

THEY ACTUALLY SEE:

3.2. Mapping the extract on the general context

As a preamble to a detailled analysis of action 140, we stipulate three main registers that are activated during the three-hour lab meeting. The registers incorporate all relevant symbols that are related to the three questions at the end of part 2:

1. The *seeing register* is an open set of clusters of symbols, centred round the question: "Are we observing precisely?" or "What do we exactly see?"

2. The *calling register* is an open set of clusters of symbols centered round the question "Do we give a correct name for what we observe?" or "How do we call what we see or analyse?"

3. The *analysing register* is an open set of clusters of symbols centered round the qustion "Shall we analyse further?" or "Shall we perform chemical tests on what we are seeing and calling?".

Related to Scheme 1, the discourse dialogue in action 140 is running over road 1:

- In line 2 Nestor initiates a specific observational statement which in a firing of the seeing-register with pointers to other registers.

- From line 3 to 24, we remark a twofold discussion with several kinds of references:

1. from line 3 to 16 the group discusses the initial statement, ending in an agreement to call it "shoots": here the calling and the seeing register are combined; the analysing register is introduced in line 11, but has no decisive impact on the dialogue;

2. from line 17 to 24 the group discusses again the agreement that ends in a conceptual refinement, here a combination of the calling and the analysing registers results in a definite agreement.

If we map the extract on our specific frame of observational discourse in Scheme 2 we come to Scheme 3:

- Statement 1 refers to their previous knowledge about the patho-genetic bacterium X which is interpreted as an announcement of a control plant. This knowledge activates some expectations as to the specific outlook of the infection.

- The confrontation of statements 2 and 3 indicates a problem, stated in 4. The problem is: they see a plant with 3 structures as a result of the infection. At first sight, the seeing register classifies this result as "shoots" based on previous observations, at least this is the case according to Nestor. But their definition of a "teratoma", nested in the calling register, fits also with what they observe. In other words, the observed object can be grasped by two concurrent concepts, represented as different clusters of symbols in both the seeing and the calling register. This no-fitness between these two registers is prelude to an observational discussion.

- In statements 5 to 10, the discussion is a calling for information to clarify the two concurrent concepts in order to create unambiguous pointers between the two registers, ending in a diagnosis of the problem: the no-fitness of "what they see" and "what they call".

- Statement 11 is a hint to the solution of the problem: Karel's first statement in this action indicates a shift to the third register concerning the analysis of the objects; but the group does not follow the hint.

- In 12 to 16 Roger recalls the problem by stressing the need for clarification of their calling register which ends in a first solution: they agree to call it "shoots", but the problem remains.

- In 17 to 20 the second general subaction starts with Roger's recalling on the problem. Again they scrutinize different slots in the three registers and this time it is more fruitful.

- In line 21 to 24 we remark the final solution of the problem, coming from Nestor's second statement: he proposes a refinement by relating a pragmatic extension to the semantic field of the concept "shoot".

This ends in a general agreement by indicating two methodological rules:
1. simplification of terminology,
2. precise observational classification.

3.3. Register analysis of the extract

We stipulate the following hypothesis: In a discourse-dialogue, the interactions can be described as knowledge-engineering processes where actors (as control structures) activate and manipulate different components of registers by several intertwined strategies (discourse rules).

This hypothesis implies that every dialogue-utterance can be represented as a list that identifies:
1. the *number* of the events in the dialogue;
2. the *actors* in the dialogue:
   - a speaker
   - the hearer(s), with differentiation of the direct and the indirect hearer
   - the silent actors which in this lab are the tested plants;
3. the *strategies* used by the actors in order to fire components in the contexts of the discourse; more in detail, discourse rules are manipulated by the actors to reach some goal or subplan in the dialogue;
4. the *contexts* which give the statement semantic and pragmatic impact in the discourse: they are represented as slots (= configurations of verbal and non-verbal symbols) in different registers (= dynamical clusters of slots).

We differentiate further among:

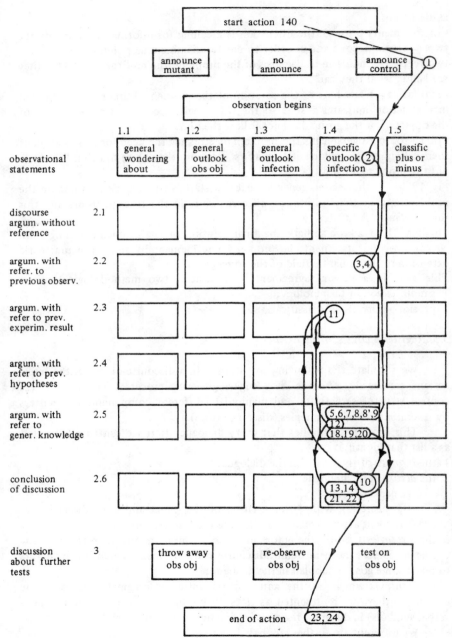

Scheme 3. Action 140 mapped on the specific frame of observational discourse

1. fired components in the context that are directly activated by the utterance of the speaker;

2. stand-by components in the context; these are slots in registers that were previously fired in the discourse but remain as a central component for understanding the utterance;

3. background components in the context are those slots that were previously fied in the dialogue but only have a peripheral character for the specific utterance. In some cases, a rule can function as a background component, as in action 140.

The combination of these three types of components, constituting the contexts, describe:

1. reasons and beliefs of the actors;

2. the actors' hypotheses concerning shared reasons and beliefs of the direct and indirect hearer(s) in the dialogue.

It helps the reader of the dialogue to identify the different motives of the speaker and the way the speaker thinks the hearer(s) can understand the speaker's statement.

An example will illustrate our approach: event 19 in action 140 is represented as:

```
(event 19
    (actors (speaker:Roger)
            (hearer   (direct:Nestor)
                      (indirect:Group))
            (silent actor:plant 5 (infected with control bacterium X)))
    (strategies (answer to event 18))
    (contexts (fired components
                (slots (teratoma)
                      (references to general knowledge
                            (definition from Braun-paper))
                      (references to contexts of other researchers
                            (Braun on plant pathology)))
                (registers (seeing)
                      (calling)))
            (stand-by components
                (slots(shoot (event 14)))
                (registers(analysing(event 11))))
            (background components
                (slots   (meta-evaluation (events 11 and 3))
                      (observational statement(event 2))
                      (references to previous observations(event 4))
```

                    (references to previous experiments(event 11))
                    (references to their own contexts (event 14))
                    (references to general research-contexts (event 12))
            (registers (nil))))))

A global representation of all relevant components in discourse during action 140 is found in the following list. The reader can remark the different pointers indicated in the contexts where the open spaces (represented by (..)) can be filled up with components of other actions. In other words, action 140 must be represented in the global contexts of the lab meeting (action 136, ..., 175) :

    (Lab–140
        (actors(Eva Ingrid Karel Nestor Omer Roger Sara Group plants))
        (strategies (A(informative statements))
                (B(conclusions))
                (C(agreements))
                (D(questions))
                (E(answers))
                (F(meta-evaluation)((no contradiction)
                                    (simplified terminology)
                                    (precise concepts)
                                    (..))))
    (contexts
                (registers ((J(seeing))
                        (pointers to K–L–G–H–N–P–U–V–W–..))
                        ((K(calling))
                        (pointers to J–L–G–H–N–R–S–U–V–W–..))
                        ((L(analysing))
                        (pointers to J–K–G–H–N–P–Q–U–V–W–..)))
                (slots (G(shoot)(pointers to J–K–L–..))
                    (H(teratoma)(pointers to J–K–L–..))
                    (N(current observational classification)
                                    (pointers to J–K–L–G–H–..))
                    (O(arguments without reference)
                                    (pointers to J–K–G–H–..))
                    (P(arguments with reference to previous observations)
                                    (pointers to J–..))
                    (Q(arguments with reference to previous experiments)
                                    (pointers to L–..))
                    (R(arguments with reference to previous hypotheses)

```
                    (pointers to J—K—L—..))
        (S(arguments with reference to general knowledge)
                    (pointers to J—K—L—G—H—N—D—P—Q—
                    R—U—V—W—(papers(braun— ..))—
                    (training books..)
        (U(their own contexts)
                    (pointers to J—K—L—G—H—N—O—P—Q—R—S—.0)
        (V(contexts of other researchers((pointers to..))
        (W(contexts of general research)(pointers to ..))
        (..))))
```

Looking at scheme 4 we remark Roger's solo-performance from 3 to 7; first by his meta-evaluation in 3, indicating the contradiction of Nestor's statement, which is the pivot for the discourse dialogue in action 140. The contradiction can only be understood by triggering the component P (references to previous observations). This means that Nestor's statement in 2 is itself not a contradiction: it is the combination of this statement with previous utterances of Nestor. In other words the pivot for the dialogue in 140 is not alone in the action 140. This leads to another hypothesis:

An adequate description of a discourse dialogue needs the dynamic combination of different interacting levels of contexts: a register approach fulfills this requirement by indicating in each register the different pointers to other registers.

Roger's question in 5 introduces the new "teratoma-slot" by his reference to general knowledge. There is no answer and he generalizes his question by referring to contexts of other researchers (in 6) and by more generalizing in leaving the seeing registers (in 7).

Finally there comes an answer from Ingrid, but the problem remains: perhaps it is her use of the ambiguous concept "structure" that does not bring the solution. It seems an inadequate way of solving contradictions (this is affirmed in statement 23).

So Roger's switching between the calling and seeing registers was not very fruitful, as is indicated in 10: with the meta-evaluation concerning plant 5, the discourse in the dialogue is switched back to its own context.

Karel's statement in 11 is important for many reasons: his meta-evaluation introduces new pointers to the analysing register with a new type of reference (to previous experiments) he stresses the importance of performing decisive chemical tests on the plants. If we confront it with Karel's second statement in 21, then we remark his *hint* to the solution.

Karel's proposal to analyse the shoots is too general, so Roger questions the problem again in 12, by focussing attention again on the calling register.

REGISTER MODEL SIMULATION

LIST of components (mnemonics refer to global representation in (Lab-140(..))

: a INFOSTAT	B CONCLUDE	: C AGREE	: D QUESTION
: e ANSWER	: F METAEVAL	: G SHOOT	: H TERATOMA
: I NIL	: J SEEING	: K CALLING	: L ANALYSING
: M NIL	: N OBS STAT	: O NO REFER	: P REF OBS
: Q REF EXP	: R REF HYPO	: S REF KNOW	: T NIL
: U US	: V THEY	: W THE	: X NIL

EVENT		2	A	B	C	D	E	F	G	H	I	H	K	L	M	N	O	P	Q	R	S	T	U	V	W
NESTOR	2	•						•			•				•								•		
ROGER	3	•					•	•		•	•			−		•							•		
ROGER	4	•				−	•			•	•			−		•							•		
ROGER	5				•	−	X	•		X	•			−		−					•		•		
ROGER	6				•	−	X	•		•	•			−		−					•		−	•	
ROGER	7				•	−	X	•		X	•			−		−					•		−	•	
INGRID	8				•	−	•	X		•	•			−		−					•		−	•	
INGRID	8b				•	−	X	•		•	•			−		−					•		−	•	
INGRID	9				•	−	•	X		•	•			−		−					•		−	•	
GROUP	10	•				•	•	•		•	•			−	•	−					•		•	−	
KAREL	11	•				•	•	X		•	X	•		−		−	•				−		•	−	
ROGER	12			•		−	X	•		X	•	X		−	−	−				•			−		•
ROGER	13	•				•	•			•	X	X		−	−	−				•			−		
ROGER	14	•				−	•	X		X	•	X		−	−	−				•			−		
NESTOR	15		•			−	X	X		X	X	X		−	−	−							−		
GROUP	16		•			−	X	X		X	X	X		−	−	−							−		
ROGER	17	•				−	X	X		X	X	X		−	−	−							−		
NESTOR	18		•			−	X	•		X	•	X		−	−	−				•			−	•	−
ROGER	19			•		−	X	•		•	•			−	−	−				•			−	•	−
INGRID	20			•		−	X	•		•	•	X		−	−	−				•			−	−	•
KAREL	21	•			•	−	•	•		X	•	•		−	−	•	•			−			•	−	
GROUP	22	•				−	X	X		X	X	X		−	−	−				−			−	−	
NESTOR	23	•				•	X	X		X	•	X		−	−	−	−		•	•			−	−	
GROUP	24	•				−	X	X		X	X	X		−	−	−	−						−	−	

Legend : • = FIRED   X = STAND BY   − = BACKGROUND

Scheme 4 : a representation of a compact simulation of action 140

Let us look more closely of Roger's kind of questions :
- his questions 5, 6, 7 and 12 always use arguments with references to general knowledge;
- his questions continuously force a clarifying of the concept of "teratoma"; he never questions the crucial concept "shoot";
- his questions shift their own contexts (in 5) to contexts of other researchers (in 6) to the general context of research (in 12) while permanently firing the calling register.

Unfortunately we have no exact data of Roger's statement in 17 where he reopens the discussion, which proves that he was not satisfied with his owns conclusion in 14, where he agrees with Nestor's proposal in 2.

The power of discourse dialogue can be illustrated by the fact that, in action 140, Roger can give an answer in 19 to a question that he himself asked toIngrid in 7. If he knew the answer in 19 why did he ask the question in 7 ?

Perhaps we find the answer in Nestor's question in 18; his introduction of new pointers in the teratoma-slot, referring to the medicine contexts, forces Roger to break through his own lab-contexts in order to shift to a related discipline in science.

A second illustration of the power of a discourse dialogue is Ingrid's two definitions of the "teratoma"-concept: the definition in 20 is more detailled more accurate than the definition in 8b because the ambiguous "structure" concept is more specified by introducing "types of tissue" (which is a pointer previously fired by Roger's answer in 19).

As already mentioned, Karel's statement in 21 gives the final solution to the problem by firing slots in the calling and the analysing registers in combination with references to previous observations and experiments, centring the proposal on their own contexts of research.

Action 140 ends with Nestor's meta-evaluation of the solution: the slots of the two concepts in the three registers have precise pointers.

His statement 23 affirms explicitly the need for simplified terminology and precise formulations. The group generally agrees in 22 and 24 because from that moment on they can stipulate their hypotheses in a more precise way by relating the use of the two concepts "teratoma" and "shoot" to a decisive physico-chemical test of the observed object: if they find no nopaline then they will call it "shoot", otherwise they will call it "teratoma".

3.4. Conclusion

- Discourse dialogues are crucial in the meetings of the researchers because the group has to agree about the results of some tests on plants. This fact forces them to clear up some ambiguous components in their registers.

- The dialogue can be described as a scanning of different slots ranging over different registers by an question-answering strategy in order to unravel the network of overlapping slots.
- The questions in the dialogue are careful tools for shifting one slot at a time centring round some main registers. Sometimes they serve as navigating elements that create pointers to newly introduced slots so that actors can answer their own questions (e.g., Roger 7 and 19), or formulate statements in a more precise way (e.g., Ingrid in 8b and 20).[4]
- As it comes out in our analysis of this extract, we remark that discovery in that lab has to be described as the construction of a new network between the introduced slots in the discourse. Nestor's statement in 21 is a conceptual innovation in terms of creating a new perspective to the problem by looking at the troublesome matter from an other plateau (the analysing register). In the extract we do not have the introduction of a new concept to solve the difficulty, it is only a refinement of pointers between their own registers. The discourse dialogue was governed by the main registers (seeing and calling) until the combination with the analysing register in 21 stipulated the solution.
- Semantic and Pragmatic components are really interwined in the lab extract. The researchers relate the meaning of their concepts indissolubly with the pragmatical results of performing chemical tests on the objects. A discourse analysis of dialogues in lab contexts has to incorporate this complexity. We think the reader can judge the adequacy of our register approach.

NOTES

(1)   See Vervenne, D., Vandamme, F., 1982.

(2)   See Vervenne, D., et al., 1983.

(3)   This phenomenon is well known by experiental psychotherapists, who call this the "explicit and implicit meanings" in communicational behaviour, and it is namely to these implicit meanings that a good therapist must respond.

(4)   As Vandamme, F., indicated during an informal talk, conceptual innovations introduce a modification of the competence of the actors.

BIBLIOGRAPHY

LECHNERT, W. G., 1978, The process of question answering.

SHINN, T., 1982, Scientific disciplines and organizational specificity: the social and cognitive configuration of laboratory activities. In: Elias, N., Martins, H., Whitley, R., (eds.), Scientific establishments and hierarchies. Sociology of the Sciences, Vol. IV, 1982, 239–264.

VANDAMME, F., DE WAELE, D., VERVENNE, D., 1981, Een projectom-schrijving van een strict-nominalistische kennisbenadering. C & C, Rep. no 38, Werkgroep Registers: kennisverwerving, verwerking en representa-tie, R.U.Gent.

VERVENNE, D., VANDAMME, F., 1982. Description of a project concerning a strict-nominalistic approach of knowledge. C & C, Rep. no 40, Werk-groep Registers: kennisverwerving, verwerking en representatie, R.U.-Gent.

VERVENNE, D., DE WAELE, D., HOFTE, M., VANDAMME, F., 1983 (in press), Some remarks on computersimulation of a working laboratory. C & C, Rep. no 58, Werkgroep Registers: kennisverwerving, verwerking en representatie, R.U.Gent.

PARADIGMS AND PROBLEM–SOLVING IN OPERATIONS RESEARCH

Ilkka Niiniluoto
University of Helsinki

Russell L. Ackoff, Professor of Systems Sciences in the University of Pennsylvania, published in 1979 in the **Journal of the Operational Research Society** two papers on the status of Operations Research (OR) (1). In the first paper, 'The Future of Operational Research is Past', Ackoff — who himself is one of the leading pioneers of OR — argues that "American Operations Research is dead even though it has yet to be buried". In the second article, 'Resurrecting the Future of Operational Research', Ackoff suggests that OR might be resurrected by adopting an "alternative paradigm to that currently used in OR".

While Ackoff already uses the term 'paradigm', which was made fashionable by Thomas Kuhn's book *The Structure of Scientific Revolutions* (1962), Dando and Bennett (1981) have suggested that "OR is now in a period of crisis analogous to that described by Kuhn in the Natural Sciences". In this paper, I shall examine the question whether such Kuhnian notions as 'paradigm' and 'crisis' are applicable to the development of OR. It is well-known that Kuhn's account of normal science and scientific revolutions has already been applied to an impressive number of fields — among them physics, chemistry, astronomy, geology, biology, psychology, linguistics, economics, sociology, political science, jurisprudence, history, theology, art and literature, folklore, education, and technology (2). One might even say that since the appearance of Kuhn's book paradigm hunting has become a favourite sport among philosophers and scientists : every scientific discipline with some self-respects seems to feel that it has to find its own 'paradigm'.

What about the claim that Operations Research is in a Kuhnian crisis ? A natural first reaction is to think that paradigm hunters have hit again — without bothering to work out the real meaning of Kuhn's basic concepts. While in a sense this suspicion is not entirely unjustified, it also turns out that Kuhn's model of science fits surprisingly well to OR. In my view, it is instructive to study why this is so, since it gives us insight into the recent 'problem-solving models' of scientific inquiry. In other words, my real aim in discussing OR is to say something about Kuhn and Laudan.

1. Ackoff's Criticism of Operations Research

The prehistory of Operations Research includes Frederick Taylor's ideas on scientific management at the end of the 19th century, A.K. Erlang's work on telephone traffic in 1908 (leading later to queuing theory), Frederick Lancaster's quantitative study of military strategies in 1916, Emile Borel's (1921) and John von Neumann's (1928) invention of the theory of games, and Abraham Wald's work on decision theory in 1939. The progress in probability theory, mathematical statistics, numerical methods, theory of automata, systems theory, and econometrics also contributed to the development of OR. It is usually said, however, that Operational Research was born in England during World War II when teams of scientists started to use mathematical methods for the planning of military operations. For example, one of the successful projects aimed at increasing the effectiveness of bombing missions. After the war OR was adopted in the civil sector as a tool of quantitative planning, and it was applied to various managerial problems in industry, business, and government.

Perhaps the most authoritative presentation of the aims and the methods of the new field was *Introduction to Operations Research* (1957) by C. West Churchman, Russell L. Ackoff, and E. Leonard Arnoff. (See also Ackoff, 1961, 1962; Ackoff and Sasieni, 1968). They defined OR as follows :

"O.R. is the application of scientific methods, techniques, and tools to problems involving the operations of a system so as to provide those in control of the system with optimum solutions to the problems." (p. 18)

Churchmann *et al.* emphasized the application of OR methods to complex industrial organizations which face "executive-type problems" of combining the behaviour of its various departments so as to yield an optimum overall result.

In his 1979 articles Ackoff complains that, after having gained a widespread acceptance by the mid 60's, OR has lost its "pioneering spirit" and "innovativeness". In his view, "academic OR and the relevant professional societies" are "primarily responsible for this decline". He argues that the current practice of OR has three major defects. First, the practitioners seek, select, and distort the problem situations so that "favoured techniques could be applied to them". Secondly, an increasing portion of OR, especially the teaching of mathematical methods, is "done by those who do not identify with the profession". Thirdly, when OR has become an isolated discipline, "the original interdisciplinarity of OR has completely disappeared".

Ackoff (1979a) gives a more detailed criticism of six points about OR. First, as the lifetime of solutions to many social and organizational problems is shorter than the time required to find them, there is a great need for "decision-making systems that can learn and adapt effectively". Secondly, OR's concept of optimality fails to take into account the aesthetic values associated with the intrinsic value of means and the extrinsic value of ends. Thirdly, managers are confronted with "messes", i.e., "complex systems of changing problems that interact with each other", and messes have to be treated holistically. Fourthly, OR's "paradigm" for problem-solving, which consists in the principle "predict the future and prepare for it", should be changed to "design a desirable future and invent ways of bringing it about". Fifthly, the treatment of messes requires an interdisciplinary approach. Sixthly, as the objectivity of science can be obtained only by taking "all possible values" into account, OR should involve "all those who can be affected by the output of decision making".

Ackoff's (1979b) "alternative paradigm" of "interactive planning" is based upon three operating principles. According to the "participative principle", "the principal benefit of planning comes from engaging in it". The "principle of continuity" requires that plans should be continuously revised in the light of their performance, unexpected problems and opportunities, and latest knowledge. The "holistic principle" states that "every part of a system and every level of it should be planned for simultaneously and interdependently" — instead of "top-down and bottom-up planning". Interactive planning should "formulate the mess", set the ideals of the organization by giving a continuously changing "idealized redesign of the system", and find the means and resources for pursuing these ideals. This new paradigm is aught in the programme of "Social Systems Sciences" that Ackoff has established at the University of Pennsylvania.

2. Is Operations Research in a Kuhnian Crisis ?

We may now ask whether Ackoff's description of the current state of OR bears any resemblance to Kuhn's account of a science in a crisis. To answer this question, let us first recall that, according to Kuhn, paradigm-based normal science will sooner or later run into *anomalies* where nature violates the expectations based upon the paradigm accepted in the scientific community. Scientific theories can be to some extent adjusted to account for such anomalies, but a persistent breakdown of the normal scientific puzzle-solving activity in important areas leads to a crisis (e.g., astronomy before Copernicus, chemistry before Lavoisier, physics before Einstein). A crisis is a "period of pronounced professional insecurity" (*ibid.*, p. 67) which begins with "the blurring of a paradigm" and with the "loosening of the rules for normal research" (*ibid.*, p. 84).

> "The proliferation of competing articulations, the willingness to try anything, the expression of explicit discontent, the recourse to philosophy and to debate over fundamentals, all these are symptoms of a transition from normal to extraordinary research". (*ibid.*, p. 90).

The period of *extraordinary research* ends with the emergence (or recognition) of a new candidate for a paradigm and its acceptance in a *scientific revolution.* Such a paradigm change begins a new period of normal science.

In his 'Postscript—1969' to the Second Edition of his book, Kuhn clarifies the notion of 'paradigm' by distinguishing between a *disciplinary matrix* (i.e., paradigm as a constellation of group commitments) and *exemplars* (i.e., paradigm as shared example). (See also Kuhn, 1977). A disciplinary matrix consists of at least four components : (i) *symbolic generalizations* (i.e., laws), (ii) *models* (i.e., metaphysical beliefs, analogies, and metaphors), (iii) *values* (i.e., methodological standards and preferences), and (iv) *exemplars* (i.e., concrete problem solutions). In normal science, the members of the scientific community try to apply the symbolic generalizations to particular cases which are similar to the accepted exemplars. These cases are structured largely through the models of the matrix, and the success of the applications is evaluated relative to the values of the matrix. In this way, we may see how good a normal-scientific tradition has been in problem-solving — and whether it is *progressive* or *degenerative* in this respect (cf. Lakatos, 1970; Laudan, 1977). Then a crisis corresponds to the degenerative phase of a scientific tradition (cf. Kuhn, 1970, p. 256).

One way of reconstructing at least some aspects of Kuhnian normal science is to treat *Kuhn-theories* as triples $\langle K, I, I_o \rangle$, where the *core* K consists essentially of a mathematical formalism (symbolic generalizations), I is the class of the *intended applications* of K, and $I_o \subset I$ is the class of paradigmatic *exemplars*. The claim associated with theory $\langle K, I, I_o \rangle$ is that K can be applied to the elements of I. Normal science consists in the gradual verification of this claim, and its crisis means the emergence of important anomalous cases $I' \subset I$ to which K cannot be successfully applied (3).

Dando and Bennett (1981) note that Ackoff is not the only person who has recently criticized OR : the optimism of the late 60's has in ten years changed to a widespread pessimism about the practical success of OR. It might be the case that this kind of feeling of insecurity is primarily a reflection of the decline in Western industry due to the oil crisis of the 70's. Such a professional crisis, generated by external reasons, should be distinguished from a crisis in

Kuhn's sense, since the latter can be characterized by terms which are internal to a scientific tradition (4).

Some of Ackoff's complaints about OR — especially his remarks against the character of OR as a "discipline", or against "academic OR" and "professional societies", and his claim that "favoured techniques" determine the problems that are studied — seem to be directed against the normal-scientific nature of current OR. In this sense — which is not Kuhnian at all — OR is in a 'crisis' because it has become normal science. Hence, it can be claimed that OR is not yet in a Kuhnian crisis — at most it may be just entering the phase of extraordinary research through the criticism of Ackoff and others.

As Kuhn has clearly shown the methodological rationale behind paradigm-based research, the criticism that all normal science is too 'dogmatic' is not justified. This criticism has nevertheless a point especially relative to those disciplines which serve as a basis for professional technologies (e.g., medicine, jurisprudence, mechanical engineering). These situations may bring about unhealthy dogmatism, since all challenges to the accepted theoretical background assumptions will be regarded as attacks against the social status of the whole profession. Perhaps Ackoff's message is that this has become the trouble with OR as well.

On the other hand, Ackoff's theses clearly imply also that in his view the current OR is in a degenerative phase, since it does not adequately treat certain important types of problems — which he calls "messes". Such messes are thus anomalies to the standard techniques of OR. This decline in the problem-solving ability of OR is due to changes in the social environment of OR (5) — the society is becoming increasingly complex as a collection of interrelated systems — and to the lack of sufficient feedback from the practice to the theory of OR.

If OR ever is to enter into a Kuhnian crisis, it first has to be based upon a Kuhnian paradigm or disciplinary matrix. Ackoff's discussion in this respect is not too clear, but in any case his own "paradigm" of "interactive planning" consists of a few general *norms* for the planning process. His criticism against OR also contains a somewhat implicit description of some general principles that he finds characteristic to the standard way of applying OR to planning problems. In other words, for Ackoff the old and new "paradigm" of OR are *theories of planning*. There are no a priori reasons why Kuhnian notions could not be applied to such theories — if they are formulated in a sufficiently explicit form (6).

Dando and Bennett (1981, 1982) interpret the situation in a different way. They agree with Raitt (1979) that

"OR has no distinctive subject matter in the way that physics has, and does not provide an accumulation of theoretical knowledge about the world."

"No one expects the history of OR to show an accumulation of models of increasing power, precision or generality. A model is constructed for practical application in a particular situation. We do not ask if it is true, only if it works ..."

They come to the conclusion that, while OR does not generate its own "scientific-empirical" paradigms "in the original Kuhnian sense", OR does have a "methodological paradigm", since OR is committed to the scientific method. They view the Ackoff debate as a controversy between "official", "reformist", and "revolutionary" paradigms, which are related to positivist, interpretative, and critical methodologies in sociology.

In my view, the idea of interpreting Ackoff's theory of interactive planning as a step from positivism to hermeneutics seems far-fletched slightly, even though Ackoff's methods for dealing with "messes" may be "softer" than the standard quantitative tools of OR. We have already seen above that there is no need to restrict the discussion of the paradigms of OR to general methodological issues, as Dando and Bennett suggest. Moreover — and this is for us the most interesting aspect of this paradigm debate — the discussion about OR has so far ignored the fact that Kuhn does not either regard scientific progress as "an accumulation of theoretical knowledge about the world". For Kuhn, science is a *problem-solving* rather than *truth-seeking* activity (cf. also Laudan, 1977). And what would be a more striking example of problem-solving activity than OR !

This observation shows that the question of the applicability of Kuhn's model of science to OR has to be reconsidered. We shall do this by looking into the nature of problem-solving in OR.

3. Problem-Solving in Operations Research

In their classical treatment (7), Churchman *et al.* (1957) outline the method of OR as consisting of the following steps :

"1. Formulating the problem.
2. Constructing a mathematical model to represent the system under study,
3. Deriving a solution from the model.
4. Testing the model and the solution derived from it.
5. Establishing controls over the solution.
6. Putting the solution to work : implementation." (p. 13).

This view of scientific method as problem-solving is largely influenced by John Dewey's *Logic : The Theory of Inquiry* (1939). For Dewey, the locus of a problem concerns "what kind of responses the organism shall make" or "the interaction of organic responses and environing conditions in their movement toward an existential issue" (p. 107). For Churchman *et al.,* a problem involves four components : (i) a decision-maker (executive) who is "dissatisfied with some aspect of the state of affairs and consequently wants to make a decision with regard to altering it", (ii) the objectives (wants) of the decision-maker, (iii) the environment consisting of the resources available to the decision-maker, and (iv) alternative courses of action among which the decision-maker has to make his choice.

When a problem has been fomulated, a mathematical model is constructed which expresses the "effectiveness" E of the whole system under study as a function of variables x_i subject to control by the decision-maker and variables y_j not subject to control :

(1) $E = f(x_1, y_j)$.

The problem is then reduced to the choice of the values of x_i which maximize (or minimize) the function (1), given the values of y_j and some restrictions on the permissible values of x_i. This optimatization problem is solved by analytical, numerical or Monte Carlo methods (simulation). The solution is then translated into a set of operating procedures, i.e., to recommendations of action for the decision-maker. This strategy is advertised as the general method of science in Ackoff (1962), p. 28.

A typical example is the *diet problem,* first studied by George Stigler in 1945. Assume that one unit of food x_i contains a_i units of vitamin A and b_i units of vitamin B, and that one unit of x_i costs c_i units of money ($i=1,...,n$). What is the minimum-cost diet which gives at least a units of vitamin A and b units of vitamin B ? This problem can be solved by minimizing the cost function

(2) $c_1 x_1 + ... + c_n x_n$

with the constraints

$x_i \geq 0$ ($i=1,...,n$)

(3) $a_1 x_1 + ... + a_n x_n \geq a$

$b_1 x_1 + ... + b_n x_n \geq b$.

152

This mathematical optimalization problem can be handled with the techniques of *linear programming* (cf. Saaty, 1959). The same method is applicable e.g. to the *transportation problem,* formulated by F.L. Hitchcock in 1941 : what is the most economical way of shipping a given amount of a product from m origins to n destinations.

Churchman *et al.* give a classification of the main types of problems to which OR is applicable :

    a) inventory problems
    b) allocation problems
    c) waiting-time problems
    d) replacement problems
    e) competitive problems
    f) combined problems.

Each type of problem is further divided into subtypes, and these are illustrated by specific applications. For example, the diet problem and the transportation problem are special cases of one important subtype of allocation problems. Some of the standard distinctions among competitive problems (where the effectiveness of a decision depends upon the decision of another party with conflicting interests) are shown in Figure 1.

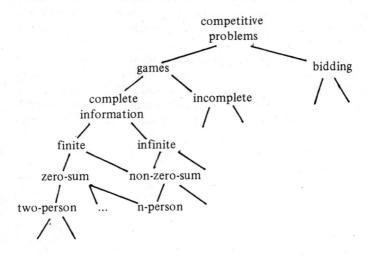

Fig. 1. Classification of competitive problems.

These classified problems are then correlated with mathematical models and techniques : for example, inventory models for inventory problems, queuing theory and sequencing models for waiting-time problems, game theory for competitive problems, linear and dynamic programming for several types problems, etc. The development of these models and techniques can be regarded as a branch of applied mathematics. In the applications of OR, they are used for finding solutions to particular decision-problems faced by various kinds of business, industrial, military, and administrative organizations.

On the basis of this survey, we can define the *disciplinary matrix* of OR as a quadruple $<T,M.P.I_o>$, where

T = a collection of mathematical *techniques* needed in the solution of optimation problems (e.g. linear programming, Monte Carlo methods)

A = a collection of mathematical *models* which can represent the structure of decision-problem situations (e.g. queuing theory, game theory, decision theory, inventory models)

P = a hierarchical classification of various types of decision-problems

I_o = a set of paradigmatic exemplars (applications of the techniques and models to particular problem situations; e.g. the diet problem).

A typical pattern of OR is to use the models in M to give structure to a particular decision-problem, to identify this problem in the hierarchy P and to apply the technique of T to this problem by imitating the procedures used for the exemplars in I_o. A disciplinary matrix of OR may be combined also with a *theory of planning* which gives more general rules for the application process of OR methods (cf. Section 3).

This notion of disciplinary matrix is close to Kuhn's corresponding concept which includes symbolic generalizations, models, values, and exemplars as its components. It is also closely related to the notion of a Kuhn-theory in Section 2 : T and M together correspond to the core K, P to the set I of intended applications, and I_o to the set of exemplars.

Normal-scientific theoretical development of the matrix $<T,M,P,I_o>$ of OR means the invention of new or more effective techniques in T, the creation of new or more comprehensive models in M, and the refinement of the structure P of problems. Ackoff's 'revolution' consists in his claim of the importance of a new class of problems — "messes" — and of the need to develop new kinds of methods for handling them.

4. Truth-Seeking and Problem-Solving

As a *problem-solving* activity, OR is oriented towards practice : it tries to use the methods of science to find optimal solutions to problems concerned with alternative courses of action. As these solutions are its primary aim, it is clear in which sense OR is not a *truth-seeking* activity.

We have also seen that the Kuhnian conception of scientific change fits quite well to OR — even though OR is not a science with its own subject matter. As this fit is so good, one may start to wonder how Kuhn's account then can be applicable to sciences at all. Is it perhaps so that all sciences are comparable to OR as problem-solving activities ? I shall argue for a negative answer by considering more closely the role of the notion of *truth* within problem-solving.

In the first place, it would be a mistake to conclude that questions about truth are irrelevant to the procedures of OR. The mathematical models that are used in OR are representations of the system under study. They may be imperfect and idealized, but still the quality of the solutions that they yield crucially depends upon their closeness to reality in the relevant respects. Thus, Ackoff points out that "the optimal solution of a model is *not* an optimal solution of a problem unless the model is a perfect representation of the problem" (Ackoff, 1979a, p. 97). But since all models are "simplifications of reality", "it is critical to determine how well models represent reality". For this reason, the models of OR have to be tested and controlled before the implementation of the solutions (cf. Churchman *et al.,* 1957, Part IX). For example, in the diet problem it is assumed that the cost of a diet is measured by function (2). If the prices c_i of food change or if some additional costs have to be added (e.g. costs for preparing the meals), then the cost equation defined by (2) has to be changed as well. In this way, OR can be said to be a *truth-using* activity : even though it is not primarily interested in the models as such, since they serve as *instruments* for finding solutions to decision-problems, *the instrumental value of these models relative to a particular application depends partly upon their degree of truthlikeness* (8). If the model is not sufficiently close to the truth, it gives nonoptimal solutions which are disappointing, since they do not relieve the decisionmaker from his initial dissatisfaction (9).

Secondly, there is a crucial distinction to be made between *cognitive problems* (What to believe ? What can be known ?) and *problems of action* (What to do ?). Cognitive problems involve hypotheses concerning alleged facts or regularities, past facts (postdiction), future facts (prediction), causes or reasons of facts (explanation). They can be expressed by WH-questions, why-questions, and how-questions — and in most cases they can be transformed to whether-questions of the following forms : Is h true or false ? Which of the alternative hypotheses h_1, ..., h_n is true ? Which of the alternative hypotheses

$h_1,...,h_n$ is it rational to accept as true ? (10) Relative to cognitive problems, one can make a distinction between *potential* answers and the *correct* answer, and between *partial* and *complete* answers. The aim of studying a cognitive problem is ultimately to find its complete correct answer. The outcome of such inquiry, viz. the acceptance of a hypothesis as true, is itself an act or a decision. Therefore, the procedure of solving cognitive problems can formally be represented as decision-making (see Levi, 1967; Niiniluoto, 1976). However, this activity is *truth-seeking* − and, hence, different from problem-solving with OR.

For scientific realists, scientific theories are the most interesting results of our truth-seeking procedures : the basic cognitive aim of science is to find true or highly truthlike explanatory theories (cf. Niiniluoto, 1980, 1983). In contrast, Laudan's problem-solving model of science is based upon the idea that all issues about truth and falsity are left outside the account of the aims of science − in spite of the fact that, in Laudan's own view, scientific theories have truth values (cf. Laudan, 1977, 1981, 1982).

Laudan claims that science is a problem-solving rather than truth-seeking activity. We have seen one way in which such a project can be effectively pursued : follow Ackoff (1962) and accept the 'behaviouralist' philosophy of OR which treats all scientific problems as problems of action ! This is not Laudan's position, however, since the problems that he discusses are not reducible to the model of OR. It is a matter of controversy what problems and their solutions are in Laudan's model − he himself has not yet made this very clear. Therefore, it is also an open question how Laudan's notion of the 'problem-solving ability' of a theory is related to such familiar concepts as systematic power and confirmation (cf. Niiniluoto, 1984).

In Laudan (1977), 'problems' are essentially why-questions of the form 'Why p ?', where p is believed to express a fact, and a theory T is said to solve a problem if p is deducible from T. As one can distinguish between potential and correct solutions to such explanatory questions, the search for their correct answers is in fact a truth-seeking enterprise.

Recently Laudan (1982) has claimed that "the *raison d'être* of science" is to put us "in a position to anticipate nature". Our theories should "shape our expectations" and yield reasonably often "correct anticipations of nature". This means that science aims at solving predictive problems of the form 'p or not-p ?' − which is again a truth-seeking enterprise (11). Moreover, this activity is also truth-using in the same sense as OR: if a theory is not sufficiently truthlike − or does not have a truth value at all, as the instrumentalists claim − it may with good luck give a correct prediction in some particular cases, but not uniformly for an indefinitely large class of empirical problems (12).

A cognitive interest in correct predictions supports the need of truthlike theories as well. For these reasons, Laudan's contrast between problem-solving and truth-seeking models of science is misleading, and the idea of science as problem-solving is fully compatible with scientific realism. In fact, it seems to me that the strategy of preferring theories which exhibit a great capacity of solving actual explanatory and predictive problems is a way of promoting truth-likeness as the aim of science.

NOTES

(1)   The term 'Operations Research' is used in America and 'Operational Research' in England. The term 'Management Science' is often used as another name for OR. I am grateful to Dr. Yrjö Seppälä for bringing the 'Ackoff debate' to my attention.

(2)   See the bibliography in Gutting (1980).

(3)   This is only a rough sketch of the formal treatment of "Kuhn-theories" and their development suggested by Sneed, Stegmüller, Balzer, and Moulines. Cf. Niiniluoto (1981).

(4)   Moreover, a Kuhnian crisis is a regular phenomenon which a discipline every now and then has to face. It is an essential element of the pattern by which scientific disciplines make progress — so that there are no negative overtones in this notion.

(5)   Kuhn notes the existence of this kind of phenomenon in Kuhn (1977), pp. 119–120.

(6)   Theories of planning which consist of *norms* (e.g. "take into account the values of all stakeholders of the organization") can be reformulated as *assertions* about rational or effective planning (e.g., "it is rational to take into account ...").

(7)   The book of Churchman *et al.* has a 'paradigmatic' status in OR — in one sense of this word in Kuhn (1962), p. 10.

(8)   For the concept of truthlikeness, see Niiniluoto (1980).

(9)   It may of course happen that an inadequate model sometimes gives satisfactory results just *with good luck,* but such a case is exceptional. For a discussion of why "truth pays", see Loewer (1980). Take again the diet problem as an example : if the decision-maker has wrong information

about the vitamins in different kinds of foods, his constraints (3) are mistaken, and the solution of the linear programming problem is not really optimal.

(10) For an analysis of cognitive problems and their relation to questions, see Niiniluoto (1976). For a question-theoretic general model of science as a problem-solving activity, see Hintikka (1981).

(11) A theory T solves a predictive problem 'h_1 or ... or h_n ?' if one of h_i is deducible from T. As a weaker criterion for a solution, one might require that one of the alternatives h_1, ..., h_n is inductively acceptable relative to theory T.

(12) One reason for Laudan's opposition to truth as an aim of science is this complaint : the realists have failed to show that approximately true theories yield approximately true empirical predictions. An answer to this problem is given in Niiniluoto (1982). See also Niiniluoto (1984).

BIBLIOGRAPHY

ACKOFF, R.L., 'The Meaning, Scope, and Methods of Operations Research', in R. L. Ackoff (ed.), *Progress in Operations Research,* vol. I, John Wiley, New York, 1961, pp. 1–34.

ACKOFF, R.L. (with the collaboration of S.K. Gupta and J.S. Minas), *Scientific Method: Optimizing Applied Research Decisions,* John Wiley, New York, 1962.

ACKOFF, R.L., 'The Future of Operational Research is Past', *Journal of the Operational Research Society* 30 (1979), 93–104. (a)

ACKOFF, R.L., 'Resurrecting the Future of Operational Research', *Journal of the Operational Research Society* 30 (1979), 189–199. (b).

ACKOFF, R.L. and SASIENI, M.W., *Fundamentals of Operations Research,* John Wiley, New York, 1968.

CHURCHMAN, C.W., ACKOFF, R.L. and ARNOFF, E.L., *Introduction to Operations Research,* John Wiley and Sons, New York, 1957.

158

DANDO, M.R. and BENNETT, P.G., 'A Kuhnian Crisis in Management Science? *Journal of the Operational Research Society* 32 (1981), 91–104.

DANDO, M.R. and BENNETT, P.G., 'Kuhnian Comments Squared ? Replies to Gault and Williams', *Journal of the Operational Research Society* 33 (1982), 100–101.

DEWEY, J., *Logic: The Theory of Inquiry,* Henry Holt and Company, New York, 1939.

GAULT, A.R., 'A Metaphysical Debate rather than a Kuhnian Crisis', *Journal of the Operational Research Soicety* 33 (1982), 91–99.

GUTTING, G. (ed.), *Paradigms & Revolutions : Applications and Appraisals of Thomas Kuhn's Philosophy of Science,* University of Notre Dame Press, Notre Dame, 1980. ·

HINTIKKA, J., 'On the Logic of an Interrogative Model of Scientific Inquiry', *Synthese* 47 (1981), 69–84.

KUHN, T., *The Structure of Scientific Revolutions,* The University of Chicago Press, Chicago, 1962. 2nd enlarged edition, 1970.

KUHN, T., 'Second Thoughts on Paradigms', in F. Suppe (ed.), *The Structure of Scientific Theories,* University of Illinois Press, Urbana, 1974, pp. 459–482.

KUHN, T., *The Essential Tension,* The University of Chicago Press, Chicago, 1977.

LAKATOS, I., 'Falsification and the Methodology of Scientific Research Programmes', in Lakatos and Musgrave (1970), pp. 91–196.

LAKATOS, I. and MUSGRAVE, A. (eds.), *Criticism and the Growth of Knowledge,* Cambridge University Press, Cambridge, 1970.

LAUDAN, L., *Progress and Its Problems,* Routledge and Kegan Paul, London, 1977.

LAUDAN, L., 'The Philosophy of *Progress* ...', in I. Hacking and P. Asquith (eds.), *PSA 1978,* vol. 2, Philosophy of Science Association, East Lansing,

1981, pp. 530–547.

LAUDAN, L., 'Problems, Truth, and Consistency', *Studies in History and Philosophy of Science* 13 (1982), 73–80.

LEVI, I., *Gambling With Truth,* Alfred A. Knopf, New York, 1967.

LOEWER, B., 'The Truth Pays', *Synthese* 43 (1980), 369–379.

MASTERMAN, M., 'The Nature of Paradigm', in Lakatos and Musgrave (1970), pp. 59–90.

NIINILUOTO, I., 'Inquiries, Problems, and Questions: Remarks on Local Induction', in R.J. Bogdan (ed.), *Local Induction,* D. Reidel, Dordrecht, 1976, pp. 263–296.

NIINILUOTO, I., 'Scientific Progress', *Synthese* 45 (1980), 427–462.

NIINILUOTO, I., 'The Growth of Theories: Comments on the Structuralist Approach', in J. Hintikka et al. (eds.), *Proceedings of the 1978 Pisa Conference on the History and Philosophy of Science,* vol. I, D. Reidel, Dordrecht, 1981, pp. 3–47.

NIINILUOTO, I., 'Truthlikeness for Quantitative Statements', in *PSA 1982,* vol. 1, Philosophy of Science Association, East Lansing, 1982.

NIINILUOTO, I., *Is Science Progressive ?* D. Reidel, Dordrecht, 1984.

RAITT, R.A., Viewpoints , *Journal of the Operational Research Society* 30 (1979), 835–836.

SAATY, T.L., *Mathematical Methods of Operations Research,* McGraw-Hill, New York, 1959.

RAMSEY ELIMINABILITY REVISITED

David Pearce & Veikko Rantala
Freie Universität, Berlin & Academy of Finland, Helsinki

Frank Ramsey's brief but incisive analysis (1929) of the conceptual nature of empirical theories has exerted a striking, if belated, impact on later generations of philosophers of science; an impact still detectable today in discussions of the so-called *Ramsey-Elimination* of theoretical terms. Above all, Ramsey influenced subsequent ideas about the ontological status of theoretical concepts and entities, the potential eliminability of theoretical terms and laws and their reduction to observational concepts and statements; issues that have remained at the forefront of debates between realists and instrumentalists over the character of scientific theories.

In this paper we briefly review some of these issues and argue that philosophers might benefit from a fresh look at Ramsey's method in the light of some new developments in mathematical logic and its application to empirical theories. On the one hand, these developments provide a tool for constructing more general logical criteria of 'Ramsey-eliminability'; on the other hand they have furnished many new and interesting results that are clearly relevant to the philosophical problem of eliminability. In conclusion, we urge that there is a case for reopening the whole question of the ontological commitment of formalized languages and theories, and its bearing on the problem of eliminating theoretical terms; for despite the lengthy philosophical discussions that took place in the 1950's and '60's, the issues raised have been by no means conclusively settled today.

0. On the elimination of theoretical terms

According to the more extreme forms of empiricism, all the descriptive (i.e. nonlogical) concepts of a scientific theory must be in some sense empirically or observationally definable. Elements of this doctrine can be found in Mach's positivism, Russell's phenominalism, Carnap's early empiricism and Bridgeman's operationalism. Logical empiricists, in particular, treated the problem of the relation of theory to experience as part of a general analysis of the language of scientific theories; in this case the links between *theoretical* language and *observational* language were at stake. Of course, successive liberalizations of logical empiricism during the thirties resulted in abandoning the view that, generally, theoretical terms are definable by means of observables, or even that theoretical laws and sentences are translatable into an observational language. After Carnap's classic account of the problem (1936–7) it was customary for empiricists to regard theoretical concepts as only in a very loose sense 'reducible' to observational concepts, and the criteria for theoretical terms or sentences to be empirically significant (Carnap, 1956) rested on grounds other than their observational definability.

This situation took a fresh turn during the 1950's. Some empiricists began to pose questions of the following kind: If theoretical concepts in science are not piecemeal redundant in favour of purely observational ones, does the total theoretical language of science still admit some sort of wholesale elimination ? Briefly: Are theoretical terms and sentences dispensible in scientific theorizing? The problem was broached by Braithwaite (1953) and analysed in depth by Hempel (1958) and others. The discussion owed much to a view of theories proposed by Ramsey (1929), a view that has subsequently become highly influential. Apparently, Ramsey's philosophy of science had little in common with logical empiricism, being closer in spirit to the conventionalist tradition of Duhem and Poincaré.[1] But a number of Ramsey's ideas, revived by Braithwaite and pursued by Carnap and others, were absorbed into the standard empiricist view of theories. Hempel, for one, accepted that Ramsey provided a method of formally replacing a finitely axiomatized theory T, containing theoretical terms, by an observationally equivalent theory R_T containing only observational terms; and Carnap (1958) proposed employing R_T to cast the entire empirical content of T in the form of a single sentence, the *Ramsey-sentence* of T. Technically, Ramsey's device looks quite simple. Let T be a first order theory axiomatized by a single sentence in a language L containing a list $\bar{R}$ of theoretical terms, and let L_O be the observational sublanguage of L possessing all terms except those in $\bar{R}$. Then the Ramsey-sentence R_T of T can be written in the form :

(0.0) $\exists \bar{R} \, \psi \, (\bar{R})$

where ψ is the L_O-sentence formed from the axiom of T by replacing each occurrence of a theoretical term by a new variable. If T_O is the set of all consequences of T expressible in L_O, i.e. $T_O = \{\phi \in \text{Sent} \, (L_O): T \mid\!- \phi\}$, then it follows that

(0.1) $R_T \mid\!- \phi$ iff $T_O \vdash \phi$

for all elementary L_O-sentences ϕ. Thus R_T axiomatizes the first order observational 'content' of the original theory T.

The problem of avoiding theoretical terms raises several complex issues. Some count as clearly methodological in character, others are ontological or semantical. A typical methodological question would be this: Can a theory like R_T, not directly involving theoretical terms, perform its scientific function of systematizing, explaining and predicting empirical phenomena ? In short, does it preserve deductive and inductive values ? Equally important are the semantical issues: What is the ontic commitment of the Ramsey-sentence ? Does the Ramsey method show that theoretical terms and entities are ontologically super- fluous ? Or are they merely avoidable in some 'technical' sense, but really in- dispensible ? Such questions, particularly those of the ontological kind, are intimately related to the controversy between realist and instrumentalist inter- pretations of scientific theories. In the widespread debates concerning the replacement procedures of Ramsey's or Craig's kind (see Craig, 1953, 1956) that ensued during the sixties, it was common for realists to attribute an instrumentalist view of theories to advocates of Ramsey's method; though the situation is by no means clear cut.[2]

Since the early seventies the discussion over the avoidability of theoretical terms has entered a further, third stage, following the appearance of Sneed's (1971) work on the logical structure of scientific theories. Sneed, like Carnap, made use of Ramsey's procedure as a device for expressing the empirical content of a theory, but Sneed's treatment expanded the subject in two interesting respects. First, Sneed defended a structural rather than linguistic notion of 'theory', and he pointed out that, from a model-theoretic standpoint, the Ramsey-sentence of a theory T is strictly stronger in general than the set of all first order observational consequences of T (the theory T_O above) obtainable, say, by Craig's method. For,

$$(0.2) \qquad \mathrm{Mod}(R_T) \subseteq \mathrm{Mod}\,(T_O)$$

holds in general. Thus it makes sense to regard the theoretical vocabulary of T as eliminable only if some further, model-theoretic conditions obtain. And with this in mind, Sneed formulated a criterion of *Ramsey eliminability,* essentially satisfied when equality holds in (0.2). At the same time Sneed relativized the notion of 'theoretical term' to the context of a given theory T in which it occurs. In consequence, his discussion involves not so much the potential avoidability of theoretical terms in favour of observables, as the replacement of 'T-theoretical' terms by means of 'T-nontheoretical' ones. Sneed provided examples of theories that are not Ramsey eliminable according to his definition, as well as a discussion of the possible elimination of concrete terms like 'mass' and 'force' in classical mechanics.

Sneed's and other concepts of eliminability were studied by a number of authors, using predominantly model-theoreticl methods (see, e.g. Tuomela, 1973; Simon and Groen, 1973; Stegmüller, 1976; Swijtink, 1976; Rantala, 1977; Simon, 1977; van Benthem, 1978). They looked at the connections between eliminability and other metatheoretical concepts like definability and identifiability, discussed the import of Ramsey eliminations for methodological and ontological aspects of the question of avoiding theoretical terms and entities, and examined purely logical properties of the eliminability concept. These papers shed a good deal of light on the whole philosophical significance of Ramsey's method and Sneed's concept of eliminability; and, in some cases, interesting model-theoretic results were obtained. But there are several reasons for feeling less than totally satisfied with the subject in its present state; let us mention two in particular.

First, consider the structuralist approach to the philosophy of science, developed by Sneed, Stegmüller, Balzer and others. For structuralists, the topic of eliminability has become an important practical component of the reconstruction of scientific theories; yet, though they have loosely agreed on the intuitive meaning of 'eliminability', a formal explication of this concept is still lacking. In this respect Sneed's own definition is quite inadequate: it is framed so as to apply to theories that are formalized, or those in which languages are made explicit, whereas the structuralist concept of 'theory' is purely set-theoretic and omits language. And even if this barrier were surmounted, it seems clear that Sneed's explication of eliminability fails to match up to his own intuitions about this notion.

Secondly, though technically sound, the various attempts to investigate eliminability from a model-theoretic perspective have left untouched a number of logical and methodological questions about the avoidability of theoretical terms. One difficulty seems to be that the definition of eliminability used up to now is just too restrictive: it applies only to first order theories, and even where applicable it fails to draw a reasonable distinction between languages that carry a genuine, irreducible theoretical commitment, and those that do not. Such problems are complex and, though we do not pretend to resolve them here, it does seem worthwhile undertaking a fresh look at the subject. In particular, if eliminability is to be a property of the logical structure of concepts and theories, then we should certainly benefit from recent, revised conceptions about the nature of logic and its role in empirical science. At the same time, we also have at our disposal many new results in extended model theory that bear on the topic of eliminability; assessing their import will be a significant philosophical task.

Below we shall review the formal definition of Ramsey-eliminability and consider some of its properties and possible shortcomings. We then propose some amended versions of eliminability that appear to be more adequate, at least in some respects. Finally, we tentatively broach the problem of the ontological reduction of theoretical terms and entities to observables, and ask what impact recent model-theoretic results might have on the question of eliminability.

1. Ramsey eliminability

As we already remarked, if T is any finitely axiomatized first order theory, then T and its Ramsey-sentence are functionally equivalent with respect to first order observational consequences. That is to say, if L, L_O and T_O are given as above, R_T and T_O have exactly the same first order theorems; expressed by

$$(1.0) \qquad \text{Th}(\text{Mod}(R_T)) = T_O.$$

A theorem of Craig (1953) implies that T_O is recursively axiomatizable, hence either R_T or T_O (axiomatized in Craigian form) can be used to capture the observational content of T. Nevertheless, there is a sense in which T may actually be stronger than T_O with respect to O-consequences; for, generally,

$$(1.1) \qquad \text{Mod}(T) \mid L_O \subseteq \text{Mod}(T_O),$$

so models of T_O are not automatically expandable to models of T. This is just another way to express (0.2), since L_O-structures that are models of R_T are just those that *can* be expanded to models of T. Thus the Ramsey-sentence captures the 'full' observational strength of T. (0.2) expresses a very well-known fact about Σ_1^1-sentences, i.e. sentences of the form (0.0) that are prefixed by a string of existentially quantified second order variables; apparently Sneed (1971) was the first to remark on the significance of this for the elimination of T-terms from an empirical theory.

For Sneed there is a clear sense in which T-terms of T cannot really be said to be eliminated unless the Ramsey-sentence of T is actually equivalent to T_O, i.e. that equality holds in (0.2). His reasoning seems to be this: An empirical theory determines a class of models Mod(T) inducing a unique class Mod(T)|L_O of structures for the observational language. Actual physical systems or empirical states of affairs can be represented by L_O-structures. Now, if Mod(T)|L_O can be specified in purely observational terms, that is to say defined by some set of first order L_O-sentences, then the theoretical vocabulary has been eliminated. Otherwise, if Mod(T)|L_O is a proper subclass of Mod(T_O), then T-terms do some 'real work' in ruling out possible observable states; so R_T (or Mod(T)|L_O), rather than T_O, captures the true empirical content of T. Essentially the same argument goes through if the words 'theoretical' and 'observational' are everywhere replaced by 'T-theoretical' and 'T-nontheoretical'.

Of course, for Ramsey and Carnap any 'work' in Sneed's sense done by T-terms could be replaced by 'work' done by the existentially quantified second order variables that appear in R_T. For Ramsey, this move was unproblematic, since he regarded only sentences of the 'primary system' (corresponding to L_O), not those of the 'secondary system' $(L-L_O)$ as fully interpreted propositions. And for Carnap, what was asserted to exist by the existential quantifiers of R_T were *not* theoretical entities and concepts, but rather new classes and relations in an abstract mathematical sense. Carnap (1963) makes this clear by distinguishing three language levels for a theory T: a strict observational language L_O whose descriptive vocabulary V_O designates directly observable properties, and possessing a restricted (elementary) syntax; an extended observation laguage L'_O, with the same set V_O of nonlogical terms, but with a much enriched logic or syntax including additional class variables and higher-order quantifiers; and, thirdly, a language $L \supset L'_O$ containing also theoretical terms. Then the sense in which R_T eliminates T-terms is that T has an observationally equivalent formulation in L'_O; and Carnap concedes, of course, that L'_O is not as completely interpreted as L_O.

For those prepared to adopt an instrumentalist, or at any rate something short of a fully realist, interpretation of the Ramsey-sentence, Ramsey's replacement procedure offers a form of ontological reduction of theoretical to observational concepts.[3] But for some realists the Ramsey-sentence provides a mere technical device that avoids T-terms in letter but not in spirit, since the ontological commitment of L_O is swelled by the addition of higher-order variables. Hempel took this view, and several other commentators (e.g. Tuomela, 1973) followed suit. For them it seems clear that the failure of ontic elimination lies in the second-order quantifiers of R_T : if these could also be affectively eliminated, presumably some kind of genuine ontic elimination would be achieved. And it is here that Sneed's criterion aptly applies, because for Sneed Ramsey elimination occurs just when the Ramsey-sentence of T (or its class of models) is definable by elementary sentences of L_O. This can be made precise for any first order theory T by :

(1.2)   *Definition:* T is R-eliminable over L_O iff $Mod(T)|L_O \in EC_\Delta$.

Apart from some minor differences that we shall ignore here, (1.2) corresponds to the main idea of T-terms being Ramsey eliminable from T according to Sneed, and is close to the definitions employed by Tuomela (1973), Swijtink (1976) and others. Clearly, if T is finitely axiomatizable (hence, possesses a Ramsey-sentence), then T is R-eliminable over L_O just in case R_T is logically equivalent to a set of first order sentences in L_O. Not all theories are R-eliminable over their observational sublanguages, and plenty of examples can be found in the literature cited above. One way of demonstrating non-eliminability is to provide a model of T_O that cannot be expanded to a model of T, since $Mod(T)|L_O$ is an elementary class if and only if it equals $Mod(T_O)$. However, it is well-known that any *finite* model of T_O can be expanded to a model of T, and any model of T_O has an elementary extension that can be expanded to a model of T. Tuomela and Swijtink have provided some conditions on L or T such that T is always R-eliminable over a given L_O; but van Benthem (1978) showed that no syntactic criterion can supply necessary and sufficient conditions to determine when theories have this property.[4] Sneed himself attempted to analyse the eliminability question for theoretical terms appearing in the main branches of classical mechanics; and in more recent developments of the structuralist programme a number of positive instances of eliminability have been claimed in theories of physics and economics (see, e.g. Balzer and Mühlhölzer, 1982; Händler, 1982). However in all these cases it seems that the authors had in mind some informal explication of eliminability, rather than the definition expressed in (1.2).

One difficulty in applying (1.2) is connected with an erroneous assumption sometimes made (e.g. in Simon (1977) and Simon and Groen (1973)), that the domain of an L_O-reduct of a model of T can be seen as comprising only observables. Recall that Ramsey eliminability is concerned with the problem of expanding L_O-models of T_O to L-models of T by adding new relations corresponding to the theoretical terms. Generally, in empirical science as well as in mathematics, this process is *not* one of simple expansion, but involves two operations: extending the domain of an L_O-structure by adding new elements, and adjoining new relations to be interpreted over the extended domain. This suggests that eliminability would be better described as relating to the process of taking *extended expansions* of models. There are many examples of this: form a vector space over a field; extend a field to a valued field; add lines and planes as new primitives to a model of elementary geometry containing only points; extend a model of Euclidean geometry to a model of classical space-time; extend a model of space-time to a model of Newtonian kinematics; and so on. In some of these cases, the new terms appearing in L are interpreted over different sorts of entities (e.g. theoretical objects); so we should assume in general that L is many-sorted language, and L_O-reducts of L-structures may omit both relations and sorts (domains).

Even within single-sorted logic we can improve on (1.2). Let P be a unary predicate of L, not in L_O, and for any L-structure m let m^P be the relativization of m to P, i.e. the substructure of m whose domain consists of all $a \in |m|$ such that $m|- P(a)$. We can then set,

(1.3)   *Definition:* T is R-eliminable over (P, L_O) iff

$$\{m_O \in \text{Str}(L_O) : \exists m \models T \ (m^P|L_O = m_O)\} \in EC_\Delta.$$

Here, the intended meaning of P is "is an observable", and for any L-structure m, the structure $m^P|L_O$ has just the "observables of m" in its domain. Of course, the notion of 'observationality' here is always relative to a given model or class of models.

There is a further, major problem with the application of (1.2). When a class of models M for an empirical theory T is specified (say set-theoretically defined), M will not usually be a (Δ) elementary class, i.e. first order definable. The requirement for eliminability, that $M|L_O$ be (generalized) elementary, is therefore much too strong in practice. But how can this difficulty be removed? Consider, once again, the intuitive meaning of eliminability. T-theoretical functions should be eliminable just in case the class of 'nontheoretical' reducts $M|L_O$ is definable without them. But what kind of definition is allowed here? Assuming we have in mind the model-theoretic definability of $M|L_O$, we face the problem: in what logic should this class be definable ? If we permit logics of arbitrary strength we risk being too generous. This would clearly apply to second-order logic, since the Ramsey method would provide us with a second-order definition of $M|L_O$. So perhaps we can achieve at best a concept of eliminability *relativized* to a logic or class of logics. Then the issue of avoiding theoretical terms, in some more absolute sense, would have to be treated *in the context* of the given logic in question.[5]

2. Eliminability Relativized

We can now draw together the points made above, to obtain a revised concept of eliminability. We shall from now on distinguish between a *logic* (in a general sense of the term) and a *many-sorted similarity type* (vocabulary plus sorts). Logics and types will be denoted respectively by the symbols 'L' and 'τ' (with or without subscripts); the relevant definitions of these notions can be found in Feferman (1974) (see also Pearce and Rantala, 1983a). We also employ the concept of *structure* found there, whereby a structure of type τ is a function m that assigns a non-empty domain to each sort of τ and a relation, function or individual of appropriate arity and sorts to each symbol in τ. Any logic L is assumed to have associated a collection Typ_L of *admitted* types, and for any $\tau \in \text{Typ}_L$, we denote by $\text{Str}_L(\tau)$, $\text{Sent}_L(\tau)$ respectively the collections of L-structures and L-sentences of type τ; $\models_L$ is the *satisfaction* relation for L. We define the L-elementary (EC_L) and L-projective (PC_L) classes in the usual way, except that we follow Feferman (1974) in allowing the PC classes to be formed by omitting sorts as well as symbols; thus if $\tau \subseteq \tau$ ' and m is a structure of type τ', m|τ denotes the τ-reduct of m, containing possibly fewer domains, similarly for classes of structures. A $\Sigma_1^1(L)$-class is the class of models of a $\Sigma_1^1(L)$-sentence; it is the projection of an L-elementary class to a subtype containing the *same* sorts (this reverses the terminology of e.g. Barwise, 1974).

Though from time we shall continue to think of a theory T as a set of statements closed under deduction in some logic L, we shall, for completeness, formulate criteria of eliminability that apply to the concept of 'theory' that we have developed in Pearce and Rantala (1983a) and elsewhere. The reader may easily adapt the definitions to suit his or her own favourite notion of 'theory'. We regard a theory as a structure

$$T = (\tau,N,M,R) \hspace{4cm} T$$

where τ is a many-sorted similarity type, $N \subseteq \text{Str}(\tau)$ is called the class of *admitted* structures for T, $M \subset N$ is called the class of *models* of T, and R is a collection of relations between elements of N. We assume that N and M are definable in some logic L, i.e. that $M,N \in EC_L(\tau)$; L is then called *adequate* for T. Below, we let 'L' range over adequate logics in this sense, and we suppose that τ_O is any fixed subtype of τ admitted by L.[6]

(2.0)   *Definition:* T is L-eliminable over τ_O iff $M|\tau O \in EC_L(\tau)$.

(2.1)   *Definition:* T is eliminable over τ_O iff T is L-eliminable over τ_O for all adequate L.

(2.0) is, of course, a straightforward generalization of (1.2). Since M is just the class of models of T in the usual sense, this definition reduces to (1.2) in the case of single-sorted first order logic.

The motivations for these definitions should be quite clear. First, the extension to many-sorted structures is highly natural in the present context, as we suggested earlier; for now a model of T may contain extra domains as well as relations, as compared with a structure for the 'observation' language τ_O. Secondly, there exists a whole range of logics that extend first order logic $L_{\omega\omega}$ but which do not admit higher-order quantifiers; e.g. the infinitary logics $L_{\kappa\lambda}$, and many logics with added quantifiers. A number of these have a relatively well-behaved syntax and semantics, and their model-theoretic properties have been thoroughly investigated in recent years. Certain of them have the great advantage over elementary logic that they can express many more mathematical properties, such as finiteness, or the Archimedian property of the reals; and they have wide potential applicability in the metatheory of empirical sciences (see, e.g. Pearce and Rantala, 1983b).

We have assumed, then, that the class of models of any empirical theory T can be defined by some sentence in a logic L that possibly extends elementary logic, perhaps in one of the senses indicated.[7] (Notice that L could also be a nonclassical, e.g. intuitionistic or many-valued, logic and the structures concerned could be Kripke models or Boolean-valued models, etc.). It follows that the class $M|\tau_O$ is also definable in some logic L' possibly different from L; whence T is L'-eliminable over τ_O. So the main interest in (2.0) lies in the case where L is chosen to be the *weakest* logic adequate for T, or the weakest logic satisfying some suitable properties, *and* L' = L. Then L-projective class $M|\tau_O$ is actually L-elementary, and we are in a position to consider whether some genuine elimination of theoretical vocabulary has been achieved.[8]

Ramsey eliminability, in the sense of (1.2), could be said to be concerned with the problem: when are $\Sigma^1_1 (L_{\omega\omega})$-classes elementary ? Analogously, the notion of eliminability introduced above is concerned with the problem: when are PC_L-classes L-elementary ? Actually, in logics L with a downward Löwenheim-Skolem Theorem the projective and Σ^1_1-classes are not very different if they contain only infinite structures. That is to say, every PC_L-class of that kind can be equivalently defined by a Σ^1_1 (L)-sentence; though naturally for the question of the elimination of a given theory, only one of the characterizations of $M|\tau_O$ will normally be appropriate.

We usually expect that a kind of eliminability obtains for the T-terms of a theory T if any of the following hold:

(i)   the T-terms are observationally definable;
(ii)   the T-sentences are translatable into O-sentences;
(iii) T is reducible to its observational subtheory.

Moreover, eliminability is understood to be a weaker notion in the sense that none of (i)–(iii) is actually implied by eliminability. Indeed, in the special case of (single-sorted) first order logic this expectation is born out. For instance, if T implicitly defines its theoretical vocabulary (with respect to its observation language), then T is clearly Ramsey-eliminable. What happens in the more general case of L-eliminability, is *it* still implied by observational definability? Two special cases should be distinguished: the single-sorted and the many-sorted. If we apply (2.0) in the case where τ is single-sorted (or τ and τ_O have the exactly same sorts), then the L-definability (in the semantic or implicit sense of definability) of T-terms trivially entails the L-eliminability of T provided that Beth's Theorem holds for the logic L in question. But the case that τ_O contains fewer sorts than τ is less trivial, and we have to employ a concept of definability that is applicable to extended domains; i.e. where new objects as well as new relations are added to a τ_O-model, unlike the situation characterized in Beth's Theorem. This type of definability has received little attention by philosophers of science (an exception is Przelecki, 1977) despite its obvious importance. However, logicians have studied such more general kinds of definability, and a number of results are available (see, e.g. Gaifman, 1974; Pillay, 1977). These show, in particular, that if T is a first order theory in which the theoretical vocabulary is implicitly definable (formally: T is a Gaifman operation with respect to τ_O), then $\text{Mod}(T)|\tau_O$ is (generalized) elementary. So, at least in the first order case, we can interpret (i) in such a way that eliminability in the sense of (2.0) is entailed by it.

As far as conditions (ii) and (iii) are concerned, it seems that their stated relation to eliminability can also be maintained for the generalized concept (2.0), though some assumptions and qualifications must be admitted. We shall not enter into the details here; though we can remark that the notions of 'translation' and 'reduction' that we discuss in Pearce and Rantala (1983d) and elsewhere (see e.g. our other contribution to the present volume) can be employed to yield a formal reconstruction of (ii) and (iii), and this can be used to check the relation between these conditions and eliminability.

3. Model Theory and Eliminability

Let us now pose a difficult question: what makes a sentence observational ? To make the question a little less perverse, suppose, for the sake of the argument, that we have already distinguished theoretical from observational primitives, and theoretical from observable entities; so that our response is to be understood *relative* to some choice of this kind. We might begin our answer in the following way:

"The degree of observationality of a sentence depends on: ....."

and proceed with a list of factors such as: (a) the degree of observationality of its primitives; (b) the observability of its ontology; (c) it syntactic structure; (d) its truth conditions; (e) its degree of testability. We can stop here because already the list is long enough to show that no simple-minded solution is likely to suffice. In fact, according to how we weigh the different factors, we might conclude, at one extreme, that all Ramsey-sentences are observational, or, at the other extreme, that not even all first order sentences in wholly observational primitives can be construed as observational.[9] However, of the factors listed, it seems that all but (a) might be invoked in one way or another against the observationality of the Ramsey-sentence.

There are two principal reasons for raising such an awkward question here. First, much of the controversy surrounding the significance of Ramsey's device, that occurred in philosophical debates during the sixties, settled on the issue of the observationality of the Ramsey-sentence. Reaction to the use of Ramsey's method was very mixed; and it was thought that one way, at least, of denying that Ramsey's device effected any kind of ontological reduction of theoretical terms and/or any genuine elimination of theoretical sentences was to deny observationality to the Ramsey-sentence itself.[10] Secondly, the formal explication of Ramsey eliminability that has appeared in the literature apparently has, at least as one of its objectives, the aim of clarifying this issue by supplying a criterion by which Ramsey-sentences or certain model classes are to be counted as observationally definable. Now if it is questionable whether even this criterion succeeds in driving a wedge between observational and non-observational sentences (or model classes), then one might begin to doubt the entire enterprise of adopting a formal concept of eliminability. To put it more succinctly: if not even eliminable theories eliminate anything, what is the point of eliminability ?

One answer is that we would be wise to distinguish two related but separate kinds of problem: the ontic commitment of the Ramsey-sentence, on the one hand, and the type of ontological reduction or elimination, if any, achieved by Ramsification, on the other. It should be clear that the Ramsey device effects no strict reduction of theoretical entities to observables; for, even when the theory T at hand is *eliminable* according to (1.2), and hence R_T has an elementary equivalent, these is no guarantee of finding a way to reduce T and its ontology to some observational subtheory. For this we would require T-terms to be observationally definable in some sense, and open theoretical formulas ranging over theoretical sorts to be translatable into observational formulas admitting only observable sorts. Yet by itself this fact does not, of course, imply that the Ramsey-sentence necessarily has a *theoretical* ontological commitment, or even that it cannot count as observational. The strongest arguments against the observationality of R_T remain those based on factors (c) and (d) : its use of higher order quantification and its semantical interpretation; so it is left for us to explore the ways in which these affect ontic commitment and observationality.

During the 1960's and indeed until very recently, philosophers customarily discussed the ontic commitment of a sentence or a logical system in terms of quantification; i.e. what kinds of variables could be quantified over (for our purposes it is unnecessary to discuss the distinctions between objectual and substitutional interpretations of quantifiers). The reason for this seems to have been that the logical systems considered shared remarkable similarities in their syntactic structure, and generally admitted only one basic type of quantifier.

At the ontological level, the distinctions to be drawn were thus between first order and higher order quantification, i.e. whether only individuals, or also classes, classes of classes, and so on, could be quantified. Accordingly, the debates over the status of the Ramsey-sentence tended to dwell on the significance of its second order quantifiers for the question of ontic commitment.

However, since the late fifties logicians have worked with systems that differ much more dramatically from elementary and second order logic (and their non-classical variants), both with regard to the kinds of quantifiers admitted and the rules of formation for connectives, as well as in other respects. Many of these systems lie somewhere between first and second order logic as to their expressive power, and for them we need to draw finer distinctions of ontic commitment than the rather crude 'quantificational' charactarization permits. Such a task awaits philosophers of logic in the future; for the present we have only some general comments to make.

First, there might be a way to approach the ontic commitment of a logic L by assessing how closely L 'resembles' first order or second order logic. The 'closer' L is to first order logic, the less its critic commitment might be thought to exceed that of first order logic. But the resemblance of one logic to another may be based on several different criteria; e.g.:

(i)   similarity of syntax and model theory;
(ii)   similarity of strength (expressive power);
(iii) similarity of metalogical properties (e.g. completeness, compactness, Löwenheim-Skolem, interpolation, etc.).

And there is no generally accepted procedure for classifying these different factors and weighing their relative importance for assessing overall resemblance; when a logician 'likens' one logic to another he may have in mind any combination of these factors, depending on context. However, the situation is not entirely hopeless. Recent work in abstract logic may not have solved problems of this kind, but it has certainly made giant strides towards clarifying the issues involved and improving our understanding of the ways in which different logical systems are related.

Suppose in fact that we could draw a 'smooth' line between first and second order logic and chart the various logics on or clustered around this line, according to their family resemblances. We might then approach the question of observationality by deciding that L-statements in observational primitives count as *observational* if L is on the first order side of some agreed point on the line, otherwise they are *theoretical*. To determine whether a Ramsey-sentence (or more generally a given Σ_1^1 or projective model class) is observational we need only then check whether it is equivalent to an L-statement (in observational primitives) on the 'observational' side of our chosen point; similarly, if a theory is L-eliminable in the sense of (2.0), the *eliminant* will be observational or not by the same criterion. Of course, even if this procedure *were* completely realistic (and we have indicated that it is not, at least at the present time), we would still face the problem of where to fix our hypothetical point on the line or, if preferred, how to assign 'degrees of observationality' along the line. On what side of the point, for instance, would fall an infinitary logic with countable conjunctions and disjunctions $(L_{\omega_1\omega})$? Does a statement in wholly observational primitives cease to be observational if it is infinitely long? The problem is not uninteresting. In particular, several of the examples of non-Ramsey eliminable first order theories discussed in the literature cited above turn out to be L-eliminable, where L is $L_{\omega_1\omega}$ or some stronger infinitary logic. So if such infinitary eliminants are to be counted as observational, then perhaps the theoretical terms in question are actually 'eliminated' after all.

We see no reason, *prima facie,* to regard an $L_{\omega_1\omega}$-sentence in observational primitives as theoretical, if an $L_{\omega\omega}$-sentence in the same type is not. For, if $L_{\omega_1\omega}$ is compared to first order logic according to factors (i)–(iii), then we find that the two logics do not differ greatly in syntax and semantics, they share many (though not all) metalogical properties, and though $L_{\omega_1\omega}$ is stronger than $L_{\omega\omega}$ there is no apparent reason for construing its ontic commitment as significantly greater. Neither can O-statements in these two logics be separated by criteria such as testability; for it is easy to invent examples of testable infinitary O-statements and similar, but less testable, first order O-statements.[11] In general, the mathematical complexity of what a sentence expresses, and the logical complexity of its syntax, are not related in any obvious way to its degree of testability.[12]

Since clearly not all theories (nor even all first order theories) are $L_{\omega_1\omega}$-eliminable over a given type, we cannot conclude from these considerations that all Ramsey-sentences are observational or that all theories have in some sense 'eliminable' T-terms. What we can do is to consult the various eliminability results for Σ^1_1 (L)-sentence or model classes that have been proved in recent work in model theory, and judge whether any overall 'patterns' emerge.

We shall postpone for the future a more detailed study of Σ^1_1-eliminability and its relevance for ontological problems of Ramsification; here, we shall just conclude with some general observations.

First, the character of such results is this: they show that any Σ^1_1 (L)-sentence $\exists\bar{R}\ \psi\ (\bar{R})$ is equivalent (model-theoretically) to some sentence ϕ not containing terms from R. Secondly, the results are *partial* in the sense that they apply in each case to a particular logic L or class of logics, and they are *local* in that the demonstrated equivalence is *relative* to some class of models.

The first result clearly of this kind is due to Svenonius (1965), who proved eliminability for Σ_1^1 ($L_{\omega\omega}$)-classes over *countable* models; but this can be improved to eliminability over all models of a given cardinality τ, for any τ (see Rantala, 1982; there are interesting comparisons here with Swijtink's notion of 'eliminability in a cardinal', Swijtink, 1976). Svenonius' result (for countable structures) was later extended by Vaught (1973) to Σ_1^1 ($L_{\omega_1\omega}$)-classes and by Makkai (1974) to some stronger infinitary languages. Thirdly, in each case the eliminant ϕ is a sentence of a rather special kind (e.g. a Vaught formula, game formula or infinitary constituent) whose interpretation is by game-theoretical rather than the usual Tarskian semantics. However, it seems that for the cases of interest to us here, one can choose ϕ to be an infinitary sentence of some logic $L_{\kappa\lambda}$.

To assess the significance of these results for the philosophical issues surrounding Ramsey-elimination, we need to focus primarily on two questions: how severe is the restriction of *local* eliminability ? What ontological commitment do the eliminating formulas carry in each of these results ? As to the first question, we can anticipate that even local eliminability may be a significant and important feature of theories, since we may well wish to focus attention on some distinguished subclass of observational structures (e.g. 'intended' models), and cardinality restrictions may be relevant here. To answer the second question, it may be fruitful to look further than the ontic commitment of a particular logical system. Knowing that a given eliminant is an L-sentence may not be sufficient grounds for determining its degree of 'observationality', even if L were to be charted on our hypothetical map of logics. We may be better off with a more direct investigation of the character of the game sentences themselves or their $L_{\kappa\lambda}$ substitutes. Ontic commitment is, after all, a property of *sentences,* not only of the logics in which they are formulated.

The generalized concepts of eliminability (2.0) and (2.1) introduced here, do not, any more than did Sneed's concept, resolve all the logical and philosophical issues concerned with the eliminability of theoretical terms and entities. Knowing that a theory is L-eliminable, for a given L, is not the same as knowing that it possesses an equivalent 'observational' formulation; and yet a theory might have a genuine 'observational' equivalent even when it is not eliminable by (2.1). In this sense our definitions yield only a coarse classification of theories. But they *are* applicable where Sneed's is not; and they do invite us to take a much more considered look at what it means to say that theoretical terms do 'real work' in a scientific theory. Moreover, they provide a general frame in which such questions may be cast.

By the same token, the model-theoretic results on eliminability do not yield compelling answers to the problem of 'observationality'. But they do suggest that the ontic commitment of the Ramsey-sentence and the philosophical import of Ramsey's device are in need of some serious re-evaluation. For one thing, an ontological argument for the 'theoreticity' of a Ramsey-sentence need not be an argument against the 'observationality' of a game formula or an infinitary sentence.

Far from being a closed chapter, just what is achieved by Ramsification is thus an open book; the correct methods for handling it are only slowly beginning to emerge.*

NOTES

(1) The similarities between Ramsey's view of theories and the views of Duhem and notably Poincaré are the subject of an extensive discussion in Giedymin (1982). In particular, Giedymin draws analogies between Ramsey's method and the relplacement procedures employed in "The physics of the principles", found in the works of Langrange, Hamilton, Fourier and especially Poincaré.

(2) Actually, Maxwell (1970), who endorses Ramsification as a means of interpreting theoretical discourse, calls his view *structural realism;* and Giedymin (1982) has labelled Poincaré's interpretation of theories (which anticipates Ramsey's method in some interesting respects) as *structuralist realism.*

(3) A word of caution: here we mean 'reduction' in the sense of avoiding or functionally replacing theoretical concepts and entities, to be contrasted with reduction in its more strict or literal sense; cf. section 3 below.

(4) van Benthem proves that the classes of elementary and generalized elementary Σ_1^1-sentence are not arithmetically definable.

(5) Some other possible inadequacies in the definition of R-eliminability are discussed in Swijtink (1976) and van Benthem (1978).

(6) For further explanatory remarks about this concept of theory, for its application and defence, the reader is referred to our joint papers listed in the bibliography.

(7) The restriction to a *single* sentence, rather than some set of sentences, is imposed here only for reasons of simplifying the presentation.

(8)   Of course, 'genuine' elimination may occur in other cases as well; see below.

(9)   Thus, Scheffler (1968) adopts the first position and van Benthem (1978) the second. The latter argues that perhaps only quantifier-free first order statements in an observational language can be considered observational.

(10) See, e.g., Hempel (1958), Carnap (1963), Maxwell (1963), Scheffler (1963), (1968), Bohnert (1967), (1968), for the range of opinions held on this point.

(11) Any example where 'finiteness' is essentially involved will suffice. For instance, an example used by Barwise (1980): "No one has more than finitely many ancestors" is an easily testable statement that requires an infinitary formula for its reconstruction. Whereas the less testable "Everyone is descended from Adam and Eve" has a first order formulation (define the ancestor relation as a partial ordering with exactly two minimal elements on the set of humans).

(12) Testability, of course, is usually taken as a property of informal statements, rather than their translations into a formal language, whereas syntactic complexity is understood here in the formal or logical sense.

(*)   The first author's contribution was completed during a fellowship held at the Netherlands Institute for Advanced study.

BIBLIOGRAPHY

BALZER, W. and F. MÜHLHÖLZER (1982), "Klassische Stossmechanik", *Zeitschrift für allgemeine Wissenschaftstheorie* 13, pp. 22–39.

BARWIZE, K.J. (1974), "Axioms for abstract model theory", *Ann. Math. Log.* 7, pp. 221–265.

BARWISE, K.J. (1980), "Infinitary logics", in E. Agazzi (ed.), *Modern Logic – A Survey*, D. Reidel, Dordrecht.

VAN BENTHEM, J. (1978), "Ramsey eliminability", *Studia Logica* 37, pp. 321–336.

BOHNERT, H. (1967), "Communication by Ramsey-sentence clause", *Philosophy of Science* 34, pp. 341–347.

BOHNERT, H. (1968), "In defense of Ramsey's elimination method", *The Journal of Philosophy* 65, pp. 275–281.

BRAITHWAITE, R.B. (1953), *Scientific explanation,* Cambridge University Press, Cambridge, England.

CARNAP, R. (1936/7), "Testability and meaning", *Philosophy of Science* 3, pp. 419–471, and 4, pp. 1–40.

CARNAP, R. (1956), "The methodological character of theoretical concepts, in: Feigl, H., and M. Scriven (eds.), *Minnesota Studies in the Philosophy of Science* I, University Press, Minneapolis, pp. 38–76.

CARNAP, R. (1958), "Beobachtungssprache und theoretische Sprache", *Dialectica* 12, pp. 236–248.

CARNAP, R. (1963), "Replies and systematic expositions", in P.A. Schilpp (ed.), *The Philosophy of Rudolf Carnap,* Open Court, La Salle, Illinois.

CRAIG, W. (1953), "On axomatizability within a system", *The journal of symbolic logic* 18, pp. 30–32.

CRAIG, W. (1956), "Replacement of auxiliary expressions", *Philosophical review* 65, pp. 38–55.

FEFERMAN, S. (1974), "Two notes on abstract model theory I", *Fund. Math.* 82, pp. 153–165.

HÄNDLER, E. W.,(1982), "Ramsey-elimination of utility in utility maximizing regression approaches", in W. Stegmüller *et. al.* (eds.), *Philosophy of Economics,* Springer-Verlag, Berlin, Heidelberg, New York.

HEMPEL, C.G. (1958), "The theoretician's dilemma", in: Feigl, H., M. Scriven and G. Maxwell (eds.), *Minnesota studies in the philosophy of science* II, University of Minnesota Press, Minneapolis, 1958. Reprinted in:
Hempel, C.G. (1965), *Aspects of scientific explanation,* Free Press, New York, pp. 173–226.

GAIFMAN, H. (1974), "Operations on relational structures, functions and classes I", in L. Henkin *et. al.* (eds.), *Proceedings of the Tarski Symposium,* AMS Proc. Symp. in Pure Math. 25, AMS, Providence.

GIEDYMIN, J. (1982), *Science and Convention,* Pergamon, Oxford.

MAKKAI, M. (1974), "Generalizing Vaught sentences from ω to strong cofinality ω", *Fund. Math.* 82, pp. 105−119.

MAXWELL, G. (1963), "The ontological status of theoretical entities", in: Feigl, H., and G. Maxwell (eds.), *Minnesota Studies in the philosophy of science* III, University of Minnesota Press, Minneapolis, pp. 3−27.

MAXWELL, G. (1970), "Structural realism and the meaning of theoretical terms", in: Radner, M., and S. Winokur (eds.), *Minnesota studies in the philosophy of science* IV, University of Minnesota Press, Minneapolis, pp. 181−192.

PEARCE, D. and V. RANTALA (1983a), "New foundations for metascience", *Synthese,* forthcoming.

PEARCE, D. and V. RANTALA (1983b), "Correspondence as an intertheory relation", *Studia Logica,* forthcoming.

PEARCE, D. and V. RANTALA (1983c), "Continuity and scientific discovery", this volume.

PEARCE, D. and V. RANTALA (1983d), "Logical aspects of scientific reduction", *Proc. of the Seventh Int. Wittgenstein Symposium,* forthcoming.

PILLAY, A. (1977), *Gaifman Operations, Minimal models and the number of countable models,* Ph.D. Thesis, Bedford College.

PRZELECKI, M. (1977), "On identifiability in extended domains", in K. Butts and J. Hintikka (eds.), *Basic Problems in Methodology and Linguistics,* D. Reidel, Dordrecht.

RAMSEY, F.P. (1929), "Theories", reprinted in D.H. Mellor (ed.), *Foundations: Essays in Philosophy, Logic, Mathematics and Economics,* Routledge, London, 1978.

RANTALA, V. (1977), "Aspects of definability", *Acta philosophica Fennica* 29, North Holland, Amsterdam.

RANTALA, V. (1982), "Infinitely deep game sentences and interpolation", forthcoming.

SCHEFFLER, I. (1963), *The Anatomy of Inquiry,* Alfred A. Knopf, New York.

SCHEFFLER, I. (1968), "Reflections on the Ramsey method," *The journal of philosophy* 65, pp. 270–274.

SIMON, H. (1977), "Identifiability and the status of theoretical terms", in K. Butts and J. Hintikka (eds.), *op. cit..*

SIMON, H. and G. GROEN (1973), "Ramsey eliminability and the testability of scientific theories", *Brit. J. Phil. Sci.* 24, pp. 367–380.

SNEED, J.D. (1971), *The logical structure of mathematical physics,* D. Reidel, Dordrecht.

STEGMÜLLER, W. (1976), *The Structure and Dynamics of Theories,* Springer-Verlag, Berlin, Heidelberg, New York.

SVENONIUS, L. (1965), "On the denumerable models of theories with extra predicates", in J. Addison *et. al., The Theory of Models,* North Holland, Amsterdam.

SWIJTINK, Z. (1976), "Eliminability in a cardinal", *Studia Logica* 35, pp. 71–89.

TUOMELA, R. (1973), *Theoretical Concepts,* Springer-Verlag, Wien, New York.

VAUGHT, R. (1973), "Descriptive set theory in $L_{\omega_1 \omega}$", *in Cambridge Summer School in Math. Logic,* (Lec. Notes in Math. 337), Springer-Verlag, Berlin, Heidelberg, New York.

THE LOGIC OF INTENTIONAL EXPLANATION *

Theo A.F. Kuipers
University of Groningen

There are two well-known theories of intentional explanation, i.e. explanation of human actions in terms of intentions or goals: the nomological and the semantic theory, with the main proponents Hempel[1] and von Wright,[2] respectively. Both theories are based on the general assumption that an intentional explanation is an argument and the specific assumption that the conclusion of this argument states that somebody performed a certain action. This specific assumption will be called the standard assumption and theories based on it standard theories.

The *nomological* theory pretends to specify the additional conditions an argument should satisfy in order to be acceptable as an intentional explanation. This normative pretension therefore starts from the standard assumption. For the nomological theory the question whether the analysis provides an adequate explication of everyday intentional explanations is of secondary importance, i.e. the explicative pretension does not play a decisive role.

The *semantic* theory is also a standard theory. Although it certainly has normative pretension the explicative pretension at least plays an equal role. One might say that the semantic theory arose as a critical reaction on the explicative value of the nomological theory. However, the semantic theory also does not dispute the standard assumption.

This paper explores the idea that the standard assumption, although it may be a legitimate point of departure for an interesting kind of explanation, is not acceptable as part of an explication of everyday intentional explanations. If this is so then there is, besides the best standard theory, room for a non-standard theory in which the explicative pretension plays the dominant role.

In Section 1 we will evaluate the explicative value of the two standard theories in some detail, leading to a number of 'explicative objections' to both. In Section 2 we will develop our 'non-standard theory': the underlying argument of an everyday intentional explanation is reconstructed as an application of the logical rule of inference called existential generalization with the conclusion that the action was intentional. It will be shown that such an intentional explanation does not have any of the explicative objections and that it is essentially weaker than a nomological explanation. In Section 3 some attention will be given to additional questions that can be raised when a true intentional explanation has been given in answer to the question of why somebody performed a certain action. Among others, it will be argued that an intentional explanation of an action leaves room for an additional utilistic explanation of the choice of that particular action out of alternatives serving the same purpose.

Finally, in Section 4 we will pay attention to the surprising aspect of our theory that essentially similar explications can be given of other types of explanation about which there is much dispute of whether they are reducible to nomological explanations: viz. functional, teleological and psychological explanations. Instead of being reducible, all these types of explanation turn out to capture the interesting part of otherwise pretentious nomological explanations.

1. The explicative value of the standard theories

In the following evaluation of the two standard theories it is impossible to do justice to all the proposed refinements, but neither is this necessary for our purposes.

The nomological theory construes intentional explanations according to the model of explanation of individual events in the natural sciences. The event to be explained is that somebody x has performed a certain action a, abbreviated as $P(x,a)$, and this should be the conclusion of the argument to be constructed. Three premises are introduced,[3] two of them being specific conditions, the third being a nomological premise. One specific condition, here called the desiderative premise, states that x desired a certain state of affairs or goal g,$D(x,g)$. The other, called the epistemic premise, states that x believed that a was necessary to approach g,$BN(x,a,g)$. Finally, the nomological premise is some kind of universal generalization (UG) of the conditional statement 'if $D(x,g)$ and $BN(x,a,g)$ then $P(x,a)$'. It should be a generalization over 'occasions' and it may or may not be a generalization over persons, actions or goals, or over a combination of these. (Note that all specific statements refer implicitly to a certain occasion.)

The result is the following :

Nomological Argument

$D(x,g)$

$BN(x,a,g)$

$\underline{UG \text{ (if } D(x,g) \text{ and } BN(x,a,g) \text{ then } P(x,a) \text{)}}$

$P(x,a)$

It is easy to see that the nomological argument is a valid argument. It is considered to be an adequate or true intentional explanation if, in addition, the premises may be supposed to be true. It is assumed that the specific premises are independent of the (specific) conclusion and hence that the verification of these premises is also independent of the verification of the conclusion[4].

Although the formulations of the specific statements are in the past tense, it would have been possible to present them in the present tense, or even in the future tense. As a consequence, the nomological argument is also a predictive argument; in the past tense it is, more specifically, a retrodictive argument. For this reason the nomological theory is said to be symmetric with respect to explanation and prediction.

In order to assess the explicative value of the nomological theory for everyday intentional explanations we need a first characterization of the latter. An exeryday intentional explanation of an action can be represented, in first approximation, in a question- and answer-scheme (QA-scheme) with a standard[5] pattern. The standard question is a 'why-question': 'Why did he/she/you/I do this ?' or, in a general form: 'Why did x perform action a ?'. Irrespective of the way in which it is obtained, the standard answer to a why-question is of the form 'x had that intention' or 'x aimed at that goal' or, more complete, 'x performed a with the intention of approaching goal g'.[6]

The answer to a why-question may also be of a different form, for instance, it may state that the behavior of x is not adequately described as (an instance of) action a. In such a case, however, we would not call it an intentional explanation. In sum, the standard pattern is given by

QA-scheme (everyday intentional explanation)
Why did x perform action a ?
x performed a with the intention of approaching goal g.

The question of the explicative value of the nomological theory can now be put more precisely as: to what extent is it possible to consider the nomological argument as the argument underlying the QA-scheme, if any ?

Let us first ask whether we can retrace the elements of the nomological argument, irrespective of their status as premise or conclusion. The desirative premise is obviously implied by the why-answer. The conclusion of the nomological argument is certainly a presupposition of the why-question and it is explicitly contained, and hence reaffirmed, in the why-answer. The epistemic premise is not explicitly stated in the QA-scheme, but it seems defensible that at least a weakened form (e.g. 'x believed that a was useful to obtain g') is a meaning component of the why-answer.

However, the fourth element of the nomological argument, the nomological premise, does not seem to be retraceable in the QA-scheme at all. Formulated as an explicative objection to the nomological theory we can put it in the following way: what does it matter what somebody (or other people) does (do) on similar occasions, the question is why somebody did what he did on this particular occasion. We will call this objection the *irrelevance*-objection to the nomological premise and hence to the nomological theory. It cannot be stressed enough that this objection is an objection to this theory only if it is (also) considered to be an explication of everyday intentional explanation.

The second explicative objection is the *symmetry*-objection. According to the nomological theory there is no essential difference between intentional explanation and 'intentional prediction' (including retrodiction). This objection may seem odd at first sight. If prediction is an important aspect of the sciences and if common sense is at least to some extent an anticipation of scientific knowledge, how is it then possible to call the transformability of intentional explanations into predictions an objection? On second thoughts, however, this is not convincing. Many historians for instance would not claim that they aim at retrodictions of human action, some of them may even be proud of that. Similarly, biologists do not aim with their functional explanations of organs in organisms at a retrodiction of the presence of these organs. Of course, this does not exclude the important role that predictions play in testing their explanations. Analogously, we seldom claim in everyday life that an intentional explanation could have predicted that the person in question would perform the particular action, notwithstanding the fact that an (hypothetical) explanation implies predictions (although perhaps only 'weak' predictions).

The third explicative objection is strongly related to the foregoing one. It concerns the standard assumption that the conclusion of the underlying argument is that somebody performed a certain action. If there is an underlying argument at all, its conclusion must be different from the standard assumption. That somebody performed a certain action is a presupposition underlying the whole QA-scheme. Although it is recognizable, it is not at all disputed. Hence, it should enter as a premise. To put in it a different way, intentional explanations are essentially explanations *ex post actu,* (hence, they cannot be transformed into retrodictions). This objection will be called the *conclusion*-objection.

The last explicative objection to be considered is the *necessity*- or *alternatives*-objection. The epistemic premise stated that x believed that a was *necessary* to obtain g. It certainly occurs sometimes that this premise may be considered to be true, i.e. situations in which people think, rightly or wrongly, that they should do *this* to achieve *that*. But it occurs more frequently that only a weaker premise can be justified, namely in the case that the actor believes that there are alternative actions serving the same purpose. Within the nomological theory a first step[7] is to introduce a 'disjunctive action' $d(a_1, a_2, ..,a_n)$ to be substituted in the epistemic premise as well as in the nomological premise and the conclusion. It is clear that this procedure weakens the explanatory (and predictive) power of the nomological argument with respect to a particular action a_i. It explains, so to speak, the particular action 'only up to alternatives'.

The objection is of course the following. In everyday intentional explanation alternative actions do not play any role, even if there are obvious alternative actions known to the actor. To the question 'Why did he open the window?' the answer 'He wanted to cool the room' provides a perfect explanation. Only if we are interested in the alternative action of, say, lowering the heating might we ask the additional question 'Why did he not lower the heating?'. But then we have a well-distinguished new why-question.

If there is a problem of non-uniqueness in everyday intentional explanations it is not the problem of alternative actions but the problem of different goals. That is, there may be different intentional explanations of the same action, leading to the problem of the relation between them.

This completes our evaluation of the explicative value of the nomological theory. In the light of the four objections we conclude in particular that the nomological argument is not the underlying argument, if there is one, of everyday intentional explanations.

We will now turn to the evaluation of the semantic theory. As has already been said this theory may be considered as a reaction to the explicative short-comings of the nomological theory. It will turn out that the irrelevance- and the symmetry-objection do not apply to the semantic theory. However, the con-clusion-objection remains (it is a standard theory), as well as the alternatives-objection. Moreover, there is a new objection, called the magic-objection.

The semantic theory is usually presented in the form of the so-called practical syllogism, i.e. the nomological argument without the nomological premise:

Practical Syllogism
$$D(x,g)$$
$$\underline{BN(x,a,g)}$$
$$P(x,a)$$

It is easily seen that the practical syllogism is, in the form presented, not a logically valid argument. But an argument may be analytically valid[8] : valid on the basis of meaning relations between the terms used in the premises and the conclusion. An analytically valid argument can be transformed into a logical-ly valid argument by adding appropriate semantic or meaning postulates specifying the meaning relations. The semantic theory states that the practical syllogism is such an analytically valid argument. The corresponding meaning postulate is, qua form, the same as the most farreaching nomological premise:

MP For all persons x, all actions a, all goals g and all 'occasions':
    if $D(x,g)$ and $B(x,a,g)$ then $P(x,a)$.

The status of MP, however, is completely different from that of a nomological premise. The truth of the latter is considered to be a matter of facts, not of meanings. On the other hand the ttruth of MP is considered to be of the opposite nature: not a matter of facts but of meaning.

Let us first of all note that the irrelevance-objection does not apply to MP even though MP is not explicitly recognizable in the QA-scheme. The reason is that meaning relations are to be expected in everyday arguments without some explicit indication. It is also clear that the practical syllogism transforms with MP into a logically valid argument.

However, we will call MP *magical* for the following reason: it presupposes that, what is in our opinion a false claim, natural language is such that particular desires and beliefs imply, as a matter of meaning, a particular action. To be sure, the problem is not that some primarily mental concepts have behavioral connotations, e.g. being hot-tempered, but that statements using only such concepts, even if they are quite specific, might imply a *specific* action.

The magic-objection becomes even more clear if we see how MP succeeds in avoiding the symmetry-objection. The predictive power of the nomological argument arose from the independent verifiability of the premises. According to the semantic theory however, sufficient verification of the premises $D(x,g)$ and $BN(x,a,g)$ is only possible, in view of the nature of a meaning postulate, by verification of the conclusion $P(x,a)$. In other words we are only justified in speaking of genuine 'desiring' and 'believing to be necessary' if the relevant action is performed. Hence, the practical syllogism cannot be used as a predictive argument.

It may seem surprising that proponents of the semantic theory like to stress this asymmetric character of their theory, appealing to the verification circularity, but are at the same time reluctant to draw the conclusion that intentional explanations are essentially *ex post actu*.

This reluctance may become understandable if we realize that they stick to the standard assumption that $P(x,a)$ is the conclusion of the underlying argument. As long as this assumption is made an explanation *ex post actu* will readily have an *ad hoc* air. However this may be, the conclusion-objection applies to the semantic theory for the same reasons as it applied to the nomological theory.

It is also not difficult to check that the same holds for the alternatives-objection. This completes the evaluation of the explicative value of the semantic theory, and we conclude that the practical syllogism is also not the argument underlying everyday intentional explanations.

If we put aside for a moment the explicative aim the **natural** question is which of the two theories presents the best account for a concept of explanation based on the standard assumption. In this respect the nomological theory seems to be the best candidate. The conclusion-objection no longer applies to either theory. The irrelevance-objection and the symmetry-objection do not now apply to the nomological theory. The alternatives-objection would, if it remains an objection at all, equally apply to both theories. But the magic-objection remains to be applicable only to the semantic theory in the following form: in concept formation we should avoid magical meaning relations of the kind of the meaning postulate assumed in the semantic theory.

2. Explication of everyday intentional explanation

In the preceding section we have already formulated the standard question and answer pattern for everyday intentional explanation. It read:

QA-scheme
Why did x perform action a ?
x performed a with the intention of approaching goal g.

It is easy to assess that we use this type of explanation frequently and easily in everyday life. Moreover, from the QA-scheme it is immediately clear that an intentional explanation will be called true if and only if the why-answer is true. There would be not much more to explicate about intentional explanations if there were not associated with it some intuitions which are not directly clear from the QA-scheme. That is, the primary task of explication is the explication of these associated intuitions.

We will consider especially two, more or less competing, intuitions: the argument-intuition and the understanding-intuition.

The *argument-intuition* we have already met as a general assumption of the two standard theories. It states that there is a valid argument underlying intentional explanations, such that the explanation is true if and only if the premises of the argument are true. We do not claim that everybody will share, or needs to share, this intuition (see below). But it is undoubtedly shared by many philosophers. On the basis of the preceding section we may already lay down some negative (related) characteristics of this argument:

1) its main conclusion should not be that somebody performed a certain action (this should be a kind of presupposition of the whole argument so that the explanation becomes *ex post actu* in an essential sense),

2) it should not be transformable into a prediction or retrodiction (i.e. it should be asymmetric with respect to explanation and prediction),

3) it should not have a (crucial) nomological premise, to avoid irrelevance,

4) meaning postulates, if necessary to obtain logical validity, should not be magical,

5) alternative actions serving the same purpose should not play a role (on the other hand, the phenomenon of different (true) explanations of the

same action should be possible).

The *Verstehen- or understanding-intuition* may be presented as a criticism of the argument-intuition. The intuition of an underlying argument, is, according to this criticism, just a prejudice, probably originating from the (false) analogy with explanation of individual events in the natural sciences. What an intentional explanation does is to make the action understandable to the questioner: although this does not seem to be an argument, this is the heart of the matter, according to the understanding-intuition. Of course, this possible motivation for the understanding-intuition does not exclude an explication of both intuitions in a harmonious way.

We will start with the explication of the argument-intuition. Let us analyse in more detail the meaning of a why-answer, or, more generally, of a statement of the form

$PI(x,a,g)$ x performed a with the intention of approaching g

where 'x' represents 'person x', 'a', 'action a' and 'g', 'goal g'.

It seems plausible to distinguish at least the following three meaning components:

$D(x,g)$ x desired g
$BU(x,a,g)$ x believed a to be useful to approach g
$P(x,a)$ x performed a.

We have already met these three components in the standard theories, albeit the epistemic component $BU(x,a,g)$ is now weaker than the epistemic premise $BN(x,a,g)$. However, this weakening is unavoidable for $PI(x,a,g)$ evidently does not imply that x believed a to be *necessary*. Neither does it imply that x believed a to be sufficient. Of course, we do not want to say that there are no occasions on which somebody believes that a certain action is necessary or sufficient for a certain goal, but only that neither of them belongs to the meaning of $PI(x,a,g)$.

In terms of probabilities it is plausible to interpret $BU(x,a,g)$ simply as the fact that, for x, the subjective unconditional probability that g will occur is lower than the subjective probability of this event under the condition that x performs action a. It is easy to check that, under very general conditions, this is equivalent to the fact that the subjective probability that g will occur if x does not perform a is lower than if x performs a.

Suppose now for a moment that x believed that a was sufficient to approach g, i.e. the subjective probability that g will occur if x performs a is 1. A special kind of this will occur if g is explicitly mentioned in the description of a, e.g. 'to open the door' and 'having the door opened'. In this case we say that $BU(x,a,g)$ and, hence, $PI(x,a,g)$ are trivial. *In what follows we will always presuppose the non-triviality of these statements.*

In our opinion the three components do not only belong to the meaning of $PI(x,a,g)$, they are, with some qualification, also exhaustive, i.e. their conjunction is equivalent in meaning to $PI(x,a,g)$. The qualification is of temporal nature. Suppose $D(x,g)$ or $BU(x,a,g)$ became true only after $P(x,a)$, i.e. x got the desire, or the belief, only after actual performance of the action. In this case we would be reluctant to call $PI(x,a,g)$ true. Hence, without mentioning it further, we will assume that the desire and the belief precede the action in a true statement of the form $PI(x,a,g)$.

In terms of the conjunction

(1) $D(x,g) \& BU(x,a,g) \& P(x,a)$

we may summarize the foregoing in the following meaning postulate:

MP.1 $PI(x,a,g)$ if and only if (1)

In the line of the nomological theory we assume also that the 'mental' components $D(x,g)$ and $BU(x,a,g)$ are independent of the 'action' component $P(x,a)$. In this way we renounce of course a variant of the crucial meaning postulate of the semantic theory, i.e. excluding $D(x,g)$ and $BU(x,a,g)$ to be true and $P(x,a)$ false. But, to be honest, due to the weakening of the epistemic component this variant lacks any plausibility. Another combination of truth-values which might seem problematic at first sight is $P(x,a)$ and $BU(x,a,g)$ true and $D(x,g)$ false. Note, however, that it makes perfect sense to talk about undesired (or even unintended) but expected consequences of an action.

An important aspect of $PI(x,a,g)$ and its components is that they are all (singular or) *specific* statements. All of them refer to a specific person and, as far as relevant, to a specific action or goal.

Now the question arises whether $PI(x,a,g)$ has also interesting *unspecific* meaning components, i.e. statements that follow from it perhaps, with the aid of some new meaning postulates, and that generalize in some way or other over persons, actions, or goals. Universal generalizations are of course out of the question. On the other hand a (large) number of existential generalizations are allowed. In the context of intentional explanation, where the why-question presupposes the truth of $P(x,a)$, one existential generalization of the additional content of $PI(x,a,g)$, i.e.

(2) $D(x,g) \& BU(x,a,g)$

will turn out to be of crucial importance, namely[9] (with y as variable for goals),

(3) $(Ey) (D(x,y) \& BU(x,a,y))$

Let us write down the conjunction of (3) and $P(x,a)$:

(4) $P(x,a) \& (Ey) (D(x,y) \& BU(x,a,y))$

The verbal formulation of (4) is of course

$PI(x,a)$: x performed a intentionally

where 'intentional' is used in the sense of 'with some intention' or 'with the intention to approach some goal'. That is, the following meaning postulate is plausible:

MP.4 *PI(x,a)* if and only if (4).

From (4) and MP.4 it is clear that *PI(x,a)* should be distinguished from '*x* intended to perform *a*' or '*a* was an intended action of *x*'. These expressions may already be taken as analytic consequences of *P(x,a)*, i.e. actions are by definition intended actions.[10] This aspect is however not relevant for us.

Consider now the statement

     IR(x,a)   : *a* was intentionally relevant for *x*

For this statement the following meaning postulate is plausible:

MP.3 *IR(x,a)* if and only if (3)

Now it is natural to introduce also the somewhat clumsy statement

     IR(x,a,g)   ' *a* was intentionally relevant for *x*'s desire *g*

with the corresponding meaning postulate

MP.2 *IR(x,a,g)* if and only if (2)

The transition from (2) to (3) is a straightforward application to (2) of the logical rule of inference called existential generalization, and the result (3) is called an existential generalization of (2). Because of MP.2 and MP.3 we may use the same terminology for the transition from *IR(x,a,g)* to *IR(x,a)*. For obvious reasons we will talk in the present context about intentional generalization (IG).

On the basis of the four meaning postulates and the standard rules for conjunction we can present now the following deductive argument

IG-argument

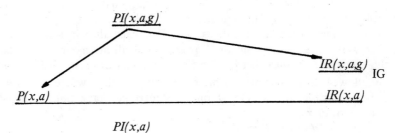

Our central claim is that the argument giving rise to the intuition that there is an argument underlying everyday intentional explanations is this IG-argument. To be precise, our claim is that the QA-scheme can be reconstrued as an IG-argument read upside down.[11]

To argue this let us start from the why-question: 'Why *P(x,a)* ?'. The apparent assumption of this question is not only *P(x,a)* but even *PI(x,a)*, i.e. *x* performed *a* intentionally. What the questioner wants to know is why this is so, i.e. *PI(x,a)*, why ? According to MP.4 we may split *PI(x,a)* into *P(x,a)* and

$IR(x,a)$. It is clear that the questioner does not dispute $P(x,a)$. Hence, the why-question is more particularly directed to $IR(x,a)$, i.e. the questioner wants to know why this is so, i.e. $IR(x,a)$, why ? The why-answer introduces now a transition from $IR(x,a)$ to $IR(x,a,g)$, which we will call an *intentional specification* (IS). Of course, IS is not a logical rule of inference (it should not be confused with the so-called rule of existential instantiation). IS introduces a specific goal about which $IR(x,a,g)$ is claimed to be true. Combining the intentional specification again with $P(x,a)$ we obtain of course, $PI(x,a,g)$. In total we get the following 'deep-structure' behind a QA-scheme :

IS-scheme

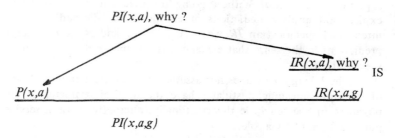

It will be clear that the IG-argument arises from reading the IS-scheme upside down or, to put it differently, the IG-argument can be attached to the IS-scheme and it brings us back to the initial assumption of the IS-scheme: $PI(x,a)$.

An obvious objection to our explicative claim is the following: it does not make much sense to attach the IG-argument to the IS-scheme for the conclusion of the former, $PI(x,a)$, is supposed to be the crucial assumption of the latter. The point is of course that this assumption, or more specifically, $IR(x,a)$ might be false in which case intentional specification and *hence* intentional generalization would not be possible.

To put it differently, verification of $IR(x,a)$ is only possible by intentional specification and subsequent generalization. In this respect the other assumption, $P(x,a)$, is different: intentional specification is certainly not the way to verify it.

Yet another way to put the crucial point is as follows: if we agree that intentional specification is the central *synthetic* (or inductive) aspect of an intentional explanation, and this seems very reasonable, then it is also quite reasonable that intentional generalization is the central *analytic* (or deductive) aspect of an intentional explanation.

We have called an intentional explanation formulated in a QA-scheme true if and only if the why-answer was true. It is clear that the deep structure, the IS-scheme, is in accordance with this definition. Consequently, this truth definition corresponds to saying that the (conjunctive) premise of the IG-argument is true.

It is easy to check that the IG-argument has all five negative characteristics specified at the beginning. The crucial one is the first: the main conclusion of the IG-argument is not that x performed a. The main part of the conclusion is obviously $IR(x,a)$. If combined with $P(x,a)$ we get the complete conclusion, but $P(x,a)$ only enters as part of the initial premise, i.e. as an assumption. In this sense the explanation is *ex post actu*, i.e. the conclusion qualifies the premise $P(x,a)$. From this it follows immediately that the IG-argument cannot be used as a prediction of $P(x,a)$. Without going into details it is clear that an intentional explanation implies predictions of another kind: the additional claim of the intentional specification $IR(x,a,g)$ (i.e. $D(x,g)$ and $BU(x,a,g)$) implies (weak) predictions in the sense that evidence may or may not be found to support this specification.

The IG-argument does not assume a nomological premise. Moreover, none of the four meaning postulates have the magical character of the meaning postulate of the semantic theory. Finally, alternative actions serving the same purpose do not play a role.

Let us now turn to the understanding-intuition. From the foregoing it is clear that we do not assume that every human action can be explained intentionally, i.e. that there is a true intentional explanation for it. This does of course not imply that no other type of explanation can be given for it, e.g. a 'psychological explanation' in terms of unconscious goals. The expression 'an action is understandable' can now be used in a strict, and in a broad sense. In the strict sense we equate 'the action is understandable' with 'the action is intentional'. In the broad sense the latter is a special case of the former, i.e. 'the action is intentionally understandable'. However this may be, from a true intentional explanation we may conclude that the action was understandable in both senses of the term. And even stronger, the intentional specification provides the grounds for saying that we have actually understood the action. Hence, the understanding-intuition can be explicated in complete harmony with the explication of the argument-intuition.

An important remaining question is the relation between an intentional explanation in our sense and explanations according to the nomological and the semantic theory. We will call explanations of the same action *corresponding* if they refer to the same goal and, hence, use the same desiderative premise.

With respect to the nomological theory there is a straightforward answer. A nomological (N-) explanation is stronger than the corresponding intentional explanation in the following sense: the premises of the nomological argument imply more than the premises of the corresponding IG-argument (and hence they imply its conclusion). First we show that the N-premises imply the three IG-premises:

- $D(x,g)$ is an explicit premise of the N-argument,
- $BU(x,a,g)$ is, without doubt, analytically implied by $BN(x,a,g)$,
- $P(x,a)$ is, by definition implied by $D(x,g)$, $BN(x,a,g)$ and the nomological premise.

But the N-premises are even essentially stronger, and even in two, quite different, respects. First, $BN(x,a,g)$ is obviously much stronger than $BU(x,a,g)$. We define the *specific additional content* (SAC) as follows: $Cn[D(x,g)$ & $BN(x,a,g)]$ $-$ $Cn[D(x,g)$ & $BU(x,a,g)]$, where 'Cn' indicates 'class of analytic consequences'.

Second, however the nomological premise *(NP)* is construed, everything implied by it, in conjunction with $D(x,g)$ and $BN(x,a,g)$, which is not implied by $D(x,g)$, $BN(x,a,g)$ and $P(x,a)$ is additional content of the N-premises, the *unspecific additional content* (UAC): $Cn[NP$ & $D(x,g)$ & $BN(x,a,g)]$ $-$ $Cn[D(x,g)$ & $BN(x,a,g)$ & $P(x,a)]$. It is not difficult to check that SAC and UAC partition all additional content of the N-premises into two disjunct classes.

Additional content restricts of course the 'domain of truth'. This explains in the first place why we can give much more true everyday intentional explanations than true nomological explanations. Secondly it explains the origin of the explicative objections against the nomological theory: this theory asks too much.

For the comparison with explanations according to the semantic theory we can now be shorter. Without the magical meaning postulate the premises of the practical syllogism (PS) only imply the IG-premises $D(x,g)$ and $BU(x,a,g)$, and with respect to these the additional content coincides with SAC of the N-premises. The PS-premises imply, in addition, $P(x,a)$ only if we accept the magical meaning postulate. Hence, *without* this postulate, PS is an *in*valid argument, incomparable to the IG-argument. *With* this postulate it is valid and stronger than the IG-argument: stronger, in two respects: SAC and the magical meaning postulate.

We conclude this section with a terminological remark. Intentional explanations are also called *rational* explanations. This terminology is however highly misleading for it is likely to confuse two things: reasons and good reasons. The term 'reason-giving-explanations' does not have this ambiguity. The crucial point is that it should be possible to call an action intentional but not (very) rational. For example, for an atheist the praying of a believer may be intentional, but not rational. The general point is that beliefs may or may not be rational. Moreover, even desires may or may not be rational.

3. Additional why-questions

A true intentional explanation of an action does not, of course, imply that there are no questions left. On the contrary, a true intentional explanation is the natural point of departure for new why-questions. To get natural formulations we will rephrase $PI(x,a,g)$ as : 'x aimed, with a, at g' and introduce the plausible existential generalization for it, i.e., 'x aimed at goal g', with z as variable for actions :

$$A(x,g) \text{ if and only if } (Ez) PI(x,z,g)$$

The first two questions now are

Q1   Why did x aim at g ?

Q2   Did x aim only at g ?

The first question leads immediately to a natural extension of intentional explanations of actions to intentional explanations of goals. In informal terms we get 'x aimed at g' because 'x desired g' and 'x believed that g was useful for g^*', i.e. $AI(x,g,g^*)$: 'x aimed at g with the intention of approaching g^*'. It is clear that the same type of IS-scheme and hence IG-argument can be formulated as before.

Suppose now that $PI(x,a,g)$ and $AI(x,g,g^*)$ are true. Does it follow that $PI(x,a,g^*)$ is also true ? It is easy to check that this new explanation of $P(x,a)$ is true if and only if, in addition to $PI(x,a,g)$ and $AI(x,g,g^*)$, it is also true that $BU(x,a,g^*)$.

Consider, however, the following principle:

PTU   if $BU(x,a,g)$ and $BU(x,g,g^*)$ then $BU(x,a,g^*)$

called the principle of transitivity of usefulness. Note that PTU can easily be extended to cases where 'a' is replaced by a third goal. Now PTU will not be a universally true principle; it comes close to the principle that people always believe the logical consequences of their beliefs, which is certainly false. Hence, $PI(x,a,g^*)$ need not be true if $PI(x,a,g)$ and $AI(x,g,g^*)$ are true.

We will say that two intentional explanations of an action, e.g. $PI(x,a,g)$ and $PI(x,a,g^*)$, are *directly related* if one of the goals can be explained by the other, e.g. $AI(x,g,g^*)$.

If two intentional explanations of an action are not directly related they need not be totally unrelated: they may be indirectly related by a third one. That is, $PI(x,a,g_1)$, $PI(x,a,g_2)$ and $PI(x,a,g_3)$ such that $AI(x,g_1,g_3)$ and $AI(x,g_2,g_3)$.

Answers to the second question ('Did x aim only at g ?') are now easy to give.[12] It may very well be that x aimed at more than one goal, and this will usually be the case. However, most of them will be related. The idea that there is *unique* intentional explanation, in many cases, can now be explicated: all goals are related in a special way.

Consider all g for which $PI(x,a,g)$ and let AI constitute a partial ordering of these goals, 'starting' with one or more goals which are even linearly ordered by AI, and so that for any of them, say g, and for any one of the remaining goals, say g^*, $AI(x,g,g^*)$ holds true. If there is such a unique 'goal-chain' at the beginning we can talk about *the* intentional explanation of the action (and of the goals in the chain, except the last one), meaning by it the specification of the first (the next) goal in the chain. But in a more liberal way of speech we will accept the specification of any member of such a chain as *the* true intentional explanation.

Returning to the first question we hasten to add that intentional explanations of goals will bring us, after some steps, to goals for which the interesting question is no longer 'Why did x aim at that goal ?', but 'How did it come about that x wanted that goal ?'. Then we get a transition from intentional explanations of goals to 'historical explanations'[13] of goals.

More or less the same transition arises in the context of the third question raised by an intentional explanation:

Q3   Why did x believe a to be useful for g ?

Analogous to intentional (or goal-) explanations of actions and goals we can construe 'belief-explanations' of beliefs of the form $BU(x,a,g)$, viz. x believes, say, B and x believes that B supports (the belief) that a is useful for g. It is interesting to note that the relation of support is, in probabilistic presentation, opposite to the relation of usefulness. Denoting the belief that a is useful for g by b it is plausible to assume that 'x believes that B supports b' implies $p_x(b) < p_x(b/B)$, whereas $BU(x,a,g)$ is probabilistically interpreted as $p_x(g) < p_x(g/a)$,, i.e. the role of B and b corresponds to that of a and g respectively, whereas we might expect the reverse correspondences.

Again we have the situation that belief-explanations of beliefs will bring us to beliefs for which the interesting question is no longer why x believed it, but 'How did x come to believe it ?', i.e. the quest for a historical explanation.

The last specific question we will consider, to which a true intentional explanation gives rise, is very crucial for our explication:

Q4   Why did x choose a among the alternatives ?

In Section 1 we saw that the two standard theories were both subject to the alternatives-objection. Our claim was that alternatives do not play a role in an intentional explanation. Our explication obviously has this negative characteristic, but it remains to be shown how alternatives should be treated as soon as they come into the picture, as is the case in Q4.

Let us start with the intentional explanation $PI(x,a_1,g)$ of $P(x,a_1)$, implying $D(x,g)$ and $BU(x,a_1,g)$. Suppose now that also for the (possible) actions $a_2, ...,a_n$ holds that $BU(x,a_i,g)$. Let a_o denote 'doing nothing' and let $BU(x,a_o,g)$ be false. Note that this is a non-trivial assumption.

From these assumptions it follows that we would be able to explain all 'positive' actions in terms of the same goal g. But x did choose a_1, why?

In order to answer this question we will postulate quantitative utilities *(u)* and probabilities *(p)* for convenience, but only use comparative relations between them.

We start with some obvious interpretations, leaving out the reference to x in quantitative terms:

$D(x,g)$: $u(g) > u(not\text{-}g) =_{df} 0$

$BU(x,a_i,g)$: $p(g) < p(g/a_i)$ $i=1,2,....,n$

$not\text{-}BU(x,a_o,g)$: $p(g) \geqslant p(g/a_o)$

In addition to these assumptions it is reasonable to assume that each of the positive actions costs more or less effort, i.e. they have, compared with a_o, negative utility

$u(a_i) < u(a_o) =_{df} 0$ $i=1,2,...,n$

One standard decision theoretic question now is whether or not the expected utility of a_i, i.e.

$$EU(a_i) = u(g)p(g/a_i) + u(not\text{-}g)p(not\text{-}g/a_i) + u(a_i)$$
$$= u(g)p(g/a_i) + u(a_i)$$

was maximal for a_1. Note that if this is so, it implies also that $EU(a_o)$ $(= u(g)p(g/a_o))$ was smaller than $EU(a_1)$.

Suppose now that x made up his mind before performing a_1, considered the alternatives $A = (a_o, a_1, ...,a_n)$, attached utilities and probabilities as suggested, and calculated the expected utilities of each action and reached the conclusion that $EU(a_1)$ was maximal and decided to aim, in choosing, at maximization of expected utility and actually chose a_1 and performed it. Now it is natural to say that the intentional explanation of $P(x,a_1)$ is still in terms of g, i.e. $PI(x,a_1,g)$, and that x's choice of a_1 out of A was also intentional, but now not directed to g but to maximizing expected utility. In other words, in this way we arrive at a natural distinction between an intentional explanation of an action and an intentional explanation of 'choosing one out of the alternative actions', i.e. of choice. Intentional explanation of choice will be called utilistic as soon as the actor uses some kind of utility decision rule.

In our opinion the success of decision theory, which is of course mainly interested in utilistic explanations of (and devices for) choice, has unfortunately led to the theoretical neglect of intentional explanation of actions. Standard presentations of decision theory do not usually start from a particular goal, but from incompatible possible outcomes, which obscures the fact that in many cases there is really one goal at stake, that will or will not be achieved. As far as this is true it may very well be that scientific interest in particular actions of human beings, e.g. in history, is more directed to intentional explanation of such actions rather than to utilistic explanations of the choice of them. On the other hand, in contexts where scientific interest is mainly directed to collective effects of individual actions, e.g. economy, sociology and politicology, it is reasonable to expect that the emphasis will be on utilistic explanations of choices.

These differences in emphasis will partly be due to the fact that there may be a true intentional explanation of an action but not a true intentional, let alone a true utilistic, explanation of the choice of that action. E.g. somebody may jump into the water to rescue someone else, without any deliberation of alternative actions serving the same purpose. Conversely, in a complex decision situation, with many possible actions and incompatible outcomes, it is hardly possible to talk about the intention with which the chosen action is performed, although the choice may be perfectly intentional in a utilistic sense.

We conclude this section with a general question raised by true intentional explanations. If, as we have suggested, there are so many true intentional explanations in everyday life, why are they not considered as belonging to our stock of scientific knowledge ? As with a lot of other (true) information (and intentional explanations just provide a special type of information) its neglect must be because this information is, in general, not considered to be scientifically interesting. An important exception is the science of history where many intentional explanations are considered interesting. As is clear from our exposition, historians should not bother about the well-known nomological criticism. If they support their hypothetical intentional explanations with evidence they explain actions in a significant and sound way. Attempts to strengthen such explanations to nomological explanations will, as a rule, not lead to interesting laws[14]. This does not of course exclude that the historian is interested in statistical information, e.g. of the form: in that period and region most people doing such and such did that with the intention of so and so. Such information may suggest intentional explanations in particular cases. Note that this use of statistical information differs from the imperfect form of nomological explanation, so-called statistical explanation.

4. Extrapolations and speculations

There is not only much dispute in the philosophy of history but also in the philosophy of other sciences as to whether the types of explanation which occur in these sciences are, or are not, of a different nature than the nomological explanations in the natural (non-life) sciences. In particular one may think of functional and teleological explanations in biology and, in addition, psychological explanations in psychology and psychiatry. Among the scientists who use such explanations, and most of them do, many have a bad conscience about it.

In this final section we will argue for the positive claim that such non-nomological explanations have a sound logical structure. In contrast to most defences of this claim we do not argue that these explanations compete with corresponding nomological explanations. On the contrary, they are, though highly informative, not so pretentious.

We will indicate only some general lines, leaving particular questions open for further research. The basic idea is of course that nomological explication of these, prima facie, non-nomological explanations will meet the same objections as intentional explanations, and that proper explication will reveal that they all have the same underlying argument as we found in the case of intentional explanation, viz. existential generalization.

Let us start with so-called functional explanation in biological anatomy and physiology. Why do certain species of animals have lungs ? Or, equivalently, what is the function of lungs (if the species has lungs) ? A rough, but essentially true, answer is that the function of lungs is to enable air-exchange between organism and environment. The argument is again existential generalization and it is obtained by reading the explanation upside down :

the (or a) function of lungs is air-exchange
lungs are functional.

Of course, this explanation leads to the question: what is the function of air-exchange ? Via a chain of related functions we will finally arrive at the function of the maintenance of life. Of course, we want such a chain to be as detailed as possible, i.e. we want as specific functions as possible.

It is clear that the most important problem for further research is the analysis of the meaning of specific functional statements, for only such an analysis can make clear how such statements, and hence how such explanations can be tested. To be sure, the articulation of the meaning of specific functional statements does not seem to be as easy as in the case of specific intentional statements. But, whatever the meaning is, it will not affect the (sound) nature of the underlying argument. Moreover, it is a safe risk to conjecture that the premises of a nomological explanation in functional terms (with the standard conclusion that certain animals have lungs) will also imply the specific functional statement. Consequently, a functional explanation will be weaker than a nomological explanation in functional terms.

It is however unlikely that the biologist will be interested in a nomological explanation (hence retrodiction) of the fact that these animals have lungs. He happens to have observed that these animals have certain organ-like parts, called lungs, and in view of the fact that most, or at least many, organ-like parts have been found to have specific functions, he asks for the specific function of lungs. Of course, our biologist will be interested in related questions, such as 'How does the process of air-exchange by the lungs work ?' and 'How did the lungs originate phylogenetically ?'. As to the first question some (causal-) nomological account can be expected. As to the second question the answer should of course be given in terms of the theory of evolution: functions (e.g. functional organ-like parts, i.e. organs) originate from genetic mutation and natural selection on the basis of survival value. In general, it will not be very interesting to lay down such a historical explanation in detail. However this may be, such a historical explanation seems to be the proper treatment of the question a nomological explanation would try to answer.

It is also clear that aspects of the answers to both questions will enter into an explication of the meaning of specific functional statements, i.e. regularities will be involved relating the operation of lungs to survival-value, but this will not bring us to a nomological retrodiction of the existence of lungs, i.e. the regularities will not (be able to) play the role the nomological premise is supposed to play in a nomological argument.

The above account can of course be extrapolated to all kinds of organs and processes in animals (and plants). In the case of processes, e.g. breathing, we are perhaps more inclined to talk about teleological explanations, but the structure of the underlying argument is the same: this process is directed to that goal, hence, this process is goal-directed.

Also the extrapolation to instinctive (outer-) behavior is plausible. If instinctive behavior happens to seem dysfunctional it is likely that the current environment differs in some relevant aspect from the environment in which the natural selection operated. The same holds true of course for rudimentary organs, etc.

There seems also to be no fundamental difference between functional explanation of instinctive behavior and learned behavior, apart from the onto-genetic origin of the latter, as opposed to the phylogenetic origin of the former. More specifically, learned behavior presupposes a mechanism of learning: the law of effect, the show-piece of behaviorism. This law of effect is itself a functional product of evolution and it produces behavior which is, as a rule, functional.

In human beings (and higher animals?) all this has culminated in the possibility of conscious functional behavior: intentional behavior, again a functional product of evolution. The capacity of intentional behavior obviously constitutes the kernel of so-called human freedom. As we have seen before, intentional explanation of actions, and hence human freedom, does not compete with nomological explanation at all.

We do not, of course, want to suggest that all non-instinctive human behavior is intentional. On the contrary, the law of effect remains to produce unconscious functional behavior: the so-called second nature, to be distinguished from the first nature of physiological processes and instinctive behavior. But, unfortunately, not all second nature behavior is only functional, especially in cases where 'unconscious goals and motives' are working which are in conflict with conscious goals. This is the domain of psychological explanation and therapy. Whereas behavioral therapy bets on the law of effect in the attempt to stop or change problematic second-nature behavior, so-called critical therapy bets on making conscious, as the proper way to increase the amount of undisturbed intentional behavior.

It is tempting to extrapolate our general diagnosis of explanatory arguments to the social level. To be sure, in the context of so-called institutional subjects, like firms and states, it generally makes sense to explain their behavior intentionally. But apart from that there is also the phenomenon of collective effects of individual intentional behavior, for example, utilistic choice-behavior. Such effects may or may not be functional on the level of groups or whole societies. However this may be, we arrive again at a type of phenomena, also occurring in non-life sciences and population-biology, where straightforward nomological explanations are feasible and interesting, namely collective results of in some respects and, as a rule, similar behavior of many individual entities of one kind or another. Such explanations will, as a rule, not postulate goals or functions at the group-level. Consequently, they do not imply intentional or functional explanations on this level.

NOTES

(1) See Carl G. Hempel, 'Aspects of scientific explanation', Section 10, in his *Aspects of scientific explanation,* Free Press, 1965.

(2) See Georg H. von Wright, *Explanation and understanding,* Routledge, 1971. See also his 'Determinism and the study of man' in *Essays on explanation and understanding* (eds. Manninen and Tuomela), Reidel 1976.

(3) We will restrict our attention to a naive version of the nomological theory. Hempel introduces the additional premise that x is a rational agent, with the corresponding change in the nomological premise. But this is not important for our explicative evaluation, i.e. all four objections to be presented remain applicable.

(4) Note that these assumptions do not imply that the two specific premises are mutually independent. In this connection Hempel speaks of the 'epistemic interdependence of belief attributions and goal attributions'.

(5) The use of the term 'standard' in the context of the QA-scheme should not be confused with the expressions 'standard theory' and 'standard assumption' defined in the introduction.

(6) Equivalent 'complete' expressions are e.g. $'x$ performed a in order to approach goal g' and $'x$ aimed with a at goal g'.

(7) To be sure Hempel transforms for this problem the nomological argument into a 'utilistic' argument where the specific goal disappears and is replaced by a number of different outcomes. In this way the explanation of an action gets confused with the explanation of the choice of an action.

(8) Although von Wright is not very clear in this respect, we take the following account as the weakest, and the least objectionable, account of what he wants to say. In general, we have much sympathy with his 'negative account', but we consider his 'positive account' as an unfortunate enterprise.

(9) In what follows it should be remembered that we announced our intention to use $BU(x,a,g)$ always in the non-trivial sense, hence also if the $'g'$ is replaced by a goal-*variable*.

(10) Similar qualifications may be made for $D(x,g)$ and $BU(x,a,g)$, now pertaining to the qualification that x's desire and belief were conscious.

(11) After writing the first version of this paper I came to know, thanks to Theo de Boer, that Rex Martin has considered the possibility that the conclusion of an intentional explanation might be that $'x$ performed a intentionally'. But he rejects it, in our opinion, mainly due to the fact that he does not see that existential generalization is involved. Cf. Rex Martin, 'The problem of the 'tie' in von Wright's schema of practical inference: a Wittgensteinian solution' in *Essays on Wittgenstein in honour of G.H. von Wright*, Acta Philosophica Fennica, Vol. 28, Nos. 1–3. (ed. J. Hintikka), North-Holland, 1976, pp. 326–363, in particular pp. 346–349. According to Martin the idea has also been considered, and rejected, by Norman Malcolm in a (as yet unpublished) paper entitled 'Intention and belief'. It should be conceded, and even stressed, that in many other publications, verbal characterizations of intentional explanation occur which are similar to our analysis. The important point is that the logical structure has not been made explicit in such presentations.

202

(12) In Section 4 we will hint upon the possibility of 'unconscious goals'.

(13) Here, and elsewhere, the intuitive notion of 'historical explanation' should not be confused with 'intentional explanation in history'.

(14) The following extended interpretation is also plausible. From our article 'Approaching descriptive and theoretical truth' (*Erkenntnis*, 18. 3, 1982, pp. 343–378) it follows that a distinction can be made between descriptive and theoretical sciences. The science of history is obviously a descriptive science; in a sense it is the only one. The nomological criticism is based on the false claim that the science of history is, or should be, a theoretical science, where nomological explanations play an important role. In constrast to this view, intentional explanations can be of crucial importance in the science of history : for it is easy to show that a true intentional explanation, conceived as the transition from $P(x,a)$ to $PI(x,a,g)$, is a (synthetic) step which brings us closer to the descriptive truth.

(*) I would like to thank A. van den Beld, Th. de Boer, T. Dehue, D. Draaisma, M. Hoekstra, M. Jeuken, J. Mooij and H. Reddingius for their useful comments on a first (Dutch) version, containing the same idea but differing a lot in presentation. I also thank Illka Niiniluoto for his stimulating critical remarks. I am very grateful to the NIAS (Wassenaar), where my stay as a fellow enabled me to write a rather new version, and to Ann Simpson of the NIAS for improving the English.

4

LOGIC OF DISCOURSE, DISCOVERY

AND

THE LOGIC OF JUSTIFICATION

A LOGIC OF DETECTION AND DECEPTION

Raymond Dacey
University of Oklahoma

1. Introduction

The economic theory of information that accompanies traditional decision theory provides the standard logic of detection. In that logic, the (economic) value of an information system increases as the reliability of the system increases. The same economic theory of information, when attached to Jeffrey's nonstandard decision theory, admits of anomalies where the economic value of an information system does not reflect the reliability of the system.

The purpose of the present paper is to report on the anomolies that appear in the application of nonstandard decision theory to the resolution of two games played between man, as the scientist, and nature. The two games are prisoners' dilemma and a truth-detection game called the scientist's game. The prisoners' dilemma game is a perverse model of scientific, or truth detection, behavior, and is examined because it is an extreme model of noncooperative behavior, and because it is a well-known model of both Newcomb's problem (4, 11) and the superpowers' arms race (4, 8). The scientist's game, due to Steven Brams (private communication), is arguably a more realistic model of scientific (i.e. truth-seeking) behavior.

In each game man has two acts, to believe or disbelieve a hypothesis about the behavior of nature, and nature has two acts, to render the hypothesis true or to render it false. Further, in each game man is endowed with equipment for (inexactly) detecting the state of nature. The economic theory of information provides a logic of optimal detection, which is also a logic of optimal (scientific) inquiry.

The anomalies reported here involve the following kind of pathological behavior. We will say that an information system, or line of inquiry, is non-trivial if the information system is more reliable than not, and we will say a play of the game is interesting if the scientist responds properly to the signals from the detection equipment. Finally, we will say that a play of the game is pathological if the nontrivial information system involved in an interesting play of the game has a lower value than the null (i.e. zero trial) information system. Interesting (nonpathological) plays of a game capture situations wherein the scientist has a guide to the selection of an optimal line of inquiry. Pathological plays of a game model situations wherein the scientist appears to have such a guide, but the guide is in fact deceptive. Put differently, pathological plays of a game model situations wherein the scientist, following good scientific practice, will deceive himself into selecting a less reliable line of inquiry.

The anomalies reported here are as follows : If the scientist is playing the prisoners' dilemma game against nature, then there are both interesting and pathological plays of the game, but the scientist can avoid pathological plays of the game by adopting a particular kind of information system. If, however, the scientist is playing the scientist's game against nature, then there are both interesting and pathological plays of the game regardless of the kind of information system the scientist adopts.

The paper preceeds as follows. Section 2 reviews the traditional theory of decision making and its related economic theory of information, and Section 3 presents the nonstandard theory of decision making required for the analysis of the prisoners' dilemma game and the scientist's game, along with the related economic theory of information. Section 4 applies the nonstandard theory directly to the prisoners' dilemma game to formulate a nonstandard decision-theoretic account of the game, and Section 5 applies the nonstandard theory to the scientist's game to formulate a nonstandard decision-theoretic account of that game. Finally, Section 6 examines the implications of the decision-theoretic accounts of the two games for the economic theory of information as a guide to scientific inquiry and scientific discovery.

2. Traditional decision theory

2.1. The elements of traditional decision theory

The basic decision problem is a triple $\Delta = \langle S, A, \beta \rangle$ composed of a set S of states of nature, a set A of actions and a benefit function β with domain SxA and range to the real numbers. The distinction between S and A is as follows: selection of an element (state) from S is beyond the control of the decision maker, whereas selection of an element (act) from A is completely under the control of the decision maker. The benefit function β evaluates the outcomes (or consequences) resulting from performing each of the acts in each of the states. (The function β is a composition of an outcome mapping and a utility function.)

The decision maker resolves the decision problem by selecting an optimal act from the set A. Traditional decision theory posits that the decision maker possesses a probability distribution P over the states of nature and announces that $a^0 \epsilon A$ is the optimal act in A for the decision problem Δ against the probability distribution P if and only if a^0 maximizes $E[\beta(a)] = \sum_s P(s)\beta(s,a)$. The act a^0 is called the initial resolution of the decision problem.

Traditional decision theory, via the economics of information, provides an account of rational inquiry about the states of nature. An inquiry, or question, about S is a set Y such that each element y of Y is an answer to the question. Similarly, Y is called an information system, and each y in Y is called a message. An information system Y is uniquely characterized by the matrix N of reliability probabilities $P(y|s)$ of the messages y given the states of nature s.

Traditional decision theory posits that the decision maker revises the initial resolution of the decision problem by selecting for each $y \epsilon Y$ the action a^y such that a^y maximizes $E[\beta(a)|y] = \sum_s P(s|y)\beta(s,a)$. The tuple $<a^{y1}, a^{y2},..., a^{yn}>$ is called the Bayes strategy and is the revised resolution of the decision problem Δ.

2.2. Properties of information systems

An information system Y is *perfect* if and only if there is a one-to-one correspondence between Y and S, i.e., if and only if Y is the complete partition $\{\{s_1\}, \{s_2\}, ..., \{s_n\}\}$ of s. An information system is *noiseless* if and only if all of the $P(y|s)$ in N are 0 or 1. If Y is a partition of S, then Y is noiseless. Clearly, if Y is perfect then Y is noiseless. If Y is not a partition of S, then Y is noisy. The foregoing concepts provide a formalization of the basic concepts from the theory of questions and answers. Specifically, a question Y is a *direct question* about S if and only if Y is a perfect information system for S. A question Y is an *indirect question* about S if and only if Y is a noiseless and imperfect information system for S. A question Y is an *indicative question* about S if and only if Y is a noisy information system for S. These latter concepts are instantiated by the following example.[1] Suppose an individual is interested in determining the state of tomorrow's weather and considers four possibilities : s_1 = dry, s_2 = rain, s_3 = snow, s_4 = hail. Let S = (s_1, s_2, s_3, s_4). The individual might ask any one of the following questions :

y^1 : Will it be dry or not ?
Y^2 : Will it be dry, will it rain, or will it be neither ?
Y^3 : Will it be dry, will it rain, will it snow or will it hail ?

Each position is a partition of S, as follows :

$$Y^1 = \{\{s_1\}, \{s_2, s_3, s_4\}\}$$
$$Y^2 = \{\{s_1\}, \{s_2\}, \{s_3, s_4\}\}$$
$$Y^2 = \{\{s_1\}, \{s_2\}, \{s_3\}, \{s_4\}\}$$

Questions Y^1 and Y^2 are indirect, whereas Y^3 is direct. An *indicative* question about tomorrow's weather is Y^4 : Is the barometer raising or falling ? Let y_1^4 = the barometer is rising and y_2^4 = the barometer is falling. The individual, upon the receipt of either y_1^4 or y_2^4, has grounds for forming a partial (or probabilistic) belief about tomorrow's weather. More specifically, y_1^4 and y_2^4 are characterized by the probability distributions $P(y_1^4|s)$ and $P(y_2^4|s)$ for $s\epsilon S$. Together with the individual's initial assignment of probabilities to the states $s\epsilon S$, these reliability probabilities provide the basis for generating, via Bayes' theorem, the individual's revised probabilities $P(s|y_i^4)$ for $s\epsilon S$ and $i = 1,2$. Note that answers to indicative questions are, in Shepsle's term, "ambiguous" answers.[2] Answers to indicative questions are interesting on a further count. Most information systems consist of detection systems that read symptoms. For example, a simple altimeter does not detect altitude, but rahter it detects air pressure. The Vella satellite does not detect the occurance of an above-ground nuclear blast, rather it detects the presence of bright white light. Symptom detectors are indicative questions and are easily deceived.

An information system Y is a *null information system* if and only if all of the rows of N are identical. A null information system is denoted Y^0 and the related matrix N is denoted N^0. If a^0 is the initial (i.e., no-information) resolution of the decision problem Δ, then the revised resolution of the problem on the basis of a null information system is the tuple $\langle a^0, a^0, ..., a^0 \rangle$.

2.3. The economics of information for the traditional theory

There are, for any decision problem, many information systems "between" the perfect and null systems. Traditional theory provides, through the economic theory of information, a complete ordering of all possible information systems. The ordering is induced by a valuation function, V, defined as :

$$V(Y) = \sum_y P(y) \max_a \sum_s P(s|y) \beta(a,s)$$

$$= \sum_y P(y) \sum_s P(s|y) \beta(a^y, s).$$

The valuation function V induces a complete ordering of all of the information systems available for the problem Δ given that the benefit function β and probability measure P are held fixed. An incomplete ordering of the information systems can be defined as follows : Y is more informative than Y' (denoted $Y \gg Y'$) if $V (Y) > V(Y')$ for all specifications of β and P. Again, the ordering so defined is a partial ordering.

The principal result in the economics of information concerns the complete ordering of information systems induced by the valuation function V. The result is stated simply as follows :

THEOREM. If Y^∞ is the perfect information system and Y^0 is a null information system for Δ and if β and P are held fixed, then $V(Y^\infty) \geqslant V(Y)$ $\geqslant V(Y^0)$ for all information systems Y. Furthermore, $V(Y^\infty)$ is finite.[3]

The foregoing theorem is relevant to the selection of an optimal question and to the selection of an optimal detection system. Since questions and detection systems are simply information systems, the economics of information systems is also the economics of question asking and detection system selection. Thus, if a problem can be modelled within the confines of decision theory, then that theory provides an account of optimal, or strategic, detection.

3. Nonstandard decision theory

3.1. The elements of non-standard decision theory

Traditional decision theory presupposes that the states of nature are (probabilistically) independent of the decision maker's acts. Non-standard decision theory does not make this presupposition.[4] If the states of nature are probabilistically dependent upon the acts, i.e., if $P(s|a) \neq P(s)$ for some $s \epsilon S$ and $a \epsilon A$, then the states are said to be *act-dependent*. Given act-dependent states, the decision maker initially resolves the decision problem $\Delta = < S, A, \beta >$ by selecting $a^0 \epsilon A$ so as to maximize $E[\beta(a)] = \sum_s P(s|a) \beta (s,a)$. Further, given an information system Y the decision maker revises the initial resolution of the problem by selecting $a^y \epsilon A$ for each $y \epsilon Y$ so as to maximize $E[\beta(a)|y] = \sum_s P(s|a\&y) \beta (s,a)$.

Decision making within the nonstandard theory parallels decision making within the traditional theory. The economics of information of the nonstandard theory, however, do not parallel that of the traditional theory. First, an information system Y for an act-dependent decision problem is characterized by a tuple $<Na_1, Na_2, ..., Na_n>$ where Na_i is the matrix of reliability probabilities of the signals $y \epsilon Y$ given the states of nature and the action a_i. More importantly, there are nontrivial information systems for which the primary theorem of the economics of information for the traditional theory, i.e., $V(Y^O) < V(Y) < V(Y^\infty)$, does not hold. The following example[5], adapted from Adams and Rosenkrantz (1), details such an instance.

3.2. A counterexample to the economics of information for the traditional theory

Suppose the benefit function β is given by the table

$\beta(a,s)$	a_1	a_2
s_1	10	0.0
s_2	−10	2.5

Suppose further that the act-dependent probability distributions are $P(s_1|a_1) = 2/3$ and $P(s_2|a_1) = 1/3$ for a_1 and $P(s_1|a_2) = .12$ and $P(s_2|a_2) = .88$ for a_2. Then $E[\beta(a_1)] = 2/3\,(10) + 1/3\,(10) = 10/3 = 3\,1/3$ and $E[\beta(a_2)] = .12\,(0) + .88\,(2.5) = 2.2$ so that $a^O = a_1$ and $V(Y^O) = 3\,1/3$.

Now, suppose the act-dependent reliability probability matrices are

$$Na_1 = \begin{bmatrix} .7 & .3 \\ .6 & .4 \end{bmatrix} \text{ and } Na_2 = \begin{bmatrix} .5 & .5 \\ .4 & .6 \end{bmatrix}$$

Then the posterior probability distributions are also act-dependent, and are as follows :

$$P(s_1|a_1\&y_1) = .7, \qquad P(s_2|a_1\&y_1) = .3$$

$$P(s_1|a_2\&y_2) = .6, \qquad P(s_2|a_1\&y_2) = .4$$

For a_1, and

$$P(s_1|a_2\&y_1) = .1456, \qquad P(s_2|a_2\&y_1) = .8544$$

$$P(s_1|s_2\&y_2) = .1020, \qquad P(s_2|a_2\&y_2) = .8980$$

for a_2.

Thus, $E[\beta(a_1)|y_1] = 4.0 > 2.136 = E[\beta(a_2)|y_1]$ and $E[\beta(a_1)|y_2] = 2.0 < 2.2.450 = E[\beta(a_2)|y_2]$, so that the Bayes strategy is $\langle a_1, a_2 \rangle$.[5] Again, following Adams and Rosenkrantz, we let $P(a_1) = .75$ so that $P(y_1) = P(y_1|a_1) P(a_1) + P(y_1|a_2) P(a_2)$, where $P(y_1|a_j) = \Sigma P(y_1|a_j\&s) P(s|a_j)$, is $P(y_1) =$

$(2/3) (.75) + (.412)(.25) = .50 + .103 = .60\overset{s}{3}$. Therefore, $V(Y) =(.603) (4.0) + (.397)(2.245) = 3.3033$. We now have $V(Y^O) = 3\ 1/3 > 3.3033 = V(Y)$, as promised.

Any attempt to provide a decision-theoretic account of the prisoners' dilemma game requires the adoption of nonstandard (i.e., act-dependent) decision theory. If traditional decision theory is employed, then the dominance present in the benefit function is maintained in the calculation of (conditional) expected benefits, regardless of the information system. The next section presents a decision-toeoretic formulation of the prisoners' dilemma game based upon nonstandard decision theory.

4. The nonstandard account of the prisoners' dilemma game

4.1. Introduction

The prisoners' dilemma game is a model of noncooperative behavior in the extreme. It is also a model of Newcomb's problem (4, 11) and the superpowers' arms race (4, 8). The prisoners' dilemma game, in ordinal form, is as follows.

Player B

		b_1 (C)	b_2 ($\overline{C}$)
	a_1 (C)	$<3,3>$	$<1,4>$
Player A	a_2 ($\overline{C}$)	$<4,1>$	$<2,2>$

where each pair $<x,y>$ represents the payoffs to players A and B, respectively, and 4 is the best payoff, 1 the worst and 3 is better than 2, for each player, and where C denotes "cooperate" and $\overline{C}$ denotes "do not cooperate". The prisoners' dilemma game is a model of the scientist's truth detection problem if, for nature, the cooperative act C ist to render the scientist's hypothesis true, and the noncooperative act $\overline{C}$ is to render the hypothesis false, and if, for the scientist, the cooperative act is to believe that the hypothesis is true, and the noncooperative act is to disbelieve the hypothesis. The payoff table reveals that the prisoners' dilemma game is a perverse model of the scientist's problem. Played game-theoretically, the prisoners' dilemma model yields the conclusion that the two players are locked in noncooperative stalemate, since the $<2,2>$ outcome is a stable equilibrium dictated by the dominance of a_2 over a_1 and the dominance of b_2 over b_1. Played decision-theoretically, via traditional decision theory, the prisoners' dilemma model yields the same conclusion, i.e., that the two players are locked in a noncooperative stalemate. The prisoners' dilemma model, played decision-theoretically via nonstandard decision theory, yields, under suitable conditions, the conclusion that bilateral cooperation is possible. However, the nonstandard decision-theoretic account of the prisoners' dilemma model also yields the conclusion that there are situations where there is no rational way to select a detection system. If, however, the model is further restricted (so that the reliability probabilities are act-independent), then the nonstandard analysis of the prisoners' dilemma model yields the conclusion that bilateral cooperation is possible and that there is a rational way to select detection equipment. This section of the paper presents the grounds supporting these claims.

4.2. Elements of the nonstandard decision-theoretic account of the prisoners' dilemma game

Let player A be the rational agent and player B be nature in a nonstandard decision theoretic play of the prisoners' dilemma game. The benefit function, in ordinal form, for player A is given by the following table.

$\beta(a,s)$	a_1	a_2
$s_1 (= b_1)$	3	4
$s_2 (= b_2)$	1	2

Without loss of generality, the benefit function in cardinal form is

$\beta(a,s)$	a_1	a_2
$s_1 (= b_1)$	u	1
$s_2 (= b_2)$	0	v,

where $1 > u > v > 0$.

The foregoing claims are pointless if they are valid only for decision problems and information systems that are themselves unimportant. To avoid rendering the claims pointless consideration will be given only to important decision problems and information systems. The concept of "important" is characterized via the following notions. An information system $Y = (y_1, y_2)$ for the prisoners' dilemma problem is *nontrivial* if and only if $P(y_1 | a_1 \& s_1)$, $P(y_1 | a_2 \& s_1) \geqslant 1/2$ and $P(y_1 | a_1 \& s_2)$, $P(y_1 | a_2 \& s_2) \leqslant 1/2$, and $P(s_1 | y_1 \& a_1) > P(s_1 | a_1) > P(s_1 | y_2 \& a_1)$ and $P(s_1 | y_1 \& a_2) > P(s_1 | a_2) > P(s_1 | y_2 \& a_2)$. Nontriviality requires that while the signals y_1 and y_2 are act-dependent, the dependence of y_1 and y_2 upon the acts does not overwhelm the capacity of the system to detect the states s_1 and s_2, respectively. A decision-theoretic play of the prisoners' dilemma game on the basis of an information system Y is *interesting* if and only if 1) Y is nontrivial, 2) $a^o = a_2$ and 3) $< a^{y1}, a^{y2} > = <a_1, a_2>$. A decision-theoretic play of the prisoners' dilemma game on the basis of an information system Y is *pathological* if and only if 1) it is interesting and 2) $V(Y^o) > V(Y)$.

The first of the foregoing claims can now be stated as follows. Claim #1 : Given a nontrivial, act-dependent information system, there are both interesting and pathological plays of the prisoners' dilemma game. The claim is easily established by the following instances of plays of the prisoners' dilemma game via nontrivial, act-dependent information systems.

4.3. Interesting and pathological plays of the game

Consider the decision-theoretic play of the prisoners' dilemma game given in tabular form below :

$\beta(a,s)$	a_1	a_2	$P(s|a_1)$	$P(s|a_2)$	$P(y|s\&a_1)$ y_1	y_2	$P(y|s\&a_2)$ y_1	y_2
s_1	.3	1.0	.2	.1	.9	.1	.5	.5
s_2	.0	.1	.8	.9	.1	.9	.5	.5

Simple calculation yields that $E[\beta(a_1)] = .06 < .19 = E[\beta(a_2)]$ so that $a^o = a_2$ and $V(Y^o) = .19$, and $E[\beta(a_1)|y_1] = .2077 > .1900 = E[\beta(a_2)|y_1]$ and $E[\beta(a_1)|y_2] = .0081 < .1900 = E[\beta(a_2)|y_2]$, so that the Bayes strategy is $<a_1, a_2>$. Thus the problem is interesting. Further calculation yields that $V(Y) = .1989 - .0042\ P(a_1)$, so that $V(Y^o) > V(Y)$ only if $P(a_1) > 2.119$. Thus the problem is *not* pathological.

Now consider the same problem as before, but alter the reliability probabilities given a_2 so that the entries in the top row of the $P(y|s\&a_2)$ table are .6 and .4. Simple calculation now yields that $a^o = a_2$ and $V(Y^o) = .19$ as before, and that $E[\beta(a_1)|y_1] = .2077 > .2059 = E[\beta(a_2)|y_1]$ and $E[\beta(a_1)|y_2] = .0081 <$

$.1735 = E[\beta(a_2)|y_2]$ so that the Bayes strategy is $\langle a_1, a_2 \rangle$. Thus, the play of the game is interesting. Further calculation, however, yields that $V(Y) = .1909 - .0086\, P(a_1)$, so that $V(Y) < V(Y^O)$ if $P(a_1) > .105$. Thus, the play of the game, for particular values of $P(a_1)$, is pathological.

The information system for the first example is $Y = \langle Na_1, Na_2 \rangle$ and for the second is $Y' = \langle Na_1, Na_2' \rangle$ where $Na_1 = \begin{bmatrix} .9 & .1 \\ .1 & .9 \end{bmatrix}$, $Na_2 = \begin{bmatrix} .5 & .5 \\ .5 & .5 \end{bmatrix}$ and $Na_2' = \begin{bmatrix} .6 & .4 \\ .5 & .5 \end{bmatrix}$. Calculation reveals that $V(Y) > V(Y^O) > V(Y')$ for $P(a_1) > .105$. Note, however, that Na_2' is systematically *more* reliable than Na_2, so that Y is systematically more reliable than Y'.

An information system Y is an *act-independent information system* if and only if $P(y|s\&a) = P(y|s)$ for all $a\epsilon A$, $s\epsilon S$, $y\epsilon Y$, i.e., if and only if, for $Y = \langle Na_1, Na_2 \rangle$, $Na_1 = Na_2$.[6] The second claim made above can be restated as follows. Claim #2 : Given a nontrivial act-independent information system, there are interesting plays, but no pathological plays, of the prisoners' dilemma game.

The first part of this claim is easily established by the following instance of an interesting play of the prisoners' dilemma game, via a nontrivial, act-independent information system. Consider the decision-theoretic play of the prisoners' dilemma game given in tabular form below :

$$P(y\,|s\&a), a = a_1, a_2$$

$\beta(a,s)$	a_1	a_2	$P(s|a_1)$	$P(s|a_2)$	y_1	y_2
s_1	.6	1.0	.3	.1	.9	.1
s_2	.0	.1	.7	.9	.4	.6

Calculation yields $E[\beta(a_1)] = .18 < .19 = E[\beta(a_2)]$, so that $a^O = a_2$ and $V(Y^O) = .19$ and $E[\beta(a_1)|y_1] = .29454 > .280 = E[\beta(a_2)|y_1]$ and $E[\beta(a_1)|y_2] = .040 < .11636 = E[\beta(a_2)|y_2]$, so that the Bayes strategy is $\langle a_1, a_2 \rangle$. Thus the play of the game is interesting. Further calculation yields that $V(Y) = .196541 + .017818\, P(a_1)$, so that $V(Y) < V(Y^O)$ only if $P(a_1) < -.036710$. Thus the play of the game is *not* pathological.

The second half of our claim, concerning the non-existence of pathologies, cannot be proven with an example, but requires an analytical proof. In the absence of an analytical proof, we advance this claim as a conjecture, supported by an exhaustive search of 160,380 plays of the prisoners' dilemma game with interesting act-independent information systems. No pathological cases were found.[7] The computer program that conducted the search was written by Richard Toelle and is presented in the Appendix.

5. The nonstandard account of the scientist's game

5.1. Introduction

The scientist's game is a model of noncooperative behavior. The preferences of the two players in the scientist's game are as follows : Nature wants most to conceal the truth of the scientist's hypothesis, and then to be believed by the scientist. The scientist most wants to discover the truth about the hypothesis. The scientist's game, in ordinal form, is as follows :

		Player B (The Scientist) a_1 (B)	a_2 (B)
Player A (Nature)	s_1 (T)	<2,4>	<3,2>
	a_2 (T)	<4,1>	<1,3>

where each pair $<x, y>$ represents the payoffs to players A and B, respectively, and 4 is the best payoff, 1 the worst and 3 is better than 2, for each player. The scientist's game involves neither dominance nor paradox. Since nature is best presumed to be passive and nonstrategic, the game has greater appeal when it is played decision-theoretically. Played decision-theoretically, via traditional decision theory, the scientist's game yields no startling conclusions. The scientist's game, played decision theoretically via nonstandard decision theory, yields, under suitable conditions, the conclusion that the scientist can rationally select optimal detection equipment. However, the nonstandard decision-theoretic account of the scientist's game also yields the conclusion that there are situations where there is no rational way to select a detection system. If the play of the game is further restricted (so that the reliability probabilities are act-independent), then the nonstandard analysis of the scientist's game yields the same conclusion, i.e., that there are situations wherein the scientist can, and situations wherein the scientist cannot, rationally select optimal detection equipment. This section of the paper presents the grounds supporting these claims.

5.2. Elements of the nonstandard decision-theoretic account of the scientist's game

The scientist's benefit function, in ordinal form is given by the following table.

$\beta(a,s)$	a_1	a_2
$s_1 \; (= b_1)$	4	2
$s_2 \; (= b_2)$	1	3

Without loss of generality, the benefit further in cardinal form is

$\beta(a,s)$	a_1	a_2
$s_1 \; (= b_1)$	1	v
$s_2 \; (= b_2)$	0	u ,

where $1 > u > v > 0$.

As before, an information system $Y = \{y_1, y_2\}$ for the scientist's game is *nontrivial* if and only if $P(y_1|a_1\&s_1)$, $P(y_1|a_2\&s_1) \geqslant 1/2$ and $P(y_1|a_1\&s_2)$, $P(y_1|a_2\&_s2) \leqslant 1/2$, and $P(s_1|y_1\&a_1) > P(s_1|a_1)$ and $P(s_1|y_1\&a_2) > P(s_1|s_2) > P(s_1|y_2\&a_2)$. Nontriviality requires that while the signals y_1 and y_2 are act-dependent, the dependence of y_1 and y_2 upon the acts does not overwhelm the capacity of the system to detect the states s_1 and s_2, respectively. A decision-theoretic play of the scientist's game on the basis of an information system Y is *interesting* if and only if 1) Y is nontrivial, 2) $a^o = a_2$ and 3) $<a^y1, a^y2> \; = \; <a_1, a_2>$. A decision-theoretic play of the scientist's game on the basis of an information system Y is *pathological* if and only if 1) it is interesting and 2) $V(Y^o) > V(Y)$.

The first of the foregoing claims can now be stated as follows. Claim #3 : Given a nontrivial, act-dependent information system, there are both interesting and pathological plays of the scientist's game. The claim is easily established by the following instances of plays of the scientist's game via nontrivial, act-dependent information systems.

5.3. Interesting and pathological plays of the scientist's game

Consider the decision-theoretic play of the prisoners' dilemma game given in the tabular form below :

$\beta(a,s)$	a_1	a_2	$P(s|a_1)$	$P(s|a_2)$	$P(y|s\&a_1)$		$P(y|s\&a_2)$	
					y_1	y_2	y_1	y_2
s_1	1.0	.1	.1	.2	.8	.2	.5	.5
s_2	.0	.2	.9	.8	.1	.9	.1	.9

Simple calculation yields that $E[\beta(a_1)] = .10 < .18 = E[\beta(a_2)]$ so that $a^o = a_2$ and $V(Y^o) = .18$, and $E[\beta(a_1)|y_1] = .4706 > .1444 = E[\beta(a_2)|y_1]$ and $E[\beta(a_1)|y_2] = .0241 < .1878 = E[\beta(a_2)|y_2]$, so that the Bayes strategy is $<a_1, a_2>$. Thus the problem is interesting. Further calculation yields that $V(Y) = .2387 - .0028\ P(a_1)$, so that $V(Y^o) > V(Y)$ only if $P(a_1) > 20.3982$. Thus the problem is *not* pathological.

Now consider the same problem as before, but alter the reliability probabilities so that the game in tabular form is as follows :

$\beta(a,s)$	a_1	a_2	$P(s|a_1)$	$P(s|a_2)$	$P(y|s\&a_1)$		$P(y|s\&a_2)$	
					y_1	y_2	y_1	y_2
s_1	1.0	.1	.1	.2	.7	.3	.9	.1
s_2	.0	.2	.9	.8	.5	.5	.1	.9

Simple calculation now yields that $a^o = a_2$ and $V(Y^o) = .18$ as before, and that $E[\beta(a_1)|y_1] = 1.346 > .1308 = E[\beta(a_2)|y_1]$ and $E[\beta(a_1)|y_2] = .0625 < .1973 = E[\beta(a_2)|y_2]$ so that the Bayes strategy is $<a_1, a_2>$. Thus, the play of the game is interesting. Further calculation, however, yields that $V(Y) = .1810 - .0163\ P(a_1)$, so that $V(Y) < V(Y^o)$ if $P(a_1) > .061$. Thus, the play of the game, for particular values of $P(a_1)$, is pathological.

An information system Y is an *act-independent information system* if and only if $P(y|s\&a) = P(y|s)$ for all $a \epsilon A$, $s \epsilon S$, $y \epsilon Y$, i.e., if and only if, for $Y = <Na_1, Na_2>$, $Na_1 = Na_2$. The second claim made above can be restated as follows. Claim #4 : Given a nontrivial act-independent information system, there are interesting plays and pathological plays of the scientist's game.

The first part of this claim is easily established by the following instance of an interesting play of the scientist's game, via a nontrivial, act-independent information system. Consider the decision-theoretic play of the scientist's game given in tabular form below :

$$P(y|s\&a), a = a_1, a_2$$

$\beta(a,s)$	a_1	a_2	$P(s|a_1)$	$P(s|a_2)$	y_1	y_2
s_1	1.0	.5	.3	.3	.7	.3
s_2	.0	.6	.7	.9	.1	.9

Calculation yields $E[\beta(a_1)] = .30 < .59 = E[\beta(a_2)]$, so that $a^o = a_2$ and $V(Y^o) = .59$ and $E[\beta(a_1)|y_1] = .7500 > .5562 = E[\beta(a_2)|y_1]$ and $E[\beta(a_1)|y_2] = .1250 < .5964 = E[\beta(a_2)|y_2]$, so that the Bayes strategy is $\langle a_1, a_2 \rangle$. Thus the play of the game is interesting. Further calculation yields that $V(Y) = .6210 + .1536 \, P(a_1)$, so that $V(Y) < V(Y^o)$ only if $P(a_1) < -.2019$. Thus the play of the game is *not* pathological.

Now consider the same problem as before, but alter the benefit function at $\beta(a_2,s_2)$ so that the game in tabular form is as follows :

$$P(y|s\&a), a = a_1, a_2$$

$\beta(a,s)$	a_1	a_2	$P(s|a_1)$	$P(s|a_2)$	y_1	y_2
s_1	1.0	.5	.3	.1	.7	.3
s_2	.0	.9	.7	.9	.1	.9

Then $E[\beta(a_1)] = .30 < .86 = E[\beta(a_2)]$, so that $a^o = a_2$ and $V(Y^o) = .86$, and $E[\beta(a_1)|y_1] = .7500 > .7250 = E[\beta(a_2)|y_1]$ and $E[\beta(a_1)|y_2] = .1250 < .8964 = E[\beta(a_2)|y_2]$, so that the Bayes strategy is $\langle a_1, a_2 \rangle$. Thus the play of the game is interesting. Further calculation yields that $V(Y) = .873 - .0932 \, P(a_1)$, so that $V(Y) < V(Y^o)$ if $P(a_1) > .1395$. Thus, the play of the game, for particular values of $P(a_1)$, is pathological.

The four foregoing plays of the scientist's game establish the two claims that, whether the scientist employs act-dependent or act-independent detection equipment, the scientist will face both interesting and pathological plays of the game. The scientist, unlike the rational agent in the prisoners' dilemma game, cannot protect himself from deception in pathological plays of the game by adopting act-independent detection equipment.[8]

6. Conclusions

The existence of pathological plays of a game has implications for the possibility of optimal scientific inquiry and self-deception. If the scientist bases his selection of an information system (i.e., his selection of a line of inquiry) on the basis of the reliability of the system, then the scientist can, in a pathological play of a game, select a system with less (economic) value than the null system (i.e., the zero trial experiment). If, on the other hand, the scientist employs the economic theory of information as a guide and selects an information system on the basis of the V-valuation of the system, then the scientist can, in a pathological play of a game, select the null system over a non-trivial system. Furthermore in pathological plays of prisoners' dilemma, the scientist who employs the valuation function V of the economic theory of information as a selection guide can select a less reliable system over a more reliable system. Interestingly, the parallel to this last result has not been observed for the scientist's game.

The anomalies reported above appear in other games, notably chicken (4) and a variant of the scientist's game. In the latter game the benefit table is as follows :

The Scientist

		(B)	$(\bar{B})$
	(T)	1	0
(Nature)			
	(T)	v	u

where, as before, $1 > u > v > 0$. Play in both games is similar to play in the scientist's game : there are both interesting and pathological plays of the games for both act-dependent and act-independent information systems.

The results reported here are those available for other games suggest that the scientist can protect himself from deception only in the (perverse) prisoners' dilemma game. The results further suggest that the scientist cannot rely on the economic theory of information as a guide to scientific inquiry. The force of the results, however, must be tempered with the observation that the computer printouts contain vastly more interesting plays of each game than pathological plays. What is required, but is yet unformulated, is a theory that accounts for the occurrence of pathological plays of each game. Such a theory would provide an estimate of the likelihood that the scientist would encounter a pathological play of the game, and therefore an estimate of the likelihood that the economic theory of information is an inadequate guide to the conduct of scientific inquiry.

NOTES

(1) The example is based upon Marschak (14), pp. 149–153. For a more detailed discussion of the theory of questions and answers based upon the theory of decisions see Dacey (7). For a discussion of alternative models of detection in game situations see Brams, et. al. (5) and Dacey (6).

(2) Shepsle's probabilistic account of ambiguity is given in (15). Note that Shepsle's notion of ambiguity is distinct from Ellsberg's notion. For the latter see (9).

(3) For the theorem see Marschak (13), p. 55.

(4) The primary nonstandard decision theory is due to Jeffrey (10). The formal foundations of the Jeffrey theory are provided by Bolker (3). Alternative nonstandard theories are due to Balch and Fishburn (2) and Luce and Krantz (12).

(5) The present example differs from the original Adams and Rosenkrantz example on two counts. First, in the present example $\beta(a_2,s_2) = 2.5$ whereas in the original $\beta(a_2,s_2) = 2.0$. Second, in the present example $Na_2 = \begin{bmatrix} .5 & .5 \\ .4 & .6 \end{bmatrix}$ whereas in the original $Na_2 = \begin{bmatrix} .50 & .50 \\ .39 & .61 \end{bmatrix}$. Both differences are minor. The changes were made to provide a less trivial example. In the original Adams and Rosenkrantz example the initial solution is $a^o = a_2$ and the Bayes strategy is $\langle a_2,a_2 \rangle$. An information system is *useless* if and only if the initial solution is a^o and the Bayes strategy for the information system is $\langle a^o, ..., a^o \rangle$. Within the confines of the traditional theory of decision making, if an information system Y is useless, then $V(Y) = V(Y^o)$, where Y^o is a null information system. (See Marschak (13), p. 52 for a discussion of useless systems.) Thus, on the basis of the traditional theory, the original Adams and Rosenkrantz example would yield $V(Y) = V(Y^o)$. That this example yields $V(Y) < V(Y^o)$ for the nonstandard theory is not very surprising. The example was changed so that $a^o = a_2$ and the Bayes strategy is $\langle a_1,a_2 \rangle$. Thus, the information system

for the revised example is *not* useless.

(6)   Adams and Rosenkrantz refer to signals from an act-independent information system as "pure observations." See (1), p. 14.

(7)   There are pathological plays of the prisoners' dilemma game given useless act-independent information systems, i.e., there are parallels to the original Adams and Rosenkrantz example, as discussed in footnote 5. An example of a pathological play of the game on the basis of a useless information system is as follows :

$\beta(a,s)$	a_1	a_2	$P(s\|a_1)$	$P(s\|a_2)$	$P(y\|s\&a)$, $a=a_1,a_2$	
					y_1	y_2
s_1	.2	1.0	.1	.2	.7	.2
s_2	0	.1	.9	.8	.3	.7

Then $E[\beta(a_1)] = .02 < .28 = E[\beta(a_2)]$ so that $a^o = a_2$ and $V(Y^o) = .28$. Furthermore, $E[\beta(a_1)|y_1] = .04118 < .43157 = E[\beta(a_2)|y_1]$ and $E[\beta(a_1)|y_2] = .01 < .18709 = E[\beta(a_2)|y_2]$ so that the Bayes strategy is $<a_2,a_2>$. Thus, the information system is useless. Calculation reveals that $V(Y^o) > V(Y)$ for all $P(a_1) > 0$.

(8)   The foregoing examples show that, within nonstandard decision theory, part of the primary theorem of the economic theory of information is false, i.e., $V(Y) \geqslant V(Y^o)$ for all Y is false. It remains to show that there are situations where the remainder of the theorem is false, i.e., where $V(Y^\infty) \geqslant V(Y)$ is also false. A perfect information system $Y = \{y_1, y_2\}$ is characterized by the reliability matrix $N = \begin{bmatrix} 1 & 0 \\ 0 & 1 \end{bmatrix}$. That is, a perfect system will signal y_1 only if s_1 is the true state, and will signal y_2 only if s_2 is the true state. The posterior probabilities of s_1 given y_1 and s_2 given s_2 are then each unity.

For the prisoners' dilemma game the perfect information system is a useless system. Due to dominance, given no information the player will select a_2, so that $a^o = a_2$. Also due to dominance, the Bayes strategy is $<a_1,a_2>$. For ease of exposition let $P(s_1|a_1) = P$ and let $P(s_1|a_2) = Q$. Then $V(Y^o) = Q + (1-Q) \cdot v$ and $V(Y^\infty) = P(y_1) + P(y_2) \cdot v$. Therefore, $V(Y^o) > V(Y^\infty)$ if and only if $Q > P(y_1)$. For a perfect system, $P(y_1) = P \cdot P(a_1) + Q \cdot P(a_2) = P(a_1) \cdot [P-Q] + Q$. Thus, $Q > P(y_1)$ if and only if $0 > P(a_1) \cdot [P-Q]$, i.e., if and only if $P < Q$. Hence, if $P(s_1|a_1) < P(s_1|a_2)$, then $V(Y^o) > V(Y^\infty)$.

For the scientist's game, the perfect information system is not a useless system. Presuming that $a^o = a_2$ (i.e., presuming that the play of the game is interesting), $V(Y^o) = Q{\cdot}v + (1-q){\cdot}u$. By calculation, $V(Y^\infty) = P(y_1) + P(y_2){\cdot}u$. As before, $P(y_1) = P(a_1){\cdot}[P-Q] + Q$ and $1-P(a_1) = P(a_2) = P(a_1){\cdot}[Q-P] + (1-Q)$.

Thus, $V(Y^\infty) = [P(a_1)(P-Q)+Q]{\cdot}1 + [P(a_1)(Q-P)+(1-Q)]{\cdot}u$
$= P(a_1)[(P-Q){\cdot}(1-u)] + Q + (1-Q)u$,

so that $V(Y^o) > V(Y^\infty)$ if and only if

$P(a_1)[(P-Q)(1-u)] + Q < Qv$, i.e., if and only if

$P(a_1)[(P-Q)(1-u)] < -Q + Qv = -Q(1-v) < 0$ since $v < 1$.

Therefore, $V(Y^o) > V(Y^\infty)$ if and only if $(P-Q)(1-y) < 0$, i.e., if and only if $P-Q < 0$. Hence, if $P(s_1|a_1) < P(s_1|a_2)$, then $V(Y^o) > V(Y^\infty)$.

Thus both the prisoners' dilemma game and the scientist's game lead to a falsification of $V(Y^\infty) \geqslant V(Y^o)$ under the simple condition that $P(s_1|a_1) < P(s_1|a_2)$. An interpretation of this condition for the prisoners' dilemma game is given in Dacey and Toelle (8), note 7.

REFERENCES

(1) ADAMS, C. and R. ROSENKRANTZ, "Applying the Jeffrey Decision Model to Rational Betting and Information Acquisition," *Theory and Decision,* 12, 1980, pp. 1–20.

(2) BALCH, M. and P. FISHBURN. "Subjective Expected Utility for Conditional Primitives," in M. Balch, D. McFadden and S. Wu (eds.), *Essays on Economic Behavior Under Uncertainty,* North-Holland Publishing Co., Amsterdam, 1974, pp. 57–69.

(3) BOLKER, E.J. "A Simultaneous Axiomatization of Utility and Subjective Probability," *Philosophy of Science,* 34, 1967, pp. 333–340.

(4) BRAMS, S.J. *Paradoxes of Politics,* The Free Press, New York, 1976.

(5) BRAMS, S.J., M.D. DAVIS and P.D. STAFFIN. "The Geometry of the Arms Race," *International Studies Quarterly,* 23, 1979, pp. 567–588.

(6) DACEY, R. "Detection, Inference and the Arms Race," in M. Bradie and K. Sayre (eds.), *Reason and Decision,* Applied Philosophy Program, Bowling Green, Ohio, 1982.

(7) DACEY, R. "An Interrogative Account of the Dialectical Inquiring System Based Upon the Economic Theory of Information," *Synthese,* 47, 1981, pp. 43–55.

(8) DACEY, R. and R. TOELLE. "Decision-Theoretic Resolutions of the Arms Race Game," presented at The 1982 meeting of the Institute for the Study of Conflict Theory and International Security, Champaign-Urbana, Illinois, September 22–24, 1982.

(9) ELLSBERG, D. "Risk, Ambiguity and the Savage Axioms," *Quarterly Journal of Economics,* 75, 1961, pp. 643–669.

(10)JEFFREY, R. *The Logic of Decision,* McGraw-Hill Book Co., New York, 1965.

(11)LEWIS, D., "Prisoners' Dilemma is a Newcomb Problem," *Philosophy and Public Affairs,* 8:3, Spring, 1979, pp. 235, 240.

(12)LUCE, R.D. and D.H. KRANTZ "Conditional Expected Utility," *Econometrica,* 39, 1971, pp. 253–271.

(13)MARSCHAK, J. "Economics of Information Systems," in M. Intriligator (ed.), *Frontiers of Quantitative Economics,* North-Holland Publishing Co., Amsterdam, 1977, pp. 32–107.

(14)MARSCHAK, J. "Information, Decision and the Scientist," in C. Cherry (ed.), *Pragmatic Aspects of Human Communication,* D. Reidel Publishing Co., Dordrecht, Holland, 1974.

(15)SHEPSLE, K. "Parties, Voters and the Risk Environment: A Mathematical Treatment of Electoral Competition Under Uncertainty," in R.G. Niemi and H.F. Weisberg (eds.), *probability Models of Collective Decision Making,* Charles E. Merrill Publishing Co., Columbus, Ohio, 1972, pp. 273–297.

APPENDIX
Prisoners' Dilemma Program, Simple Model

(This program was written by Richard Toelle, College of Business Administration, The University of Oklahoma, Norman, Oklahoma, 73019)

```
1000   REM   LIST OF VARIABLES
1010   REM
1020   REM
1030   REM
1040   REM   U                                    B(A1&S1)
1050   REM
1060   REM   V                                    B(A2&S2)
1070   REM
1080   REM   P   PRIOR PROBABILITY                PR(S1\A1)
1090   REM
1100   REM   Q   PRIOR PROBABILITY                PR(S1\A2)
1110   REM
1120   REM   R   RELIABILITY.                     PR(Y1\A1&S1)
1130   REM
1140   REM   S   RELIABILITY.                     PR(Y1\A1&S2)
1150   REM
1160   REM   T   RELIABILITY.                     PR(Y1\A2&S1)
1170   REM
1180   REM   W   RELIABILITY.                     PR(Y1\A2&S2)
1190   REM
1200   REM   A                                    PR(Y1\A1)
1210   REM
1220   REM   B                                    PR(Y2\A1)
1230   REM
1240   REM   C                                    PR(Y1\A2)
1250   REM
1260   REM   D                                    PR(Y2\A2)
1270   REM
1280   REM   E   POSTERIOR PROBABILITY            PR(S1\A1&Y1)
1290   REM
1300   REM   G   POSTERIOR PROBABILITY            PR(S1\A1&Y2)
1310   REM
1320   REM   S   POSTERIOR PROBABILITY            PR(S1\A2&Y1)
1330   REM
1340   REM   H   POSTERIOR PROBABILITY            PR(S1\A2& Y2)
```

```
1350   REM
1360   REM
1370   REM
1380   REM   M                              PR(A1)
1390   REM
1400   REM
1410   REM
1420   REM
1430
1440
1450   PRINT TAB(121);
1460   PRINT "CRITICAL"
1470   PRINT TAB(123);
1480   PRINT "RANGE"
1490   PRINT "STATUS     U     V     P   Q     ";
1500   PRINT "PR(Y1\A1&S1)   PR(Y1\A1&S2)   PR(Y1\A2&S1)     ";
1510   PRINT "Pr(Y1\A2&S2)         M";
1520   PRINT CR;
1530   FOR I = 1 TO 130
1540   PRINT " - ";
1550   NEXT I
1560   REM
1570   DIM FLAG$(1)
1580   DIM INED$(2)
1585   DIM INFIN$(1)
1590   REM
1600   FOR V = 0 TO 1 STEP .1
1610   FOR U = V TO 1 STEP .1
1620   REM
1630   REM
1640   FOR P = .1 TO .9 STEP .1
1650   FOR Q = .1 TO .9 STEP .1
1660   REM
1670   IF P*U >= Q + (1−Q)*V THEN 2170
1680   REM
1690   FOR T = .5 TO 1 STEP .1
1700   R = T
1710   FOR W = .1 TO .5 STEP .1
1720   S = W
1730   REM
1740   REM
```

```
1750   REM
1760   REM
1770   REM
1780   A = (P*R) + ((1–P)*S)
1790   B = (P*(1–R)) + ((1–P)*(1–S))
1800   C = (Q*T) + ((1–Q)* W)
1810   D = (Q*(1–T)) + ((1–Q)*(1–W))
1820   REM
1830   E = ((P*R))/A
1840   F = (P*(1–R))/B
1850   G = (Q*T)/C
1860   H = (Q*(1–T))/D
1870   REM
1880   If P > E THEN 2150
1890   IF P < F THEN 2150
1900   IF Q > G THEN 2150
1910   IF H > Q THEN 2150
1920   IF G + (1–G)*V > E*U THEN 3150
1930   IF H + (1–H)*V < F*U THEN 2150
1940   REM
1950   FLAG$ = "    "
1955   INFIN$ = "   "
1960   REM
1970   IF (–D*H –D*V + D*V*H – C*E*U +A*E*U+B*H +B*V
                                        –B*V*H)=0  THEN 2000
1980   M = (–D*H  –D*V +D*V*H–C*E*U+Q+V–V*Q)/(–D*H –D*V
              +D*V*H  –C*E*U  +A*E*U +B*H +B(V –B*V*H)
1990   GOTO 2020
2000   INFIN$ = "e"
2010   M = O
2020   K = (((M+1)*(A–C)+C)*E*U)+((M+1)*(B–D)+D)*(H+(1–H)*V)
2030   L = (((M–1)*(A–C)+C)*E*U)+((M–1)*(B–D)+D)*(H+(1–H)*V)
2035   IF (–D*H – D*V + D*V*H – C*E*U  +A*E*U  +B*H  +B*V
                    –B*V*H) = 0  AND K < Q+V–V*Q THEN FLAG$ = "*"
2038   IF INFIN$ = "e" THEN 2100
2040   REM
2050   IF M< 0 AND K < Q+V–V*Q THEN FLAG$ = "*"
2060   IF M > 1 AND L < Q +V–V*Q THEN FLAG$ = "*"
2070   IF M >= 0 AND M <= 1 AND K <Q+V–V*Q THEN FLAG$ = "*"
2080   IF K < Q+V–V*Q THEN INEQ$ = ">="
2090   IF L < Q+V–V*Q THEN INEQ$ = "<="
```

```
2100   IF FLAG$ = k" " THEN 2150
2110   REM
2120   PRINT USING "  'R   #.### #.###   #.### #.###", FLAG$,U,V,P,Q;
2130   PRINT USING "       #.###           #.###          #.###",R,S,T;
2130   PRINT USING "         #.###          'C##.###",W,INEQ$,M;
2140   PRINT INFIN$
2150   NEXT W
2160   NEXT T
2170   NEXT Q
2180   NEXT P
2190   NEXT U
2200   NEXT V
2210   END
```

ON THE LOGIC OF KEPLER'S EVOLVING MODELS

A. Phalet

1. A general characterisation of dynamic logic as an aspect of a logic of discovery

A logic of discovery should, as a logic, be a definition of a validity-preserving relation between propositions; in the case of a logic of deduction, a proof of a proposition P from axioms A conveys the validity of A, their truth say, to P, and establishes the relation just mentioned from A to P. In a general way, a logic considers closure conditions for classes of sentences, with respect to a validity-preserving relation, such that their complementary classes are not empty. For example, the complementary class of the class K of sentences, which is closed with respect to the consequence relation, is the class of sentences to which the value "false" is conferred by at least one interpretation that assigns the value "true" to the sentences of K. An interpretation I of a sentence or formula F is an assignment of meanings to symbols of F such that F is assigned a truthvalue. For example, there is an interpretation I_N of the formula $(x)(x' \neq O)$, called F_1, in the domain of natural numbers such that the interpreted formula, (I_N, F_1) is the proposition : "the number O has no immediate successor" (in the series of natural numbers), which is a true proposition.

Let T be a class of sentences and (I,T) a theory which is intended as a partial description of a physical system such as, for example, the solar system. Then I is an interpretation of the sentences of T in a domain or structure S, which is a representation by means of a mathematical structure, i.e. a model, of an aspect or part of the physical system concerned. In order to augment our knowledge of the physical system, i.e. of a specific domain of investigation or aspect of reality, the theory (I,T) has to be supplemented by propositions (I',F), which are not already derivable in the theory (I,T). Such a completion of the theory (I,T) results in a theory $(I+I', T \cup \{F\})$, where $I+I'$ is an interpretation of the sentences of $T \cup \{F\}$ in a structure S' of which S, the structure associated with the interpretation I of T, is a substructure. Thus, to a proper completion of a theory corresponds a proper extension of the structure to which the interpretation refers. Such an extended structure or model S' can, possibly, be a more adequate representation of the physical system under investigation than the structure or model S. So far only structural or mathematical truth-values which are assigned by an interpretation to sentences F have been considered. An empirically justifiable truthvalue is a (numerical) value which characterises, not a sentence F, but a proposition such as (I',F). As explained later on, it is assigned on the basis of verification by observation or measurement.

The proposition (I',F) is a proper completion of the theory (I,T) if (I+I', T∪{F}), is also a (mathematically) true theory and F is not a consequence of T. A logic of discovery does, of course, not consider a validity-preserving relation from axioms to theorems within the same theory. Let (I*,F*), where F* is not a consequence of T, be a true proposition with respect to the structure S*, and let F be a consequence of F*. Then the relation R_D exists from F* to F if there is an interpretation I', which assigns the value "true" to F with respect to a structure S' such that (I',F) is a true completion of the theory (I,T), i.e. (I',F)+(I,T) = (I+I',T∪{F}) = (I'',T'), where (I'',T') is true with respect to the extended structure S''. Consequently, the validity of F* is preserved throughout the transformation of I* into I' which is a subinterpretation of I+I' (= I'') or through the transformation of S* into S' which is a substructure of S''.

The fundamental problem, however, is not so much a specification of R_D as a formulation of the applicability conditions of the relation R_{DE}, which is thought of as preserving also empirical validity. The preservation of mathematical validity does not entail preservation of empirical validity; preservation of the latter, however, entails preservation of the first. The domain of application of R_{DE} ranges from the ascertainment of an event – the simplest case of discovery – where R_{DE} = I (dentity relation) and (I*,F*) = (I',F) = (I'',T'), to the complexity of the discovery of an empirically valid proposition, outside the theory, but able to be integrated in it with preservation of mathematical and empirical validity. The integration of an empirically valid proposition requires structural or interpretational transformations and brings about a transformation of the theory on the level of empirical content and validity. The conditions of this transformation, which are, a fortiori, also conditions of the integration of a proposition – which integration completes the discovery of a new truth, a law say – are the subject matter of that aspect of the logic of discovery, which, in the following paragraphs, is called dynamic logic. The reason why we start with dynamic logic in our attempt to investigate the formal structure of discovery, is that the history of sciences places at our disposition, as facts on which to base our attempt, aspects of such transformations of theories.

As a logical theory, dynamic logic is, essentially, a description of the conditions which define the applicability of a validity-preserving relation. This relation, R_{DL} say, defines a – possibly partial – order on the elements of classes of theories, $\{Tr_1, Tr_2, ...\}$, such that the sequence $(Tr_1, Tr_2, ...)$ approaches, in a sense determined by the definition of R_{DL}, a theory (or class of theories) the empirical validity of which is maximal. The relation R_{DL} preserves this maximal validity as the limit of the sequence of empirical validities — an infinity of possible "truthvalues" will be considered — to which corresponds the sequence of theories $(Tr_1, Tr_2, ...)$. Only theories Tr_i of a quantitative nature seem to provide the necessary means, viz. numerical values as the results of measuring or predictive calculation, to determine the said approximation. Hence, dynamic logic is a formal theory of the approximation of truth by mathematical means. This approximation is attempted in science by means of theories (M,R) which consist 1) of a description of a mathematical structure M wherein the parameters, considered explicitly in the theory, such as distinaces, orbits, etc., occur as mathematically definable entities, and 2) of a set R of relations, the theory's equations, and, possibly, of numbers — for example numbers n_i characterising masses m_i — which enable one to calculate, i.e. to predict, numerical values for some parameters when the values of others are determined by measurement.

A dynamic logic is itself, formally speaking, intended as an (M,R)-theory which attempts to achieve, not only mathematical, but also factually based objectivity, or objectivity referring to events, by means of quantification — of course, the more one endeavours to shield the logical system from unaccountable psychological or sociological interference, the more it approaches the status of an empirically independent, purely mathematical structure, if it approaches anything at all. Consequently, the elaboration of dynamic logic should be based on investigations of actual adjustments or structural alterations which bring about a change of the logical connections between the propositions of the theory involved and of their truthvalues, or of the truth-estimating systems themselves. Thus, the elaboration of this logic requires 1) a systematic representation of the events, such as adjustment or structural change, which occur in the domain of investigation which is the factual basis of dynamic logic, and 2) a systematisation of the effects of the said events on the level of the logical aspects of language, especially the factors that concern truth and consistency. The logical theory itself culminates in the formulation of the conditions of the approach of truth, which concern mathematical structures, the structures M of the theories involved, and measurable or computable parameters such as uncertainties or truthvalues. The structures which are supposed to belong to limiting theories, i.e. theories which are thought of as the limits of sequences $(Tr_1, Tr_2, ...)$ of theories, are the results of a validity preserving transformation of "non-standard" structures, such as, for example, the structure of infinitesimals, considered by Archimedes in his method by which he states to have discovered mathematical theorems[1]; in this case, the transition proceeds from the structure of infinitesimals to the mathematical structure defining integration. Consequently, a full account of dynamic logic requires the elaboration of the logic of mathematical discovery.

2. Adjustment or structural change considered as events brought about by the problem-solving activity of a knowledge-acquiring system

The events, adjustments or structural changes, are considered as decided and performed by a knowledge-acquiring system PS. The decision of PS to accept a proposition p — proposing a solution to a problem — as an element of the theory (M,R) about some aspect of the world, depends on the result of the measurement of the truthvalue of p and on the determination of the level of tolerance which represents the "scientific strength" of the theory (M,R). The truth-measuring, or rather truth-estimating function f_k, mapping sentences in the real interval [1,0] or in the set of subintervals of [1,0], and the level of tolerance, measured by a real number r, are liable to adjustment by a subsystem AS—to simplify the representation,empirical truthvalues are assigned to sentences F instead of propositions (I,F). The truth-estimating system to which f_k and r belong, can be closed or open. The openness of the system in question amounts to the circumstance that there are propositions p such that, if $f_k(p) = a$, the unknown correct truthvalue of p is an element of the interval [a+s,a−s],where s is the measure of the possible deviation of the truthvalue in either sense; measurement is, as a rule, only more or less accurate. A truth-estimating system is, so far, definable as a triple (f_k, s, r), where s is the parameter whose value determines the maximal deviation of the effectively computed result $f_k(p)$, and r the measure of the theory's strength. Actually, s is only really important in the neighborhood of r; for, if $f_k(p)$ (=a) is an element of the interval [a+s, a−s], and r is an element of [a+s,a−s[, then we cannot know whether p should be accepted, or tolerated, in the theory (M,R) or rejected. According to whether the truthvalue of a proposition p is either greater than or equal to r, $f_k(p) \geqslant r$, or smaller than r, $f_k(p) < r$, where $0 < r \leqslant 1$, p is either admitted or cannot be considered for admission in the theory; now if $a > 0$ and r is an element of [a+s,a−s[a decision on acceptance or rejection is impossible; it has to be suspended.

Let V be the set of sentences which are mathematically valid or true under an interpretation I in the structure S. Then the set of sentences E such that $f_k(p) \geqslant r+s$, where $p = (I,E)$,which are the propositions accepted in a theory Tr_k, is a subset of V. The quadruple (V,f_k,s,r) is the truth-estimating system of the theory Tr_k. Adjustment concerns either the parameters r or s, or the means of observation or measuring, represented by k; structural change concerns the structure S and hence V. When Tr_k is the theory (M,R) then S = M. The system

(V, f_k, s, r) determines the so-called empirical truthvalue.

Acquisition of knowledge aims at the reduction of uncertainty about a domain of investigation. A state of uncertainty $u \neq O$ of the knowledge-acquiring or problem-solving system PS is the expression of the non-functionality of a subsystem of PS. This non-functionality concerns the quantification procedures : 1) the same thing is measured twice under the same circumstances with different results, and 2) measurement, of a planet's velocity say, and predictive calculation of the same quantity yield different results. We are only interested in the uncertainty the reduction of which is the measurable correlate of the approach of truth.

The measure of the non-functionality of an equation or law, element of the class R of a theory (M,R), is, tentatively, defined as the least upper bound of all possible differences $|m_i - c_i|$, where the m_i are the results of the measuring procedure mp, applied to events e, at times t in order to measure the invariants, lengths say, q_i carried by aforesaid events, and the c_i are the results of predictive calculation, by means of equations of R, i.e. the c_i are the predicted quantities which measure at times t the magnitudes q_i carried by events e. For example, if the mean distance of Saturn from the sun is taken to be 1000, then Jupiter's mean distance from the sun is 572, according to Copernicus' measurements, whereas this same distance is 574, according to Kepler's equation : $r_1/r_2 = \dfrac{T_1}{(T_1 + T_2)/2}$, where r_i is the distance of planet P_i from the sun, and T_i its periodical time, i.e. the time needed to cover the whole length of the orbit of P_i.[2] The difference $|m - c| = |572 - 574|$, which is the relative error of 0,003 (= 2/572) or 0,3 %.

That a least upper bound, as defined above, exists, means that the possibility of error or deviation is bounded, i.e. the mathematical structure of the theory (M,R) by PS and the structure of the domain of investigation or physical system which PS proposes to represent by means of (M,R), are commensurable. The relation of commensurability between structures, a relation induced by a relation between results of measuring and computation, is a fundamental aspect of the approximation of truth, and has, consequently, to be clarified. According to Kepler's explicit formulation in *Mysterium Cosmographicum*, chapter XX, one approaches truth when the set of differences between the results of measuring, viz. m_i, and of calculation, viz. c_i, displays some regularity or structure. Thus, reduction of uncertainty means approach of truth by a definite or mathematically definable — at least in principle: the mathematical theory wherein the definition concerned should be formulated may not yet be disclosed — operation of adjustment of the structure of the model described by the theory (M,R). These operations are transformations which leave some definite characteristics of the structure concerned invariant, such as projection, homeomorphism, etc. In his letter of 11 october 1605 to Fabricius,[3] Kepler argues that the orbit of Mars is an ellipse — this was first published in *Astronomia Nova,* 1609.[4] He starts from the proposition that the orbit of Mars lies (nearly) in the midst between a circle C and an inscribed ellipse E such that the distance from the center O to a point of C, i.e. the length of OC, and the corresponding distance to a point of E, i.e. the length of OE, where OE is a segment of OC, are, respectively, too large and too small by (nearly) the same length. The circle and the ellipse, Kepler says, are figures of the same kind and the figure which is in the midst between them is, thus, an ellipse, i.e. their transformation, resulting in the orbit of Mars, has to be such that, for each pair of corresponding points (C,E), the distances (OC−OE)/2 are diminished proportionally, i.e. in the same proportion which is the — elliptical — invariant, mentioned above.

Since the components of the mathematical structure M of the theory (M,R) are abstract entities or relations whereas those of the domain investigated are physical events, the following problem arises: which is the foundation of the identity of the quantity which is calculated on the basis of a set of equations connected with a mathematical structure, and the quantity which is measured by applying measuring instruments to events of the physical domain of investigation ? How do we know that m_i and c_i are numbers to be attached to the same quantity ? What must be added to PS in order that PS is able to perform, if only approximately, the identification in question ? PS must be able to correlate the entities or relations of its mathematical structures M with a representation of the events of the physical domain of investigation on the one hand, and, on the other, the results of its measuring with the mathematical entities of its theory (M,R).

To begin with, PS has at its disposal a system of conceptual systems CS_i to which belong models M_j; they are liable to adjustments by AS — in the next paragraph a description of Kepler's models M_i will be attempted. The systems CS_i are devices which generate the meaningful propositions of PS. They are required to formulate the problems P, the problem conditions PC, and the hypotheses H. The systems CS_i supply, consequently, the conceptual means for stating a problem P, for specifying the conditions a possible solution H of P has to satisfy, and for proposing solutions of P. To a CS_i belongs a model M_i with respect to which a sentence generated in CS_i can, possibly, be given an interpretation. A special instance of such an M_i is the mathematical structure M of a theory (M,R) which is conceived by means of the system CS. It is this system CS which produces the definitions of the mathematical entities, the components of M.

Such mathematical entities are invariants with respect to sets of transformations or operations in a mathematical structure. For example, if we consider a system of Euclidean geometry, based on the notion of distance, the straight line segment AB is an invariant with respect to the replacement of d(A,B), the distance from A to B, by d(A,C)+d(C,B) for every point C on AB. If we prefer to leave numbers out of account – the distance d is a function mapping pairs of points into the set R of real numbers – we may choose a system based on the relation "the point Y is between the points A and B" [AYB]; this system is equivalent to the first and enables the determination of the straight segment as an invariant with respect to the order relation, mentioned above, as defined, for example, by Forder's axioms.[5] Mathematical entities such as lines, points, etc. can, in turn, carry invariants – of an higher order – such as length, or localise a velocity, the velocity of a flowing liquid in a point, represented by a vector $(\dot{x}_1, \dot{x}_2, \dot{x}_3)$. A length l is an invariant with respect to transformations of lines; all the lines defined by the differentiable functions $f(x) = y$ such that $\int_a^b \sqrt{1+\left(\frac{dy}{dx}\right)^2}\, dx = c = F(l)$, are transforms produced by the transformations that identify or constitute the invariant l.

Now, let us describe observation as the execution of a set of transformations in order to identify invariants carried by the events of a physical domain or system. The only condition the support which carries the observed entity, has to satisfy is that the transformations executed to identify the entity concerned leave the support undisturbed. An accurate measuring instrument is an observation device which realises that condition to a satisfactory extent – later on the same instrument may be considered as inaccurate. The application of an accurate measuring instrument to an event is expected to result into the localisation and identification of the mathematical entity which carries the invariant l, length say, which is mapped on an element of the set of real numbers. Consequently, a measuring instrument has 1) to execute the transformations that define the mathematical entity which carries the second order invariant or quantity l, and 2) to map this second order invariant on a real number.

3. Kepler's system and construction of models M_i

In the historically important chapter XX of *Mysterium Cosmographicum*, 1596, Kepler proposes, as a law, the statement that the velocity of a planet is inversely proportional to its distance from the sun, $y = c.1/x$. He adds that the same relation is known, in optics, to hold between the distance from a point, the source of light, and the intensity of the illumination of the object at the said distance from that point. Later on, in *Epitome Astronomiae Copernicanae*, 1618, although he knew the correct relation between distance and luminosity, viz. $y = c.1/x^2$, he states nevertheless that the same relation, viz. $y = c.1/x$, proved in optics, is accepted on the basis of analogy – per analogiam

– in astronomy, and is found to be in accordance with the empirical data in astronomy.

Kepler's source of optics were the *Opticae Libri Decem,* 1270, of Vitello[6], where the following proposition 22 is proved in the second book: the illumination of a body from a point is stronger than the illumination of a body which is farther off that point. In Vitello's optical model M_{op} there occur 1) physical entities, i.e. abstract or imaginative representations of physical events which are observed or supposed to exist in the domain of investigation, such as forces, substances, properties, etc., and 2) mathematical entities which are used in order to quantify the physical entities. Light is spread over a triangle, abg or aht, the area of which represents the quantity or "force" of light, radiating from a source of light, the point a. The force of light impresses the light in a body, the segment bg or ht. Note that Vitello considers the luminosity over a one-dimensional "body"; as a result the luminosity is inversely proportional to the distance, whereas, if the luminosity of a surface is considered, this luminosity is inversely proportional to the square of the distance. The force of

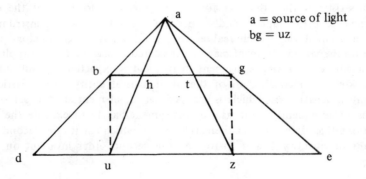

a = source of light
bg = uz

light produces the luminosity of the impression of light in the body and, therefore, the variation of the luminosity depends on the variation of the force. There is, however, in Vitello's model no mathematical entity the variation of which expresses the variation of the force of light, which is measured by the area of a triangle; the variation of the triangle cannot, however, represent the variation of the force. He cannot consider straight lines the lengths of which represent the distances from the point a to the bodies bg or uz; for, in a physical model, such a straight line must have a carrier, i.e. a physical support, viz. a ray of light. But, according to Vitello's theory of light, the force of light is constant over the whole length of the ray of light. This state of affairs compelled Vitello to consider the force of light on ht and the resulting luminosity on uz, i.e. he was forced to disconnect cause and effect. Kepler will endeavour to restore the connection by disconnecting the physical and the mathematical model in the following way. He distinguishes 1) a physical model M_1, 2) a model M_2 wherein the mathematical entities are related to each other by causal production relations, and 3) the mathematical model or structure M wherein the mathematical entities are related to each other by functional relations which replace the causal production relations of M_2.

A naive physical model M_1 — rather a physically intended imagery — assembles sometimes quite heterogeneous, possibly living or divine, things and forces into a machinelike imagery that is meant to reproduce the phenomena under investigation. In *Astronomia Nova*[7] Kepler considers, as elements of his model M_1, immaterial, magnetic fibres, flowing from the sun's "anima" which is something divine and which makes the sun rotate on its axis. Those immaterial fibres are outstretched to the planets and swing them around as the fibres themselves, linked to the sun, revolve with it. This model is meant as a physical device which executes an algorithm and produces in this way the representation in that model of the events observed in the domain of investigation. Note that Kepler, to ensure that his representation is a working device, i.e. that it is coherent, is compelled to suppose that the sun turns around its own axis. A few years later this supposition will be verified by observation.

In the second model M_2, the causal-mathematical model, the objects are mathematical entities: so far the model is homogeneous. But, the variations of some of the entities of the model "bring about" variations of other entities. This is the "heuristic" model on which the solutions of problems, such as the laws of astronomy, are planned. M_2 is the solution Kepler proposed to solve Vitello's problem, as explained above: either cause and effect are disconnected or the variation of a mathematical entity — strictly speaking, of a second-order entity carried by a first-order mathematical entity or transform — produces a variation of a physical event, viz. illumination, which is the impression caused by the force of light: "virtus imprimens lumen in corpus". For Kepler, however, force of light is the same as luminosity or density of light rays — *Paralipomena ad Vitellionem, I, propositio IX*, 1604 — and the density, the number of rays divided by the illuminated area, depends on the distance from the point a, the source of light (figure 1) — *propositio IV*.

The transfer of the relation of inverse proportionality from the optical model to the astronomical model required an implementation of that aspect of the astronomical model, which is represented by the model M_1. At the time when *Mysterium Cosmographicum* was written this model consisted of sun and planets without the connecting immaterial magnetic fibres. They were added to the model in *Astronomia Nova,* 1609, under the influence of W. Gilberts' *De Magnete magnetisque corporibus et de magno magnete Tellure Physiologia* *nova,* 1600. In his letter of 3 October 1595 to M. Mästlin,[8] he writes that motion is to the sun what creation is to God. As the creation of God, the planetary system is a representation of (the structure of) the Holy Trinity: Father — sun, Son — fixed stars, creation — motion (mediated by) the Holy Spirit — the ether (aethra), wherein the planets move. The implementation proceeds in such a way that it results in isomorphy between a substructure of M^*, the divine or the optical model, and a substructure of the implemented model M_1. The relation between source of light, rays of light and illuminated body- is transferred to sun, magnetic fibres, moved planets. Rays and fibres carry straight lines as mathematical entities, whose lengths are the distances to be measured — the straight lines are localised in the domain of investigation by means of the representation of events in the model M_1, and identified and measured by measuring instruments. The variation of the length of a straight line carried by a ray or fibre is, however, not the expression of a variation of a physical characteristic of the physical support: the force of light or moving force is the same in every point of ray or fibre. This variation has only mathematical existence.

In his causal-mathematical model M_2, the difference r_2-r_1 between the mean distances r_2, r_1 of the planets P_2, P_1 from the sun, brings about 1) an augmentation of the time of revolution due to the greater length of the orbit of the planet P_2, and 2) an augmentation of the time of revolution due to the smaller mean velocity of P_2, such that both augmentations are equal, i.e.

$\frac{2\pi(r_2-r_1)}{v_2} = (2\ \pi\ r_2/v_2) - (2\ \pi\ r_2/v_1)$, where v_i is the mean velocity of planet

P_i. From this it follows that $v_1/v_2 = r_2/r_1$, i.e. the mean velocity v is inversely proportional to the mean distance r. Since Kepler did not have at his disposition the notion of velocity in a point — the velocity of the planet varies, actually, from point to point on the orbit — he used the notion of periodical time T, which is the time needed by a planet to complete a revolution round the sun. He should have obtained the formula $r_1/r_2 = \sqrt{T_1/T_2}$, which is equivalent to $v_1/v_2 = r_2/r_1$. He proposed, however, the formula $r_1/r_2 = \frac{T_1}{(t_1+T_2)/2}$. (see par. 2). These formulas express functional relations and are, consequently, connected with the third, mathematical model M; the formulas belong to the set of equations R of the theory (M,R).

Kepler's incorrect formulation of the inverse proportionality by means of the periodical time, seems to result from an erroneous representation of the mean velocity of P_2 — in the model M_2 this representation, which has to take the time variable t into account, is left to the imagination. His formula is derivable from the assumption that the mean velocity of P_2 over $2\ \pi\ (r_2-r_1)$, the difference between the greater orbit of P_2 and the orbit of P_1, is v_1, which is, however, the mean velocity of P_1 : from $\dfrac{2 \pi (r_2-r_1)}{v_2} = ((2 \pi r_1)/v_2) -$ $((2 \pi r_1)/v_1)$ the formula of Kepler, viz. $r_1/r_2 = \dfrac{T_1}{(T_2+T_1)/2}$, can be derived.

The risky appeal to imaginative representation, which seems to be responsible for Kepler's mistake, can be avoided either 1) by supplying the deficiency of the model M_2, viz. by the addition to the components of M_2 of the instantaneous velocities — since the class of these velocities in M_2 is infinite a fundamental problem of model construction appears to be the conception of an infinite variation, an infinite collection of transforms, as a mathematical invariant — or 2) by the consideration of the fictitious model M'_2: the mean velocity v_i of planet P_i is a fiction with respect to the model M_2, which represents the orbit as an eccentric circle, i.e. the sun is not in the center of the circle representing the orbit, or, later as an ellipse; mean distance and mean velocity require, besides the genuine models M_2, M, the auxiliary constructions or fictitious models M'_2 and M', wherein the correct formula $r_1/r_2 = \sqrt{T_1/T_2}$, as the expression of inverse proportionality, is derivable as shown above.

The completion of the model of type M_2 seems to proceed as follows. In the first stage, the variation of an element of the physical model M_1 is represented as dependent on the variation of a mathematical entity, occurring in M_2. In a second phase, the original varying element of M_1, luminosity or velocity, is also represented by a mathematical invariant in M_2; for example, velocity is represented as a vector. Between the first and second stage, auxiliary constructions may occur: the infinite variation which ranges over an interval I is "approached" by a finite variation $v_1,...,v_n$, where v_i is a mean value for the subinterval I_i of I. Finally, the variation of the mathematical representation of the physical event under investigation, is represented as an invariant, for example, uniform acceleration. Consequently, model completion in M_2 proceeds according to the laws of mathematical objectivation, viz. the determination of invariants with respect to a set of transformations. The objectivation of change or variation consists in the determination of a class of transforms, i.e. a class which is closed with respect to a defining set of transformations, as explained in par. 2. To the process of objectivation must correspond, in M_2, and a fortiori, in M, a procedure of quantification: a function F(f, —), mapping the new entities, the classes of transforms, in the real numbers, defined from f, the function mapping the transforms in the same set of numbers, where the primitive transforms, primitive with respect to quantification, are lengths.

Kepler's model, as explained in the following section, did not reach the third stage, viz. the determination of the invariant in the case of infinite variation of distance and velocity.

4. The preservation of empirical validity

In par. 1 it has been said that a logic defines a relation, called a validity-preserving relation, such that, if a class of sentences is closed with respect to this relation, its complementary class is not empty. Let K be such a class, closed with respect to a validity-rpeserving relation R, and CK the complement of K, with respect to the class of all sentences. That a sentence p is provable means that the addition of p to K does not result into the emptiness of the complementary class $C(K \cup \{p\})$. A proof is either direct or indirect. In the first case a proof establishes the existence of the relation R from p_A, an element of the class K, to a sentence p: a direct proof is a validity-preserving procedure which realises a transition from p_A to p. An indirect proof, i.e. a demonstration by reductio ad absurdum, establishes the appartenance of p (= not q) to the class K by making explicit a procedure which realises a validity-preserving transition from q, possibly together with p_A, to an arbitrary sentence, which means that the addition of q to K would result into an empty complementary class.

The possibility of a logic of discovery now amounts to the affirmation of the possibility of establishing the existence of a validity preserving relation by means of a finite procedure which realises a transition from the first to the second argument of the relation concerned. Let us represent that relation by means of the schema $F^* \frac{T}{T'}$, where F^* is a sentence, and T, T' are theories — on the syntactical level, a theory is considered as a class of sentences; the same notation is used as in paragraph 1. Moreover, let (V, f_k, s, r) and $(V', f_{k'}, s', r')$ be the truth-estimating systems associated with, respectively, T and T', as explained in 2, and let F be a consequence of F^*, but not a consequence of a sentence belonging to T. Then the empirical validity-preserving relation R_D from F^* to F, $R_D(F^*, F)$, holds, if 1) $V \subset V'$, 2) $F \in V'$, i.e. F has an interpretation, I'', in the structure S'' with respect to which the elements of V' all have a mathematically true interpretation, 3) $f_{k'}(F) \geq r'$, i.e. F is acceptable in T' as empirically true, 4) $r \leq r'$, and 5) $s \geq s'$. The conditions 1), 4) and 5) are sufficient for the relation R_{DL}, a validity-preserving relation between theories (cf. par. 1), to hold between T and T' in that order; the existence of R_{DL} is a necessary condition of the existence of R_D in the schema $F^*/\frac{T}{T'}$. The conditions 1)–5) are only a specification of the most simple case of the existence of an empirical validity-preserving relation R_D : if 1)–5) hold, then $F^* \frac{T}{T'}$ holds, which entails the discovery of F as an acceptable empirical truth of the theory T'. Actually, the definition of R_D must be based on the specification of the class of procedures which realise effectively the validity-preserving transitions from F^* to F and from T to T', i.e. on the class of so-called proofs.

In the situation described by $F^*/\frac{T}{T'}$, viz. the validity of F^* is transferred to F the addition of which to T results in a richer or more accurate theory T', the acceptance of F as empirically true in T' depends on the existence of R_{DL} from T to T'. This relation depends, in turn, on the insertion of the mathematical structure S' and interpretation I', which makes F mathematically true, or realises F, in S', in the structure S and interpretation I for which the sentences of V in (V, f_k, s, r) are mathematically true: there must exist a procedure to combine S' and S (I' and I) into S" (I"), the mathematical structure (interpretation) associated with T". Let us represent such a procedure by the symbol Pr_i, i.e. $Pr_i: (S', S) \rightarrow S$", and the corresponding procedure for interpretations as IPr_i, i.e. $IPr_i: (I', I) \rightarrow I$".

Let DPr_i ($IDPr_i$) represent a procedure which transforms the structure S* (interpretation I*) associated with F* into S' (I'). Now, the problem of discovery consists in the determination of a pair $(Pr_i(IPr_i), DPr_i(IDPr_j))$ such that $F^*/\frac{T}{}$ holds; for the time being, the schema is supposed to hold when the conditions 1)–5) above are satisfied.

The simplest DPr-procedure is DPr_1, where $DPr_1(S) = S'$ if S and S' are isomporhic. The simplest Pr-procedure is Pr_1, where $Pr_1(S', S) = S$" if S' and S are substructures of S"; $(D, R_1, ..., R_m)$ is a substructure of $(D', R'_1, ..., R'_n)$ if $m \leq n$, $D \subseteq D'$, $R_i \subseteq R'_i$ for $1 \leq i \leq m$.

Next we consider Pr_2, where $Pr_2(S', S) = S$" if S' and S are substructures of S", making exceptions of some elements of the domain D of S, which have in S" to be replaced by elements of the domain D' of S', which are themselves structures; for example, a primitive object, element of the domain D of S, is replaced in the domain D" of S", by a space which is an element of the domain of S'.

The procedure which establishes $F^*/\frac{T}{}$ is a direct procedure – or a direct "proof" – if a pair (Pr_i, DPr_j), where i = 1,2 and j = 1, is found and if F* is empirically true, i.e. is acceptable as empirically true in some theory T*. For, if these conditions are satisfied, the mathematical representation of events in the structure S*, associated with F*, is such that computation or measurement are guaranteed, at least in principle: their measurement is conceivable if not materially realisable, as far as the representation of the events by the substructure of S", which corresponds to S' and S* – both are supposed to be isomorphic – is concerned. Moreover, S* is thought to be commensurable with the structure of the domain of investigation of the theory T*. As explained in par. 2, the supposition of this so-called commensurability is based on the existence of a least upper bound of errors or deviations, which is a measure of bounded non-functionality or bounded uncertainty on which, also, the assignment of empirical truthvalue is based. The transfer of the commensurability of S*, and, consequently, of the empirical truthvalue of F* to, respectively, S' as a substructure of S", and F' as an element of the theory T", is based on the

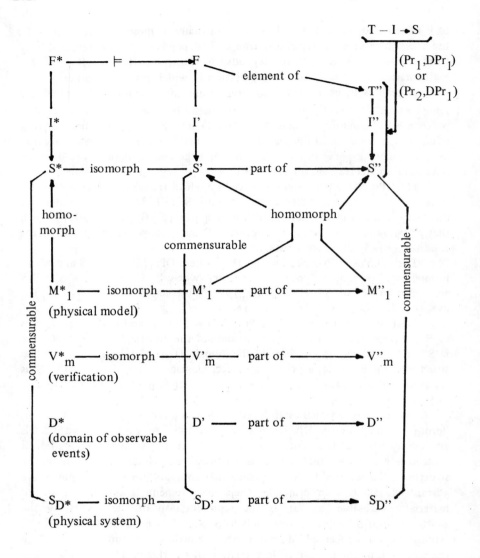

isomorphism of the physical models of type M_1, M^*_1 and M'_1, associated respectively with F^* and $F - M'_1$ is a part of M''_1, the physical model associated with T". As explained, the components of a model of type M_1 are the supports or carriers of the mathematical entities of the mathematical model of type M, which are, in turn, the carriers of measurable quantities. This results in the existence of a homomorphism from a model of type M_1 into the corresponding model of type M, i.e. from M^*_1 into S^*, etc. Then the set V^*_m of measurements in D^* according to the representation in M^*_1 of the observable or measurable part of the physical system S_{D^*} is isomorphic with the set V'_m of measurements, which is a subset of V''_m, the set of measurements in D'' according to the M''_1.

Consequently, the conditions which determine in the system $(F^*,I^*, S^*,M^*_1,V^*_m,D^*,S_{D^*})$ 1) the mathematical validity, 2) empirical truthvalue of F^*, 3) the commensurability, i.e. the adequacy of the mathematical model S^* with the exception of the application of a definite set, possibly a structure, for example a group, of transformations, to the structure S^*, 4) the structure of the set V^*_m of verifications by measurement, are transferred to the subsystem $(F,I',S',M'_1,V'_m,D',S_{D'})$ of $(T'',I'',S'',M''_1,V''_m,D'',S_{D''})$ such that the corresponding results 1)–4) are determined for the first, and conditions 1)–5) are realised with respect to the truth-estimating system (V'',f_k'',s'',r'') of the second system.

The indirect procedure is applied when F^* has not been assigned an empirical truthvalue. Actually, the indirect discovery is the most fundamental procedure, since it realises a transition from mathematical validity to empirical validity. The indirect method proceeds as follows: 1) completion of M_1 by M'_1 which is isomorphic with M^*_1, so that M''_1 is obtained, 2) consideration as starting point of the (false) supposition q, where $q \models$ not F, where $F^* \models F$, i.e. not F is a consequence of q and F of F^*, 3) application of a finite set V_m of verifying measurements to q and to F, 4) if conditions 1)–5) are satisfied with respect to (V'',f_k'',s'',r''), then F is accepted, and a fortiori discovered, as an empirical truth.

5. Kepler's procedures of discovery and dynamic logic.

As explained in par. 3, Kepler realised the transfer of the relation of inverse proportionality from optics to astronomy by a completion of his physical, astronomical model of type M_1; as a result, his new physical model, $M_1(As)$, was isomorphic with the model in optics, $M_1(Op)$. However, neither luminosity nor (instantaneous) velocity were represented in $M_1(Op)$ or $M_1(As)$ as supports of mathematical entities which should themselves be the carriers of measurable quantities or second-order mathematical entities. As a consequence the relation of inverse proportionality could not be assigned an empirical truthvalue, neither in optics nor, to begin with, in Kepler's astronomy. His method of discovery had to be indirect.

Let F(ip) represent the formula expressing the relation of inverse proportionality. In chapter XX of *Mysterium Cosmographicum*, Kepler considers, to begin with, the (false) supposition F(s) that the velocity of the planets is the same on each orbit. The negation of F(ip) is a consequence of this supposition: $F(s) \models$ not $F(ip)$.

The great advantage of the indirect procedure is the freedom of choice of the false supposition which is only restricted by the condition that it has to entail the negation of the genuine proposal, $F(ip)$. This freedom enables the proposal of a formula with an interpretation in a quantifiable model, i.e. a model wherein the entities concerned represent measurable events of the domain of investigation. Kepler's choice of $F(s)$ is such that measurement becomes possible and empirical truthvalues can be assigned, since $F(s)$ states that, whatever the mean distance from the planet to the sun, the mean velocity of each planet is the same. The consideration of the instantaneous velocity requires that an infinity of distances, each with the corresponding instantaneous velocity, is taken into account. $F(s)$ reduces this infinity to five mean distances and, at the most, five mean velocities. $F(s)$ is confronted with a consequence $F'(ip)$ of $F(ip)$, viz. the mean distance is inversely proportional to the mean velocity of each planet. $F'(ip)$ is represented, incorrectly as explained in par. 3, by the formula $r_1/r_2 = \dfrac{T_1}{(T_1 + T_2)/2}$. The errors or differences $|m - c|$ between measurement and predictive calculations according 1) to $F(s)$ as expressed by the formula $r_1/r_2 = T_1/T_2$, are a) 169, an error of 29,5 % , in the case of Jupiter, b) 131, an error of 45,2 % , for Mars, c) 126, or 19,1 % for Earth, d) 104, or 14,5 % for Venus, and e) 108, or 21,6 % for Mercury; and according 2) to $F'(ip)$: 2, or 0,35 % for Jupiter, b) 16, or 5,5 % for Mars, c) 36, or 5,5 % for Earth, d) 43, or 6 % for Venus, e) 4, or 0,7 % for Mercury.[9]

A reduction of the differences $|m - c|$, which measure non-functionality or uncertainty, is an approach of truth if the set of all possible differences has a least upper bound; this condition is significant if the set is infinite — in this case the elements of the set can be arranged in a monotonic, non-decreasing sequence of which there exists a unique limit, a number assigned to a quantity, supported by a mathematical entity which has to be produced by a definite set of, generally, continuous transformations, to be applied to components of the mathematical model of type M in order to adjust this structure, e.g. from circle to ellipse. The condition is less significant, to say the least, when the set of differences is finite. For adjusting transformations are no longer directed to the realisation of a structure the components of which carry quantities measured by numbers which are determined by means of or as limits of sequences, since these numbers are now only mean values. Mean values of what ? Of the distances in a circle, or an oval or an ellipse, or a triangle ? Now, Kepler considered the following construction: the five solids fit between the spheres of the planets: the cube between Saturn and Jupiter, the tetrahedron between Jupiter and Mars; the dodecahedron between Mars and Earth, the icosahedron between Earth and Venus, and the octahedron between Venus and Mercury[10]. The mean distances, on the other hand, are determined in the following way: $r_1 = (r_1/r_2) \times 1000$, where r_2 is the mean distance of the planet whose sphere circumscribes a solid, and r_1 the mean distance of the planet the sphere of which is circumscribed by that same solid; for example, if r_1 is the mean distance of Jupiter from the sun, then r_2 is the mean distance of Saturn, and, where $r_2 = 1000$, $r_1 = 574$, according to his formula F'(ip), and, according to (Copernicus') measurement, $r_1 = 572$; the difference $|m - c|$ is 2. According to Kepler the set of the five differences has a significant structure: the smallest differences, 2 and 4, concern the mean distances of the planets Jupiter and Mercury, whose spheres are inscribed within, respectively, the cube and the octahedron, two similar figures, viz. if the radius of their circumscribed sphere is 1, then the radius of their inscribed sphere is $(1/3)\sqrt{3}$; the greatest differences, 36 and 43, correspond in the same way to the similar solids dodecahedron and icosahedron, where the radii are as 1 to $(1/15) \sqrt{15(5+2\sqrt{5})}$ — the numbers given by Kepler are less exact, but show the same similarity. Moreover, to the greatest differences between the radii correspond the smallest differences $|m - c|$ and to the smallest, the greatest differences $|m - c|$. Kepler endeavours to insert his mathematical model of the planetary system into a — fictive — construction consisting of the five solids, and to show the commensurability of quantitities of the first with corresponding quantities of the second, viz. of the length of radii, which determine the distances considered. As already noted, to adjust mean values in order to obtain correct mean values does not direct the adjusting construction, to be applied to the erroneous model, towards a unique solution. Therefore the problem of the correct form of the planets' orbits could only be solved in the second phase of model completion (cf. par. 3) — the consideration of mean values has been characterised as an auxiliary construction which reduces an infinite variation to a finite variation, viz. a finite set of mean values. In the second phase the variations which are infinite in number are shown to be the transforms of an invariant. Historically Kepler's so-called first law that the planets' orbits are ellipses came after his — correct — so-called second law, actually the first, about the relation between distance from the sun and velocity. The correct formulation of this relation in the so-called area law runs as follows: the ratio between the times a planet needs to cover equal segments of the (circular) orbit is the same as the ratio between the areas, ADS and SCD, formed by the respective segments or arcs and the radii that join the two endpoints to each arc with the point S, the sun.[11]

The problem of infinite variation of the distances arose from the sun's position, which did not coincide with the center of the circular orbit. The first method Kepler proposes is, again, a reduction of the infinite variation to a finite variation: the orbit is divided into segments of 1° and with each such segment he associates one radius.[12] This method amounts to the consideration of 360 mean

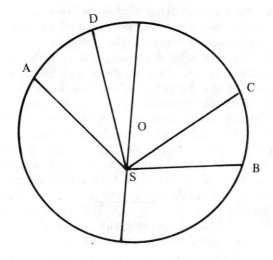

values for distance and velocity for one orbit. Kepler discarded this method as unsatisfactory; it was, as he put it, mechanical and tedious. He intended to verify, by means of this method, that the ratio between the times a planet needs to cover equal segments of the eccentric (circular orbit) is the same as the ratio between the distances of the respective segments from the sun. Thus, if the equal segments AD and BC are, for example, 20° the ratio between two sums of the lengths of 20 radii, viz. the length of SA + ..., and the length of SB + ..., has to be considered. This method lead nowhere in the following sense: a refinement of the method approaches an infinite sum of lengths of (an infinite number of) radii; such an infinite sum, however, is not something definite, i.e. refinement of the "mechanical" method does not direct the adjustment towards a definite mathematical entity. Only the mathematical approximation of a limit can direct the adjusting transformation of a structure to another, corrected, structure. His second method was based on the consideration of infinitesimals: the radii from S to the points — actually infinitely small arcs — of the arc AD fill up the area SAD, said Kepler; and therefore it seems to me, he said, that if one should compute the surface of SAD, he would obtain the sum of the infinite number of radii from S to AD.[13] This transfer of the relation of inverse proportionality to a non-standard model, wherein the class of definite entities is closed with respect to infinite summation, in order to solve the problem of infinite variation, resulted into the formulation of the correct second area law. Consequently, this law was discovered in a non-standard mathematical model. Since the arguments of the relation, viz. the times needed to cover the segments

AD or BC and the areas ADS and BCS, were classical, mathematical entities, the relation could be transferred to the classical mathematical model of the planetary system. The assignment of an empirical truthvalue to the law required, in principle — the areas considered were not easily calculable without the aid of integration calculus — the transfer of infinite summation to the standard structures, wherein the entities are definable as invariants with respect to sets of transformations in such a way that identification and assignment of real numbers to the mathematical entities carried by the events of the domain of investigation, by measuring instruments, are possible.

NOTES

(1) *The Works of Archimedes with the Method of Archimedes,* T.L. Heath, editor, Dover Publ., New York, pp. 13—14.

(2) J. Kepler, *Gesammelte Werke I, Mysterium Cosmographicum,* M. Caspar, editor, München, 1938, p. 71.

(3) *G.W.,* IX, ed. M. Caspar, München, 1951, p. 247.

(4) *G.W.,* III, ed. M. Caspar, München, 1937, chapter 59 : "Demonstration, quod orbita Martis ... fiat perfecta ellipsis..."

(5) *The Foundations of Euclidean Geometry,* (1927), Dover Publ, New York, 1958, p. 42 ff.

(6) ed. F. Risnerus, 1557, pp. 69—70.

(7) Chapters XXXIII and XXXIV.

(8) *G.W.,* XIII, ed. M. Caspar, München, 1945, p. 35.

(9) *G.W.,* III, p. 73.

(10) *G.W.,* I, Tabellae III et IV.

(11) *G.W.,* III, p. 265.

(12) op. cit., p. 263.

(13) op. cit., p. 264.

A CONNECTION BETWEEN MODAL LOGIC AND THE LOGIC OF DIALOGUES IN A PROBLEM—SOLVING COMMUNITY

Jean Paul Van Bendegem
Senior Research Assistant NFWO
Rijksuniversiteit Gent

I

Suppose you have to solve a problem and a solution is not in sight. Surely, one of the following strategies will come to your mind (as a matter of fact, mathematicians are trained to do so) :

(1)   do I know a related problem such that a solution to that problem implies a solution to the original problem
(2)   could it be that the problem considered in its entirety is too complex. Can I split it up in parts such that each of the parts is (perhaps) easier to solve (and such that the conjunction of all the partial problems is equivalent to the original problem)
(3)   do I know another method for handling the problem.

Of course, all this is hardly new. After all, George Polya spend a great deal of his life convincing his audience that these strategies are worthwhile and important as ingredients for a logic (or heuristic) of discovery. But what I do believe is that an important element of those strategies has been overlooked (or at least not stressed often enough) : *problem-sharing.* Suppose you have a community of problem-solvers. According to the first strategy, if, e.g., n different but equivalent formulations of the problem have been found, each problem-solver may focus his attention on one of them. In short, the different problems can be distributed over the community. In the case of (2), each member of the community may select a subpart of the original problem and in the last case, trivially, each one of them may select a different method. It then follows that, if a problem has been distributed over a community, then it becomes necessary to establish some kind of communication channel between the members. Hence, dialogues of some kind will take place in the network to regulate the problem-solving process. What do these dialogues look like ? That is the question this paper tries to answer.

Note : in other papers[1], I have tried to show that assuming certain complexity considerations, a community of problem-solvers is always making a "profit" by distributing a problem. This implies that there is a certain degree of necessity to distribute problems. But once a distribution takes place, dialogues become necessary. Hence, if we want to control complexity, dialogues are necessary and thus, dialogue logic is of prime importance. A conclusion of this kind supports the thesis that no matter what your ideas or beliefs are about the nature of logic, any logic will have to deal with the logic of dialogues.

II

Let us imagine a problem-solving community C. Each member c is busy solving problems. If some c suceeeds in solving a problem p, he will send round a message informing his colleagues of this fact (at least, those he can reach). This message will say: "I have solved p". Let us abbreviate this sentence by :

(4) $$\Box p$$

The use of this notation will become clear in the sequel of this paper. The question of this paper can be reformulated in terms of the elementary message (4) : what kind of dialogues involving sentences like (4) are possible and what are the underlying rules for conducting such dialogues ? To guide our ideas, let us return briefly to the strategies mentioned. What does (1) state ? Suppose c wants to solve q. He does not succeed. He looks around at his fellow problem solvers to see if anybody has found an equivalent problem, say, p. Suppose further that c' has been able to show that $p \supset q$. If he has actually solved that problem, he informs c that

(5) $$\Box (p \supset q)$$

c now knows that if anybody, including himself, succeeds in solving p, the original problem is solved as well. The rule that is at work here, can be summarized thus :

(6) $$(\Box p \ \& \ \Box(p \supset q)) \supset \Box q$$

What does (2) state ? Suppose it has been shown by some member that

(7) $$p \equiv p_1 \,\&\, p_2$$

Then if two members each solve one part – i.e. they announce that $\Box p_1$ and $\Box p_2$ – then the original problem may be considered solved. The rule in this case, is :

(8) $$(\Box p_1 \,\&\, \Box p_2) \equiv \Box p \quad \text{, given (7)}$$

The third strategy is of a quite different nature and will be the subject of part III.

Up to now, I have discussed connections between statements that are of the form "I have solved p". But we also need some kind of relation between problems being solved and the problems themselves. It seems quite reasonable to suppose that (9) should hold :

(9) $$\Box p \supset p$$

What (9) says, is that if p has been solved by someone, then p should be added on the list of results. In other words, since it has been shown that p can be solved, we may safely assume p.

Anybody familiar with modal logic,[2] will have noticed that (6) and (9) are precisely the two modal axioms of the system T. But in order to have T itself, we still need the rule of necessitation :

(10) $$\text{if} \vdash p \text{ then } \vdash \Box p$$

But surely this is acceptable. If p is a theorem, then every problem-solver will accept p. Hence p may be considered solved, thus $\vdash \Box p$. Or, to put it differently, since p is a theorem, there is a proof of p. Such a proof does count as a solution to the problem p.

Therefore, we have T. (8) is derivable in T, so no extra assumption is needed. But T is a rather weak modal system and it is quite natural to wonder if perhaps one of the stronger systems, S4 and S5, is acceptable. In fact, it is easy to see that S5 will do the job. The additional axiom is :

(11) $$\Diamond p \supset \Box \Diamond p$$

The interpretation of this sentence requires that the interpretation of $\Diamond p$ should be stipulated. Given the definition that

(12) $$\Diamond p =_{df} {\sim}\Box{\sim}p$$

◇p will mean that "p is solvable", i.e. it is not permitted to accept ~p as being solved.

The axiom says that if it is solvable that p then it has been solved that p is solvable. This is hardly surprising as one would expect that iterated boxes and diamonds should collapse to a single box or diamond. If, e.g., p has been solved then obvious it has been solved that p has been solved.

So far what has been said, is not strikingly novel. After all, most logicians and philosophers are familiar with the provability interpretation of the box.[3] And one would expect that "p has been solved" and "p is provable" should share many, if not all properties. But from a semantical point of view, the matter is quite different. A standard model for S5 consists of a set W of worlds and a relation $R \subset W \times W$, the accessibility relation. In terms of the interpretation presented here, W is replaced by C, the community of problem-solvers and R tells us what communication channels exist between problem-solvers. The semantical clauses can be interpreted in problem-solving terms in a straightforward way. As an example, I take the clause for □p :

(13)   c ⊨ □p iff for all c' such that Rcc', c' ⊨ p

If c has solved p, than he sends a message to all his colleagues he can reach and they all add p to the list of accepted results. Conversely, if all problem-solvers in contact with c (including c himself, of course) have p as an accepted result, then it must be because p has been solved.

S5 is a very nice logic : its semantics is quite simple, decidable and intuitively extremely pleasing. This decision method can be easily adapted to a dialogue situation as the following example shows :

consider the following inference

(14)   □p, □(p ⊃ q) ⊢ □q

It is well-known that for S5, R has to be an equivalence relation. Let us assume for simplicity that the model has three elements :

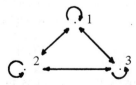

Suppose 1 claims □p, and 2 claims □(p ⊃ q), but 3 denies □q, hence he assumes ~ □q. The following dialogue (which is a direct transcription of the tableaux method) will take place[4]. I have been somewhat elaborate in phrasing the dialogue, for the sole purpose of a real-life imitation.

1 : Since I have solved p, I must inform my colleagues that they must add p to their list. I will do the same.

2 : I accept p.

3 : I accept p too.

2 : But I have solved p ⊃ q. Hence you should add p ⊃ q to your list. I will do the same.

1 : I accept p ⊃ q.

3 : I accept p ⊃ q. However I have shown that ~q is solvable. Hence one of you has to accept ~q.

1 : I will do that. But that is impossible ! I have already accepted p and p ⊃ q, hence I must accept q, but now you ask me to accept ~ q. Sorry, I cannot do that.

In answer to the question of this paper, we can now state that the dialogues of a problem-solving community correspond to the semantical S5-tableaux. Although this is a nice result, it may not seem very impressive. But this way of looking at the S5-semantics opens up a rather intriguing line of research. The problem-solving community corresponding to the S5 rules is really *a perfect community* : every member is in touch with every other member. What would happen if we changed the structure of the community. If the structure ceases to be perfect, we will lose some theorems. Which ones ? In other words, the question I am asking now, is this : start out with a particular problem-solving community C. Stipulate a communication relation R over C. What is the problem-solving capacity of this community. We already know that S5 is the strongest system around (unless we want a collapse into PC). This corresponds nicely to the fact that the associated community C is indeed perfect. Let me present three examples to show what the idea is worth :

example 1 : suppose we have a highly centralized structure

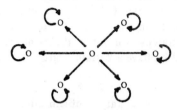

R is such that for all c, Rcc and there is a special c, such that for all c', Rcc'. R is by definition reflexive, it is trivially transitive, but it is not symmetric. We

must lose something in comparison with S5. As a matter of fact, in this structure the following inference is not valid :

(15) $\qquad\qquad\qquad\qquad \Diamond\Box p \vdash \Box p$

Suppose c in the center claims $\Diamond\Box p$ and that c' on the outside claims $\sim \Box p$. The following dialogue will take place[5] :

c : Since I have shown $\Box p$ to be solvable, I will tell someone that he has to accept $\Box p$. I will take c" (on the outside)

c" : I accept $\Box p$. Hence I know that p has been solved and hence I add p to the list of my results.

c' : I have shown that $\sim p$ is solvable. Hence I must tell someone to accept $\sim p$. But the only person I can reach is myself. Therefore I must accept $\sim p$ myself.

And here the dialogue stops since c" has no way to communicate with c' and vice versa. The problem really lies in the center since on the outside nothing can go wrong. Suppose c' accepts both $\Diamond\Box p$ and $\sim \Box p$. The entire dialogue will turn into a monologue of c' in which he convinces himself that he has to accept both p and $\sim p$.

example 2 : suppose we have two perfect communities, $PerfC_1$ and $PerfC_2$. They are linked together by a two-headed arrow, connecting a member c_1 of the first community to a member c_2 of the second community. Although this type of community is very close to the perfect community, it is not identical to it. Once again, the same inference that has been studied in example 1, fails. The failure arises at the special member c_1 (or c_2 because of symmetry). I will not present the dialogue, but c_1's strategy is quite obvious. On the one hand, he accepts $\Diamond\Box p$ and tells a member of his community to accept $\Box p$. This member in its turn will inform his community that p has been solved. But c_1 also knows that $\sim p$ is solvable. This information he passes on to c_2 who will accept $\sim p$. And no problem has occurred. For any other member in one of the communities this strategy will not work. As in example 1, the problem lies in the fact that c_1 and c_2 have a certain degree of freedom in distributing the information.

example 3 : the case of the solitary problem-solver. In this model, $p \vdash \Box p$ is valid (trivially so). Hence it follows that the solitary problem-solver has the freedom to claim that, if he accepts anything (p), he may consider it solved ($\Box p$). This need not amaze us, since in this particular model, S5 collapses into

PC. Hence, for an isolated problem-solver, the problem-solving task becomes in a certain sense, redundant. He only has to be careful in selecting what he will accept (in order to avoid inconsistencies).

Speaking in more general terms, it should be added that the semantics for the various modal systems have been very well studied[6]. A problem in this connection that deserves a lot of attention is precisely to find out what axiomatic system matches a given model (which reduces to stipulating the properties of R). Here we have a treasury of results that can be translated in a straightforward way in terms of a problem-solving community and its associated communication channels.

A quite different argument to sustain the claim that these models may prove to be interesting, is because of their connection with Jaakko Hintikka's question-answer approach[7]. He considers a game between myself and Nature. The novelty of his approach lies in the fact that I can ask questions to Nature. The connection is quite simply this : for a problem-solver c in a community C, the rest of the community, i.e. $C - \{c\}$ plays a role similar to that of Nature in Hintikka's games. If c has not succeeded in solving p, he can ask around to see if anybody else has succeeded. Another similarity that is quite striking, is Hintikka's insistence on model-oriented dialogues[8]. Roughly speaking, this means that we are interested in the validity of certain dialogues given some additional information (usually referred to as the background knowledge). Clearly in the approach presented here, we too take a model-oriented stance. We start out by presenting a particular community which corresponds in modal terms to selecting a particular model. Hence we are not looking at the broad class of all models. If this connection turns out to be more than a weak comparison, as I believe it will, this would have the interesting consequence that, as different communities are considered, a problem-solver will play against different types of "Nature". The question then arises what kind of dialogue partner Nature is : is it perfect or not ?

III

At the beginning of part II, I mentioned that the third strategy is of a quite different nature and requires an altogether different treatment. But as I will show, a conservative extension of S5 will do the job.

The intuitive idea is once again rather straightforward. In the system presented up to now, $\Box p$ only states that p has been solved. But the third strategy has precisely to do with the specific way to solve p. Hence we must succeed in incorporating information of that kind into the formalism. One way of doing this, is to include that information in the box and I will write

(16) $$[\alpha]p$$

for "p has been solved using the method α".

It seems quite evident to accept the two following statements :

(17) $$\Box p \supset [\alpha]p$$

if p has been solved, then it must have been solved by using some method α,

(18) $$[\alpha]p \supset \Box p$$

If p has been solved using some method α, then surely p must be considered solved. Thus we have the equivalence. But combining this with the rule of necessitation, leads us straight into problems, for now it follows that :

(19) $$\text{if} \vdash p, \text{then} \vdash [\alpha]p$$

This must hold for any α ! But that means that if p is accepted, any method may be used to obtain p. Such a result is clearly not acceptable. Hence some modification must be made. I propose the following : instead of writing $[\alpha]p$, I will write

(20) $$\{\alpha\}p$$

where $\{\alpha\}p$ stands for "there is a method α such that α solves p" or, if quantification over methods is allowed for, $\exists\alpha[\alpha]p$.

There is no harm now to accept, instead of (17) and (18) :

(21) $$\Box p \equiv \{\alpha\}p$$

We can still substitute β for α in (21), but this causes no problem as it is existentially bounded. We therefore add (21) as an axiom to our system.

To make the picture complete, we have to stipulate what happens on the semantical level. Only a slight modification is needed. Besides the relation R we introduce a new relation M over the set of couples consisting of sentences and methods. Mpα means that α is a method for solving p. A problem-solver c will now have to deal with couples of sentences and methods. The semantical clauses not involving methods remain unchanged and the clause for $\{\alpha\}p$ consists of two conditions :

(22) if c $\models$ p, then there exists a α such that Mpα

(23) c $\models$ {α}p iff for all c' such that Rcc', Mpα and c' $\models$ p

The two conditions combined show clearly the semantical equivalence of $\Box$p and {α}p, hence (21) is satisfied.

Let us call the resulting system S5$_M$. This is a rather nice system, since it has the following properties :

(24) S5$_M$ is consistent

This follows straight away from the consistency of S5,[9] a well-known fact in the literature. Any formula involving methods can be translated equivalently into a formula not involving methods, hence the consistency of S5$_M$ is reduced to that of S5.

(25) S5$_M$ is complete, i.e. $\vdash_{S5_M}$ p iff $\models_{S5_M}$ p

If $\vdash_{S5M}$ p then $\vdash_{S5}$ p^o, where p^o results from p by replacing all occurrences of methods by boxes. Because of axiom (21) p^o must be a theorem. Hence $\models_{S5}$ p^o because of the completeness of S5.[10] Translating p^o back to p results in an equivalent formula, hence $\models_{S5_M}$ p. The other direction runs along similar lines.

As far as the dialogues corresponding to the S5$_M$ decision method are concerned, there is no problem in writing out the necessary additions and changes, the only difference being that if a problem-solver informs someone that he has solved a problem, then he must also inform him of the method used. Although one might expect that few new interesting facts about S5$_M$-dialogues will arise – since it is a conservative not proper extension – the following example may illustrate the opposite view.

Consider once again the perfect community. Suppose one half of them knows that Mpα, i.e. α is associated with p. Note that this does not imply that p has been solved. To obtain that we must have either $\Box$p or {α}p, but both cases require that p is present. Hence I have used the expression "associated with". Suppose further that the other half knows that Mpβ. Someone, say c, may now safely conclude that $\Box$p or, equivalently {γ}p, because what the semantical clause stipulates, is that there must be *some* program. It is not required at all that everybody should be using the same method. Which is precisely what the third strategy expresses. It is interesting to note that the third strategy is much harder to follow in the centralized community if you happen to be on the outside. Because you will be unable to tell anybody else about the method you have used. On the other hand, the center has the unique position of being able to force its methods on the other members. This is another reason for rejecting the centralized community as a community model since it reduces its problem-solving capacity.

Note : in earlier versions, I actually used dynamic logic as a language.[11] But that was not without its problems. For a start, dynamic logic lacks $[\alpha]p \supset p$. It does have the rule of necessitation, but precisely in the form (19) which turned out to be not acceptable. Furthermore, its semantics, although quite nice on its own, does not mix with a S5-type semantics. In fact, what is left over is the idea of expressing "p has been solved using a method α" by (16). What we do lose however by not adopting dynamic logic, is the idea of composition of methods. In dynamic logic, two operations are considered $\alpha;\beta$ (first β is executed an then α) and $\alpha \cup \beta$ (either α or β is executed). Two axioms are formulated for reducing such composite methods :

$$[\alpha;\beta]p \equiv [\alpha][\beta]p \quad \text{and} \quad [\alpha \cup \beta]p \equiv [\alpha]p \,\&\, [\beta]p$$

Take e.g. the first axiom. In our approach this turns out to be very un-informative. Suppose we have a method $[\alpha; \beta]$, because of the axiom this is equivalent to $[\alpha][\beta]$. But this in its turn is equivalent to two boxes, which can be reduced to one box. Hence one method will do the job of the composite method. Since this procedure always works, there is very little interest in having an axiom like the one consicered.

IV

There is however an important objection that might be raised against this proposal. Although it is clear that we are able to talk about problems, problems being solved and methods used for solving them, if we look at the dialogues themselves, we see that the most interesting part of the dialogue is still missing. For, in the present formulation, if someone claims that $\Box p$ or $\{\alpha\}p$, then anybody that can be reached by the original problem-solver will simply accept p and that is it. Should not one at least expect a dialogue about that ! After all, if someone has solved a problem, I am not only interested in knowing this fact, but I will only be convinced of that fact if I have had the opportunity for checking the solution. Is it possible to incorporate such a type of dialogue in the present framework. I think it can be done.

In the first place, it must be emphasized that dialogues about the correctness of problem-solving methods will take place at a particular point in the global dialogue. To be precise, a correctness dialogue will take place if a c claims

□p and c' (such that Rcc') wishes to examine the solution first before accepting p. This suggests that the subdialogues can be easily inserted in the global dialogue.

In the second place, the shortcoming must reside in the fact that the only thing we know about problems and methods is that you need the latter to solve the former (formally expressed by Mpα). We need to know more about the relationship between p and its associated method. One possibility is this : if p is a problem then the following holds if there is a method α such that Mpα :

(26) $$[d \ ? \ ; \alpha] \ s$$

d stands for the initial data and s for the final answer. Since α is a method for solving p, this must imply that α is capable of transforming the initial data of the problem into a solution, which is exactly what (26) tries to express. In another paper,[12] I have tried to formulate a logic for dialogues about statements like (26). From the viewpoint of that paper, the system presented here, can be interpreted as an extension.

The nice thing about this line of approach is that we recover the full richness of dynamic logic. As one can see, in (26) the composition of methods already occurs. d? is called a test-program. To be sure, the resulting logic is once again not equivalent to dynamic logic itself. One example may illustrate the problem. In terms of the interpretation of (26) we would like the following to hold : if [d? ; α]s and the solution s can be used as the initial data for a new problem, thus [s? ; β]t, then we also have a solution for the combined problem, viz. [d? ; α;β]t. Alas, a result of that kind is not valid in dynamic logic.[13] I will not present the formal details of the solution I have worked out. Suffice it to say that it is not without problems some of which are still open to me. Semantically however, the model is quite nice and fits in rather easily with the modal-type semantics. This is of some importance as the models are what we want to have knowledge about in the first place.

A final remark concerns the use of PC as "base" logic. This does lead in $S5_M$ to some debatable results the most striking of which is of course :

(27) $$\Box p \ v \sim \Box p$$

In terms of the interpretation presented here, this means that any problem is either solved or cannot be solved. That surely is a very strong claim as any intuitionist will gladly inform us. Obviously it is a minor technical problem to replace throughout the whole presentation PC by IPC, since the latter has (almost) as nice properties as PC (though harder to prove).[14] Let there be no mistake : I do agree with the intuitionists, but I did use PC to keep the formal part of the paper as simple as possible, since the idea of this paper was to read on an informal level formulas that are extremely well-known.15

NOTES

(1) The present paper is a continuation of a line of research I started in "Pragmatics and mathematics or how do mathematicians talk ?", *Philosophica* 29, 1982, pp. 97–118. See also "Dialogue Logic and Problem Solving", to be published in *Philosophica* 35, 1985. The complexity issue is explored in "Dialogue Logic and Complexity", preprint, Ghent, 1985.

(2) All information about modal logic has been extracted from G.E. Hughes & M.J. Cresswell, *An introduction to modal logic,* Methuen and Co., London, 1968 and the recently published *A companion to modal logic,* Methuen and Co., London, 1984 by the same authors.

(3) There is of course the famous paper by Kurt Gödel, "An interpretation of the intuitionistic sentential logic" reprinted in Jaakko Hintikka (ed.), *The Philosophy of Mathematics,* Oxford University Press, Oxford, 1969, pp. 128–129. In present-day logic, most well-known is G. Boolos, *The unprovability of consistency,* Cambridge University Press, Cambridge, 1979. Of special interest are two articles by Raymond Smullyan, "Modality and Self-Reference" and "Some principles related to Löb's Theorem" both in Stewart Shapiro (ed.), *Intensional Mathematics,* North-Holland, Amsterdam, 1985 (resp. pp. 191–211 and pp. 213–230.)

(4) To be precise, it is one type of dialogue resulting from the corresponding tableaux for that inference. Therefore this one dialogue is not sufficient for concluding that the inference is valid. One would have to look at the set of all dialogues resulting from the given tableaux. The dialogue selected here is the most interesting one that will occur.

(5) The same remark as above should be made (note 4). For it is obvious that c also knows that $\sim$p is solvable. But so formulated, the dialogue turns into a monologue of c, where he only needs his colleagues to tell them what to accept. It works in this case because adding $\sim\square$p to c's knowledge does not generate a contradiction.

(6) See note 2.

(7)   See e.g. "Sherlock Holmes Confronts Modern Logic : Toward a Theory of Information-Seeking through Questioning" and "Sherlock Holmes Formalized" (the former in co-authorship with Merrill B. Hintikka). Both are to be found in Thomas A. Sebeok and Umberto Eco (eds), *Dupin, Holmes, Peirce : the sign of three,* Indiana University Press, Bloomington, 1983, resp. pp. 154–169 and pp. 170–178. A very interesting article is "Information-Seeking Dialogues : Some of Their Logical Properties" (co-author Esa Saarinen) in *Studia Logica,* 32, 1979, pp. 355–363.

(8)   See e.g. Jaakko Hintikka, "A Spectrum of Logics of Question", in *Recent Developments in Dialogue Logics,* Jean Paul Van Bendegem (ed.), *Philosophica,* 35, to be published 1985.

(9)   See Hughes & Cresswell, *op. cit.,* p. 59.

(10) See Hughes & Cresswell, *op. cit.,* p. 121.

(11) An excellent introduction to dynamic logic is David Harel, *First-Order Dynamic Logic,* Springer, Heidelberg, 1979 and R. Parikh, "Propositional Dynamic Logic of Programs : a Survey", in E. Engeler (ed.), *Logic of Programs,* Springer, Heidelberg, 1981.

(12) See note 1, especially "Dialogue Logic and Problem Solving".

(13) This has to do with the fact that $[\alpha]p \supset p$ is not an axiom (nor a theorem) of dynamic logic. Hence in a model, there is no restriction on the accessibility relation. In fact, if the programs are ignored (i.e. replaced by boxes) then the resulting modal logic is K.

(14) It is worth mentioning here that Dov M. Gabbay is involved at the present moment in a related field. In "Negation as Inconsistency", (co-author M.J. Sergot), *Research Report DoC 84/7,* 1984 (presented at the 2nd BAAI-meeting on deductive databases, Leuven, June 29, 1984) he proposes to interpret negation intuitionistically : $\sim$p is the case if adding p to the database can be shown to lead to problems. In terms of our approach, claiming $\sim\square$p stands for claiming that if it is assumed that p has been solved, this can be shown to lead to inconsistencies.

(15) When finishing this paper, I discovered an article by R. Parikh and R. Ramanujam, "Distributed Processes and the Logic of Knowledge", in: Parikh, Rohit (ed.): *Logics of Programs,* Springer, Heidelberg, 1985,

pp. 256–268. There are many similarities with the approach outlined here requiring a more detailed study.

DYNAMIC DIALECTICAL LOGICS AS A TOOL TO DEAL WITH AND PARTLY ELIMINATE UNEXPECTED INCONSISTENCIES

Diderik Batens

It is well known that inconsistencies play an important role in the context of discovery. This paper is about a new kind of logics, viz. logics which I devised specifically for theories that were intended to be consistent and that were believed to be consistent during some time, but that later turned out to be inconsistent. I shall also present some variants of dynamic dialectical logics which lead to the elimination of some inconsistencies and, as a consequence, to an enrichment of the theory.

Dynamic dialectical logics display essentially the following property: if an inconsistency occurs at some point in a proof, the rules of inference are changed and, as a consequence, some statement that was derivable at a previous point in the proof may not be derivable any more, whereas some statement that was not derivable at a previous point in the proof may become derivable after the inconsistency has been arrived at.

As we shall see, some dynamic dialectical logics have a further property: they eliminate certain inconsistencies, or lead to the decision to accept some inconsistency rather than another, and, as a consequence, they lead to an enrichment of the theory. I do not claim, however, that the latter "enrichment" logics are adequate in all cases. In some cases the removal of an inconsistency leads to a new conceptual system. This problem is a heuristic one and falls beyond the scope of deductive logics.

The reason I call these logics dialectical is that there are some similarities with Hegelian dialectics: we have to confront *inconsistencies* which derive from a given theory (or set of premises); these inconsistencies constitute a *problem;* the occurrence of inconsistencies leads to changes to the logic, i.e. to the rules of inference, and leads to changes to the set of derivable statements; and for some dialectical logics, inconsistencies are eliminated and this elimination results in an enrichment of the theory. Moreover, I call these logics dynamic in order to stress the difference with Routley and Meyer's static dialectical logics.

263

I do of course realize that the dynamic properties of the logics sound rather extravagant. This is why I shall first try to describe informally where this kind of dynamics comes in and how it may be justified intuitively. I want to stress from the outset, however, that the logics I am considering here are decent formal logics, which I have formulated in an exact way both syntactically and semantically, and for which completeness proofs and soundness proofs are available. In general, any claim I shall make about the formal properties of these logics has been proved as a metatheorem[1]. But let me first explain the matter intuitively.

Consider a very simple case: a theory T was intended as a consistent theory and for this reason was formulated with classical logics as its basis, but after some time it turns out to be inconsistent. As a concrete example one might think of Russell discovering his paradox in Cantor's set theory. As T is inconsistent, any statement is a theorem of T. But obviously nobody will start deriving all statements from T. Strictly speaking the theory is also false. But it is not in general an acceptable decision simply to reject the theory. If no rival theory is available, rejecting T would leave us with no theory at all in the domain. And even if rival theories are available, it is possible that T, except for its being inconsistent, is in several respects better than its rivals, or that it is worthwhile pursuing it for other reasons. In order to live with T after it has been shown to be inconsistent, we clearly need something other than classical logic. Moreover, in order to find a consistent improvement of T, we need to distinguish between the important theorems of T, which we want to keep as much as possible, and those theorems of T which we are ready to give up. But of course, in order to make sense of the expression "important theorem *of T*" we need something other than classical logic, for according to classical logic everything is a theorem of T.

I have already shown that to derive everything from T or simply to reject T is a bad course of action. Which other courses of action are available ? In the first place we may refer to the machinery described by Nicholas Rescher in *Hypothetical Reasoning*[2] (and in many other places). The disadvantage of this machinery is that its outcome is extremely dependent on the way in which the theory is axiomatized. There are some further disadvantages which are connected with the fact that the machinery cuts the theory in pieces, viz. in consistent subsets of axioms, but I shall not deal with these here.

As another possible course of action one might replace classical logic by some paraconsistent logic. A logic is paraconsistent if it does not in general lead from inconsistency to triviality, i.e. if

$$A, {\sim}A \nvdash B$$

for at least some negation $\sim$. Most relevant logics are paraconsistent; other paraconsistent logics are based on the intuitionistic implication or on some many-valued implication or even on material implication[3]. As an example I mention the propositional logic PI which I studied in a recent paper[4] and which I consider as a minimal paraconsistent logic with respect to the propositional calculus.

Syntactically

A1 $p \supset (q \supset p)$
A2 $(p \supset (q \supset r)) \supset ((p \supset q) \supset (p \supset r))$
A3 $((p \supset q) \supset p) \supset p$
A4 $(p \& q) \supset p$
A5 $(p \& q) \supset q$
A6 $p \supset (q \supset (p \& q))$
A7 $p \supset (p v q)$
A8 $q \supset (p v q)$
A9 $(p \supset r) \supset ((q \supset r) \supset ((p v q) \supset r))$
A10 $(p \equiv q) \supset (p \supset q)$
A11 $(p \equiv q) \supset (q \supset p)$
A12 $(p \supset q) \supset ((q \supset p) \supset (p \equiv q))$
A13 $(p \supset \sim p) \supset \sim p$

Modus Ponens and *Uniform Substitution*

$\alpha \vdash A$ and $\vdash A$ as usual.

Semantically : $v \in V$ iff

C0 $v : F \rightarrow \{0,1\}$ (F is the set of all formulas)
C1 $v(A \supset B)=1$ iff $v(A)=0$ or $v(B)=1$
C2 $v(A \& B)=1$ iff $v(A)=v(B)=1$
C3 $v(A v B)=1$ iff $v(A)=1$ or $v(B)=1$
C4 $v(A \equiv B)=1$ iff $v(A)=v(B)$
C5   If $v(A)=0$, then $v(\sim A)=1$ (not conversely)

$\alpha \models A$ and $\models A$ as usual.

Incidentally, this paraconsistent logic will prove useful for the articulation of dynamic dialectical logics.

I was considering the course of action which consists in replacing the underlying logic of T, viz. classical logic, by some paraconsistent logic. This, however, has the disadvantage that the resulting theory is in general *extremely poor*. Paraconsistent logics sanction as invalid all inferences which presuppose that the world is consistent (e.g., disjunctive syllogism: AvB, $\sim$A$\vdash$B). As a consequence, paraconsistent logics not only avoid that every statement be derivable from the inconsistent theory T, they also avoid a large number of other consequences of T, which are not in any way related to the specific inconsistency which is derivable from T. (Strictly speaking any inconsistency is derivable from T, but if we replace classical logic by some paraconsistent logic this situation is changed). What we need, both in order to live with the inconsistent theory and in order to determine the set of interesting theorems *of T,* is *the theory T, in its full richness, except for the pernicious consequences of its inconsistency.* This is *exactly* what dynamic dialectical logics give us, and no other logic gives us the same thing.

Intuitively speaking we now proceed as follows. After we derive both A and $\sim$A from T, we shall refrain from making any inference which presupposes the consistency of A. E.g., for all B, we shall avoid making the following inferences :

AvB, $\sim$A / B
B$\supset$A, $\sim$A / $\sim$B
$\sim$(A&B),A / $\sim$B

but we shall continue to derive, e.g., D from DvC and $\sim$C. In other words, we *localize* the inconsistency, and then restrict the rules of inference *locally,* i.e. with respect to statements that have been shown to behave inconsistently. Still in other words, we go paraconsistent with respect to some statements (viz. those that behave inconsistently) and keep the full classical logic with respect to other statements.

In proceeding in this way, we may arrive at the following situation: we discover that B behaves inconsistently, whereas we have relied on the consistency of B in order to derive A. But this means that A is not derivable in the way in which it was derived, i.e. that we erroneously relied on the consistent behaviour of B. In view of the fact that A is still derivable and that A is not derivable any more, A behaves consistently and hence the following inferences become valid again :

AvB, $\sim$A/B
B$\supset$A, $\sim$A/$\sim$B

Needless to say, we want to exclude certain forms of dynamics, e.g., perpetual circles, and such forms of dynamics will be excluded indeed.

In view of the fact that dynamic dialectical logics localize inconsistencies and that the rules of inference become only restricted with respect to those statements that behave inconsistently, they may also be considered as *adaptive logics*. They "adapt themselves" to the specific inconsistencies of some theory.

I shall now show how the intuitive approach may be made exact. Let us start from PI. We have the following theorem (PC is the propositional calculus):

$$\vdash_{PC} A \supset B \text{ iff there are (zero or more) } C_1, ..., C_n \text{ such that}$$

$$\vdash_{PI} (C_1 \& \sim C_1) v ... v (C_n \& \sim C_n) v (A \supset B)$$

Examples : $\vdash_{PI}(p\&(p\supset q))\supset q$, $\vdash_{PI}(p\&\sim p)v[(\sim p\&(pvq))\supset p]$, $\vdash_{PI}(q\&\sim q)v$ $[((p\supset q)\&\sim q)\supset\sim p]$.

To the first example corresponds the (unconditional) inference

$$p, p \supset q / q$$

The other two examples may be turned into *conditional* inferences as follows :

$\sim p, pvq / q$ provided p behaves consistently
$p\supset q, \sim q / \sim p$ provided q behaves consistently

and these may be paraphrased, e.g., as follows :

(*)   if $\sim p$ and pvq are derived, then q may be derived, provided p and $\sim p$ are not both derivable from the premisses (i.e. $\sim p$ is and p is not).

It is readily seen that this statement is circular in view of the (usual) definition of "derivability". This is why I shall stick to the *pragmatic* idea that is present in the intuitive formulation of the dynamic dialectical logic and modify (*) to:

(†)   if, *at some time* both $\sim p$ and pvq occur as steps of the proof and p does not occur as a step of the proof, then q may be added as a new step to the proof.

In order to take the dynamic character of the proof into account, I stipulate that we *delete,* at any given time, all steps of the proof that are no longer derivable at that time. This means that, as soon as both A and $\sim A$ occur in the proof, we delete all steps that were written by relying on the consistent behaviour of A. I shall not give an exact formulation of the present dynamic dialectical logic, but merely offer an example of a demonstration which the reader will easily follow.

(1)	~p&q	premiss	—	$\emptyset$
(2)	r⊃p	premiss	—	$\emptyset$
(3)	~svr	premiss	—	$\emptyset$
(4)	q⊃s	premiss	—	$\emptyset$
(5)	q⊃p	premiss	—	$\emptyset$
(6)	~p	(1)	A&B/A	$\emptyset$
(7)	q	(1)	A&B/B	$\emptyset$
[(8)	~r	(2),(6)	A⊃B,~B/~A	p] deleted after (11)
[(9)	~s	(3),(8)	AvB,~B/A	p,r] deleted after (11).
(10)	s	(4),(7)	A⊃B,A/B	$\emptyset$
(11)	p	(5),(7)	A⊃B,A/B	$\emptyset$
(12)	r	(3),(10)	~AvB,A/B	s

Each line consists of five elements: (i) a line number, (ii) a formula, (iii) the numbers of the formulas from which the second element is derived, (iv) the rule by which the second element is derived, and (v) the set of formulas the consistent behaviour of which is presupposed. The fifth element of line (9) contains p, because ~r is employed for the inference of ~s and ~r was derived by relying on the consistent behaviour of p. After line (11), ~r and ~s are not derivable any more and r becomes derivable (r is not derivable after line (10), because at that time both s and ~s occur in the demonstration).

If we were to continue the demonstration, nothing interesting would happen: no further inconsistencies may be derived and all further steps will be trivial PI-consequences of { p,~p,q,r,s }. In general, we may define "A is an ultimate consequence of α" as follows: there is a demonstration S of A from α and this demonstration *may be extended* into a demonstration S', in which A has not been deleted, and which is such that A will not be deleted in any further extension of S'.

The present dynamic dialectical logic has the following property: both p and q *are* ultimate consequences of {~p,~q,pvq}, but p&q is *not* an ultimate consequence of this set. In such cases I say that p and q are *connected with respect to their consistency*.

For some purposes the aforementioned property is troublesome. It turns out, however, that the logic may easily be adapted in order to avoid this trouble. There is an easy way to get hold of connections between the consistency of sentences. There are some related complications which I skip here but which are resolved in a perfectly intuitive way. If we adopt the following policy :

> If it has been demonstrated that either A_1 or ... or A_n behave inconsistent-
> ly, and nothing more specific (e.g., that A_1 or ... A_{n-1} behave incon-
> sistently) has been demonstrated, then do not rely on the consistent
> behaviour of A_1 or of ... or of A_n.

This policy leads to a logic in which the aforementioned trouble is avoided (and nothing else has been changed, e.g., the premises (1)–(4) have the same set of ultimate consequences as earlier). This logic is called DPI and has the following properties :

For any finite set α :

(i)   the notion of an ultimate DPI-consequence of α may be defined in a systematic way (i.e. without referring to dynamic proof);
(ii)   any finite number of ultimate DPI-consequences of α may be ultimately derived within some extension of any DPI-proof from α;
(iii)   the set of ultimate DPI- consequences of α is decidable.

By referring to the notion of an "intelligent extension" (i) and (ii) may be generalized to infinite α, and (iii) may be generalized to infinite sets α for which $Cnp_I(\alpha)$ is decidable.

Before proceeding to some variants of DPI, I make some short comments. 1) With respect to the type of application I am considering, PI is to be preferred in general to other paraconsistent logics as a basis for a dynamic dialectical logic. 2) There is a decent two-valued semantics for DPI; completeness and soundness are provable. 3) If a theory which has PC as its underlying logic is shown to be inconsistent, the replacement of PC by DPI not only leads to "the theory in its full strength, except for the pernicious consequences of its in-consistency", but this replacement is also natural. What we were doing before the inconsistency was discovered, viz. applying the full PC, is justified from the point of view of DPI : as long as no inconsistency has been derived, DPI validates the same inferences as PC.

The last part of this paper contains some remarks on the problem of the "enrichment" of an inconsistent theory that is caused by the elimination of inconsistencies.

Dynamic dialectical logics eliminate an infinite number of inconsistencies in comparison to classical logic and if applied to inconsistent but nontrivial sets of premises. On the other hand there is an obvious sense in which trivial theories are extremely poor — they give no information at all[5] — and in this sense dynamic dialectical logics lead to an enrichment.

Let us denote the PI-axiomatization of the set of ultimate DPI-consequences of a by §a and split up §a into one or more consistent subsets, either by deleting one "half" of each inconsistency on nonlogical grounds, or by deleting both halves of each inconsistency, or by simply splitting up §a into consistent subsets which are maximal with respect to §a. In each case it may be readily demonstrated that we arrive at one or more sets which are richer than the sets arrived at by performing the analogous procedure to α itself or to the set of PI-consequences of α. In other words, after DPI has been applied the elimination of inconsistencies leads to an enrichment with respect to the corresponding consistent subtheories of the original theories.

The most dramatic enrichment is arrived at under the following circumstances. Suppose that $A_1, \ldots, A_n$ are connected with respect to their consistency and that we decide to choose for the inconsistent behaviour of one of them. As a consequence all other A_i will behave consistently (in general), and this elimination of "potential" inconsistencies may be proved to result in general in an enrichment of the theory. If we are merely interested in an optimal enrichment (i.e. if we have no nonlogical grounds for preferring another one), we may on this ground decide which inconsistency we choose.

My main aim in writing down these remarks was to show that the notion of an enrichment can be captured in terms of a deductive logic. The most interesting enrichments do of course arise if an inconsistency is eliminated by introducing new concepts, but this problem is typically a heuristic one and is probably beyond the reach of any deductive logic.

It was suggested at the conference that dynamic dialectical logics rely on syntactical considerations only, and that they would have at best a merely technical semantics. As may be easily seen from my paper, referred to in the first note, both statements are false. The semantic idea behind dynamic dialectical logics is to define the consequence relation in terms of the set of worlds (model sets, etc.) in which *all premisses* are true and that are *as consistent as possible* [6] The adaptation of this idea to the forms of enrichment discussed is both straightforward and intuitive.

NOTES

(1)   For the exact formulation of the logics, the semantics, the metatheorems and more information in general, I refer to my "Dynamic Dialectical Logics" in G. Priest and R. Routley (eds.), *Paraconsistent Logic,* in print.

(2)   Amsterdam, North-Holland, 1964.

(3)   For a good overview of paraconsistent logic see A.I. Arruda, "Aspects of the Historical Development of Paraconsistent Logic", in G. Priest and R. Routley (eds.), *Paraconsistent Logic,* in print.

(4)   "Paraconsistent Extensional Propositional Logics", *Logique et Analyse,* 90–91, 1980, pp. 195–234.

(5)   Simple-minded classicists say that contradictions give maximal information, that they are maximally rich, that they "explain" everything, etc.

(6)   It is instructive to compare this with Rescher's approach, which refers to the set of *consistent* worlds in which *as many premisses as possible* are true.